Acknowledgments

This is the page where I get to say thanks. Thanks to my fantastic bosses and co-workers at ESPN and ESPN.com who were kind enough to hire me, support me, edit me, brainstorm with me, and literally make it possible for this book to exist.

Thanks to all my incredible, talented, always-energizing baseball editors at ESPN.com—Dave Kull, David Schoenfield, Scott Ridge, Matt Szefc, Matt Meyers, Nick Pietruszkiewicz, Christina Kahrl, Eric Ortiz, Michael Knisley, and my favorite concierge, Marty Bernoski. I hope, when they read this book, it doesn't cause them to try to count up all the hours of sleep I've cost them every October and all the hours of their life they'll never get back waiting for me to file that third take in the middle of the night.

Thanks to Tim Kurkjian, Peter Gammons, Jerry Crasnick, Jim Caple, Buster Olney, and all the fantastic people I've been lucky enough to cover baseball with at ESPN over these last 13 years. These guys are more than just my co-workers in this gig. They're among my best friends on earth.

Thanks to Steve Hirdt, Ken Hirdt, Rob Tracy, Randy Robles, Kevin Hines, Frank Labombarda, and the amazing crew at the Elias Sports Bureau, for all the incredible nuggets they've dug up for me (and all of us at ESPN) over the years. And thanks to Sean Forman, for inventing baseball-reference.com's addictive and indispensable Play Index, and to Lee Sinins, for bringing the awesome Complete Baseball Encyclopedia to life. A lot of my famous trivia questions are a direct result of having those works of genius at my disposal.

Thanks to so many of the cool, funny, insightful people in this sport who have made me laugh, made me think, made me wiser, and made me never stop driving to do my job better every day, just the way they do.

Thanks to my editors at Triumph Books, Tom Bast and Adam Motin, for convincing me this was a book that needed to be published, and for working so enthusiastically to make it everything I'd hoped it would be. And thanks to ESPN's all-knowing stats guru, Mark Simon, for always finding time to help me dredge up a never-ending supply of Useless Information, and for all he did to keep me from botching up about 700 facts in this book.

And thanks, especially, to my beautiful, special family, for always understanding why I have to disappear into that overstuffed office of mine for all those hours, and for lifting me to never stop reaching for the sky in everything I do, in work and in life.

Wild
Pitches

Rumblings, Grumblings, and Reflections on the Game I Love

Jayson Stark

TRIUMPH
BOOKS

To Lisa, Steven, Jessica, and Hali,
my amazing family, whose love, passion, and support
have been a greater source of inspiration
than they'll ever know.
They probably think they're the presidents of my fan club,
but in truth, I'm the president of theirs.

Library of Congress Cataloging-in-Publication Data
Stark, Jayson, 1951-
   Wild pitches : rumblings, grumblings, and reflections on the game I love / Jayson Stark.
      pages cm
      ISBN 978-1-60078-942-7 (hardback)
1. Baseball—Miscellanea. 2. Baseball—History. 3. Baseball—Records. I. Title.
GV867.5.S78 2014
796.357 '64—dc23   2013050911

This book is available in quantity at special discounts for your group or organization. For further information, contact:
   Triumph Books LLC
   814 North Franklin Street
   Chicago, Illinois 60610
   (312) 337-0747
   www.triumphbooks.com

Printed in U.S.A.

ISBN: 978-1-60078-942-7

Design by Sue Knopf

Contents

Foreword

When my Hall of Fame ballot arrived with the names of Barry Bonds and Roger Clemens on it for the first time, a difficult assignment became significantly harder, so perplexing, in fact, I needed to talk to a rational, clear-thinking friend about what to do with my vote. So I called the person that I always call in times of need or confusion, Jayson Stark, because he is so generous with his time and information, and because he is the voice of reason.

In this age of social media, where we rush to judgment, and value getting it first over getting it right, Jayson Stark has not betrayed his journalistic roots—fairness and accuracy first—from Syracuse University and the *Philadelphia Inquirer*, where I met him 30 years ago. It is hard to be the voice of reason these days, but he remains it, and so much more, to baseball writers across America. I have had great mentors—Dan Shaughnessy, Randy Galloway, Peter Gammons—but I've learned more from Jayson Stark than from anyone in the business about where, and how, to look for things of interest.

He has been, for so long, the voice of so many things in baseball, which you will read in this book. He is the voice of the funny quote. For years and years, he has always found the smart, amusing guys in the game, and gone to them when humor is needed to describe a game, a play, or a predicament. There are too many of his guys to name, but Larry Andersen, Jim Deshaies, Andy Van Slyke, Casey Candaele, Dann Bilardello, and Adam Dunn have made me laugh so many times over the years because Jayson went to them when a joke was needed. My contribution to that humor has been Rich Donnelly, who was a coach in the Texas Rangers system when I met him 30 years ago. I'd tell Jayson, "You have to call this guy. He is so funny." And now Rich's laugh runs through Jayson's columns.

Jayson is the voice of the great statistic. He has presented these numbers in different ways, under numerous titles, be it his Zero Heroes, Box Score Line of the Week, or his Department of Useless Information, which is never useless and always entertaining. He once told me that he kept track of every non-pitcher who pitched in a major league game for about a decade, and made it a goal to talk to every one of them about their experiences on the mound. And he has memorized some of the great lines in box score history.

"I have stuff rattling around in my brain that I can't get out," he once told me. "I can still remember Bob Forsch's pitching line from 1989: 7-18-10-10-0-3. I remember a writer asking him, 'But at least you didn't walk anyone,' and Forsch said, 'Why would anyone want to?'"

Jayson is the voice of the trivia quiz. In many of his columns, especially his famed Rumblings and Grumblings, he would insert a trivia question. It became so popular, the *Mike and Mike* morning radio show has him present a trivia question every Tuesday. (I don't know if they've ever gotten one right.)

Jayson is the voice of historical context. When someone retires, or is eligible for the Hall of Fame, or is in the running for the Most Valuable Player, or Jayson's own yearly award, the Least Valuable Player, no one puts a career or a season in perspective better than Jayson. His fascination with the history of the game makes him a must-read when comparisons are made between players of 100 years ago and players of today. His work the last two years on the achievements of Miguel Cabrera tell us exactly how great he has been. And we now know just how great Mariano Rivera was, based on Jayson's great research.

Jayson is the voice of the unusual play or situation. In a game in 2013, Brewers shortstop Jean Segura stole second base. Then, with runners at first and second base, he tried to steal third, got caught in a rundown, and wound up back at first base! Then he tried to steal second (again!) and was thrown out—all in a span of five pitches. It was one of the strangest base running maneuvers in the history of baseball, and no one took more glee in researching it than Jayson. Of course, he has all his guys at the ready for such a play, be it Dave Smith at Retrosheet or SABR historian David Vincent. They know when something strange happens, a play that demands an explanation, the first call is going to be from Jayson.

And yet this is where Jayson has always separated himself: when it comes time to write something serious, or take on someone in the game, be it the commissioner or Scott Boras, Jayson can do that, too. That hard edge was developed not just at Syracuse, but from the late '70s and early '80s, when he covered the Phillies, who were a rough group of guys to be around. When Phillies center fielder Garry Maddox lost another ball in the sun, and Jayson wrote that Maddox had more trouble with the sun than Icarus, the two ended up in a utility closet together, with Maddox pointing an angry finger at the beat guy from the *Inquirer*. And yet, Jayson never backed down with the Phillies, and he doesn't today.

Now he is the voice of ESPN.com. When a big news story breaks, Jayson usually writes it. And, during the postseason, Jayson writes game stories during each round of the playoffs, including the World Series. He is the last guy to leave the press box every night in October, usually dragging out around 3:00 AM. "I was still looking stuff up at 2:30 in the morning," he said after Game 3 of the 2013 World Series. "I guess I could just mail it in at that time of night, but I can't. This stuff is too good, it's too important. I won't do that."

That's my friend—Jayson Stark, one of the great voices of baseball.

> *Tim Kurkjian is an analyst on ESPN's* Baseball Tonight *and* SportsCenter. *He is also a contributor to* ESPN The Magazine *and ESPN.com.*

Introduction

Hanging on my office wall is a framed photo, of two little kids walking home from the school bus on a sunny Philadelphia afternoon, a long, long time ago. One of those kids was me. The other was my beautiful sister, Karen. I have to say, we looked pretty darned ecstatic to have made it through another day of elementary-school madness. I sure hope we didn't mess up any big multiplication tables that day. Or anything else equally momentous.

At the time, by our calculations, I was in fifth grade, and she was in fourth grade. I wasn't aware at that very moment that she considered me to be some sort of all-knowing fount of baseball wit and wisdom. But then she had to go and write 17 words which I still find totally amazing, to this day:

"If you wanted to know a lot about baseball, my brother would be able to tell you."

She wrote that in a "composition" for a fourth-grade English assignment. Many years later, she framed those words, along with the photo of that joyous walk home, and gave them to me for a birthday gift. One of the best presents I've ever gotten in my life.

All these years later, I still look at that photo, and the words below it, and wonder how I then, somehow, got to live this incredible life. How did I get this lucky? How did it all turn out just the way I dreamed it, back when I was 10? C'mon. That never happens.

I didn't want to grow up to be a baseball player, even then. I wanted to grow up to be a baseball writer. My mom, the late, great June Herder Stark,

was a writer—an incredible, quick-witted, phrase-turning genius of a writer, I might add. And that's what I wanted to be. But none of us can figure out how the baseball part of this story came to happen, because it wasn't as if I was raised in the Northeast Philadelphia equivalent of the Boone or Ripken house. I was really the one and only sports fan living in it.

My dad, Ed Stark, was a brilliant guy, with a love for bourbon, barbecued steaks, and the perfect white sand on the beaches of Ogunquit, Maine. And he liked sports enough that he took me to games and played catch with me in the backyard. But he was a much greater threat to comb through every detail of his bank statement than a box score. I can't tell you how many times he'd shake his head, as I sat in front of the TV, watching The Biggest Game of the Year (since yesterday), and tell me: "Jayson, I saw that game 20 years ago."

My mom, meanwhile, loved *reading* sportswriters, because Philadelphia was the home of many of the best who ever lived. But I can't remember her ever really following sports—not until her son got hired by a reputable employer to start covering them, anyway. Whereupon she quickly turned herself into such a baseball expert, naturally, that she could debate Dick Allen's Hall of Fame credentials with me until the day she died.

Meanwhile, my sister's worst nightmare, as she wrote in that very same "composition," was that I had so many baseball photos and posters splattered on every wall, she was sure that "each night, I think I'm going to dream about baseball." Reading between the lines, I'm getting the impression she had other, more important dreams in mind. I can't imagine what. But suffice it to say that while she survived an entire childhood with me, she never wanted to grow up to be, say, Linda Cohn.

So that was my family. Looking back, I have no clue now how I turned into the sports-loving nut case I became at an early age. But by the time I was nine years old, I was hooked. And the really crazy part of my sports addiction was that I did such an excellent scouting report on myself as an athlete that long before I got cut by my high school baseball team, I'd already fixed my sights on the coolest job ever—sportswriting. I'd go to games as a kid and bring my binoculars—not to get a closer view of the field, but to look up into the press box (seriously) and try to figure out what the heck everybody was doing up there. It couldn't actually be described as "work." Could it?

Well, now I know better, obviously. When people ask me about my job these days, I like to tell them it's a labor of love…and it's a good thing, because there's a lot of labor. But I can honestly say that, in more than three decades of covering baseball, first at the *Philadelphia Inquirer* and then, for the last 14 seasons at ESPN and ESPN.com, it's never felt like "work" to me. Every day, I get to wake up and do something I love. And I hope it shows, in every word in this book.

What you'll find, in the pages to follow, is a selection of my favorite columns from those ESPN.com years. Many of them have been tweaked slightly, to account for the fact that innocent people like you find yourself reading them now, years later. So some needed to be updated. Some had a few now-unimportant details surgically removed. Some required a little clarification here and there. But as I put them all together, I felt like Marty McFly, taking the DeLorean on a journey back through time, to ballparks and press boxes and spring training complexes where I've spent some of the most memorable days (and nights) of my life.

And behind so many of those stories, there's another story. So let me guide you through the book you're about to transform into a nationally celebrated best seller. Heck, if you've gotten this far, there's no point in turning back now. I promise the time you spend rummaging through these pages will be vastly more rewarding than doing the dishes, or vacuuming, or whatever else you had planned.

If you've been reading me for more than just the last 13 paragraphs, you know that, among other things, I'm a big-picture kind of guy. I love to take a step back and look at baseball life from afar, from the top row of the upper deck, and examine why things are The Way They Are. And that led us to a chapter that we're catchily calling "The Big Picture."

Why does baseball history matter? You don't need to ask Ken Burns. Just join me on a visit to Camden Yards, on Cal Ripken Jr. Passes Lou Gehrig Night in 1995, and to Tiger Stadium, on its last day as a major league venue in 1999. We just have to remind ourselves why the tears flowed as Ripken orbited the warning track, and why a grandson took his grandfather to that final game at Tiger Stadium, and it all becomes clear. No other sport connects past and present, with such deep human meaning, the way baseball does.

But baseball is so much more than just a nostalgia trip these days. I walk through clubhouses and see players fiddling with their iPads. And if I'd never stopped to ask about it, I never would have known the technological miracles that are allowing them to dial up numbers and video that are changing the sport before our eyes, every night. So I'll take you on a visit inside baseball's incredible Information Age, and let the likes of Joe Maddon explain some of the futuristic reasons that it seems like nobody can hit anymore.

You'll find a lot of October in this book, too. I love October. I don't sleep much. And I work so deep into the night that I cause my poor, innocent ESPN.com editors to sleep even less. But I get to see stuff, in person, that people talk about for, like, a thousand years. I sometimes stumble across lists of the greatest games ever played, and I get chills when I realize how many of them I was in the ballpark for. And now, thanks to the ingenious decision to publish this book, we get to travel back to those moments in time together.

Back to Yankee Stadium in the autumn of 2001, to watch Derek Jeter turn himself into baseball's first-ever Mr. November…Back to the North Side of Chicago in October of 2003, on an evening when I still vividly remember looking around Wrigley Field during the seventh-inning stretch, more convinced than Ernie Banks that I was going to be able to tell my grandchildren that I was there the night the Cubs finally made it back to the World Series… Back to Busch Stadium in 2011, for what just might have been the greatest World Series game ever played, where David Freese's walkoff home run will be floating through the October sky for the rest of time.

And back, too, to the nights when championships were won. To an epic evening in 2004, when the Red Sox set the ghosts free…Back to October of 2009, when four iconic Yankees stood on a podium in the middle of Yankee Stadium, sharing one final championship moment together…Back to October of 2010, when one of the most unlikely title teams ever did for San Francisco what the Giants of Mays and McCovey and Bonds never could.

In the midst of that journey back in October time, though, I was forced to recall what an all-powerful jinx I can be. Why did the Cubs lose the Bartman Game in 2003? You really shouldn't be blaming Steve Bartman. Obviously, they lost because, just the day before, I'd made the mistake of writing what a life-changing event the people of Chicago, and the Cubs themselves, were about to experience when their World Series dreams came true. Oops! And what cosmic event was responsible for the Rangers becoming the first team ever to blow five leads in one World Series game in 2011? Uh, that was me, too. All because I'd written only 24 hours earlier about what it would mean to their fans to win a World Series for the first time in the half-century-long history of that franchise. So take Neftali Feliz and Nelson Cruz off the hook. I'm guilty. Sorry!

I could have kept those ill-fated pieces stuffed in my secret archives, you realize, and you never even would have known. Instead, I'm including them in this collection as a reminder that, in baseball, it's never safe to assume anything, no matter how logical or inevitable it might seem. But just so you remember I'm not a dope all the time, I also included a couple of astonishing prognostications that I somehow got right. I'll let you guess (for now) what they were—because, judging by the tweets I get when I'm wrong, I'm certain no one on earth has any recollection that I was ever right about anything. Ever.

This literary journey also took me back to many awesome stops beneath the spring training palm trees…Back to Fort Myers in 2005, when the great James Taylor strolled into the Red Sox clubhouse while I was standing there talking to David Ortiz. And I then cajoled him into reflecting, without even bursting into song, on what kind of bizarre, uncharted universe we suddenly found ourselves living in, now that the Red Sox had somehow won the World Series…Back to Sarasota in March of 2007, when a phenom named Josh Hamilton walked out of the tunnel of oblivion and into a Dairy Queen—with his Reds uniform on. When he told me the story of how he'd driven home from the game in that uniform, then laid it out on the bed just to "take in the moment," I felt like calling Hollywood. Immediately. *Hello? Is this Mr. Coppola? Got one for ya.*

And the journey led me back to probably the most historic spring training park ever built, Al Lang Field, right in the middle of downtown St. Petersburg, Florida, where the ghosts of Babe Ruth and Stan Musial still echoed. In March of 2008, as Al Lang approached its final days of Grapefruit League life after more than 80 springs under the Florida sun, I couldn't understand why no one other than me seemed to be grasping the significance of the era that was about to end. So I began collecting Al Lang memories, for weeks, until I found myself one day spending an entire afternoon at the house of the legendary Cardinals baseball professor, George Kissell. We both had tears in our eyes as he tried, voice cracking, to digest the thought that baseball would never be played again in a place where he said he could still hear the cheers of the crowd, even on days when this "museum of baseball" was empty and still.

I admit I never mind a little weeping over the stuff I write. I'm mushy like that. But I never mind a lot of laughing, either. So there's a whole chapter in this book of pure, unadulterated fun. (I'm not big on adulterated fun, so it's a good thing.) For something like 15 years, I've been trying to figure out why grown baseball players attempt to speak through their gloves to foil all the secret agents in the stands. So I launched a major investigation into this important topic. And the Pulitzer Committee can thank me later—for leaving out all the bad-breath stories these guys told me, if nothing else.

And back in 2007, as Barry Bonds was chasing a hallowed record that America was so delighted to see him break, I found it ironic that the man who was about to call Historic Home Run No. 756 for the viewers in San Francisco was a man who had hit exactly one home run—in 12 years in the big leagues. That man was one of America's true broadcasting treasures, Duane Kuiper. So I convinced him to tell me all about his one, his only, homer. It's a story Duane Kuiper doesn't spin to just anybody, because a lot of people use it to poke fun at him. So I was honored that he told it. And I was more honored that a few years later, at the 2010 World Series gala, he told my brother-in-law, devoted Giants fan Bill Bernstein: "You know who wrote the best story ever written about my home run? Your brother-in-law." Cool!

Then there's a project I embarked on about a decade ago—to compile the goofy, incomprehensible Strange But True Feats of every year. A team gets five hits in a row but doesn't score a run? A pitcher gets ejected but still throws a complete game? Another pitcher strikes out a hitter he never actually threw a pitch to? This is stuff that's supposed to be impossible. But the independently minded sport of baseball never got that memo. So in baseball, of course, something like it happens every day. My mom always told me I should write a book and call it, *I Never Saw That Before*. I never did write that one. But in this book, I did include a bunch of Strange But True Feats of the (whole darned) Millennium. And as a very special bonus, they include lots of comic commentary from two of the most hilarious baseball humorists of all time—Astros/Cubs broadcast-quipmeister Jim Deshaies and a man who really should have his own show on Comedy Central, longtime coach-witticist Rich Donnelly.

Along the way, as I was spending my career searching for those goofy little feats, those big-picture epics, and those October moments I'd never forget, I got to spend some time with a bunch of baseball men who fit the definition of *legends*. So there's a chapter on them, too. What was it that drove Bobby Cox to get himself thumbed out of more baseball games than any manager who ever filled out a lineup card? Somebody (besides the umpires) had to get to the bottom of that, right? And where did Cox's favorite player ever, Chipper Jones, rank in the annals of the greatest third basemen and switch-hitters of all time? When I sat with Chipper for 45 minutes one day and told him what the numbers said, even he found it all too mind-boggling to comprehend.

But not all the stories turn out happily ever after, even when they involve men who soar to heights no one before or after them has ever reached. So how could I not reflect on the sad story of one of the most fascinating people I ever covered, Pete Rose, and how I inadvertently turned into one of the reasons that his Hall of Fame election day never came. And then there was the Hit King's partner in baseball exile—the Long Ball King, Barry Bonds. How appalled was Bud Selig in 2007 by the idea that Bonds was about to hold the most exalted record in his sport? More than the commish could ever bring himself to put into words. And the more I listened to him avoid saying those words, the more I realized the powerful point he was trying to make by not uttering them.

Finally, as I think I mentioned once or twice, I'm a Philadelphian. I'm not sure why I never got around to moving to, ohhhh, Maui. But shockingly, I didn't. I've stuck around Philly for most of my life. So I was pretty much required by law to include a chapter for all my fellow Philadelphians—both of them—who keep trying to convince me I'm their Favorite. Sportswriter. Ever. (Shhhh. Don't mention how we're related.)

Only in Philadelphia could millions of people grow misty-eyed at the demise of that giant round slab of concrete (complete with concrete turf) which we knew, affectionately, as the Vet. So you can all reminisce one last time about the Vet's final day of life. And only in Philadelphia could a team lose its 10,000th game (not in one year) and inspire its fair city to throw a party to "honor" it. But that happened, too. Really. I always felt that 10,000th loss should have inspired an awakening, not an excuse to drink more beer.

So you can reflect on that uplifting message here, too.

But Philadelphians aren't really the cold-hearted, mean-spirited, wing-gobbling, cheese-whiz-slobbering boobirds they're made out to be by so much of non-215-area-code civilization. They fall in love way more easily than they're given credit for. With a man named Harry Kalas, for instance, a fellow who became so much more than just the ultimate, heaven-sent voice of baseball. I really believe that on the day he died, he was easily the most beloved Philadelphian since maybe Benjamin Franklin. But there was a similar sort of love affair with a fun-loving, screwball-snapping October hero named Tug McGraw. And even with a career .161 hitter named John Vukovich. So those men, all gone too soon, are remembered in this book, too. Couldn't do a Philly chapter without them. Could I?

Oh, and there's one more surprise feature you'll find in these pages, by popular demand. Yeah, yeah. *Of course* I snuck a few trivia questions into this book, too. Since my good friends, Mike and Mike, have somehow turned me, totally by accident, into the Alex Trebek of baseball trivia, or something like that, I knew you'd want me to scatter an occasional trivia stumper throughout these chapters. So you'd better get all the questions right. There's going to be a quiz.

You know, when my sister wrote that fourth-grade composition, way back when, about her beloved big brother and his hopeless case of baseball fever, I'm sure she never imagined what a visionary she would turn out to be. Or that we'd still be laughing about her eloquent words all these years later. But every time I read them, I wonder if some things in life truly are meant to be. Those dreams I had, at 10 years old, launched me on this journey of a lifetime.

And what a journey. It was at a baseball game that I first saw the remarkably smart and gorgeous woman I was crafty enough to marry, the incredible and inspiring Lisa Stark. It was in baseball where all three of my kids—Steven, Jessica, and Hali—would wind up working, or interning, or both, as they began exploring what they wanted to do with their lives: Steven pointing a TV camera in the Phillies' dugout, Hali as social-media genius for Major League Baseball, Jessica as a jack-of-many-trades summer intern who then moved on to other, amazing pursuits. In other words, baseball actually became, sort of, the family business. Wow. How cool is that?

So obviously, this sport has been so much more, in my world, than just something to write about. It has shaped my entire universe for more than 30 years. And now, as I look over this collection of all these tales I've been fortunate enough to tell, about the greatest sport there ever was, I'm reminded again of how much fun I've had telling them (even when it was 4:00 AM and I was the last guy left in the stadium). Hopefully, you'll have just as much fun reading them.

Chapter 1
The Big Picture

June, 2006

Why Baseball's History Matters

Why Baseball's History Matters, Scene 1

The place: Camden Yards in Baltimore. The date: September 6, 1995.

There are moments in baseball that couldn't possibly happen in any other sport. This was one of them.

Most baseball history is made with no notice, with no warning. But not on this night.

On this night, 46,272 spectators arrived at Camden Yards knowing exactly what they were about to witness—and even *when* they would witness it.

Halfway through this game, the second it became official, Cal Ripken Jr. would finally break Lou Gehrig's legendary Iron Man record. He knew it. His teammates knew it. Everyone in America knew it.

There was no reason for this particular moment to turn into one of the most powerful and emotional experiences in the lifetimes of those who witnessed it. But somehow, it did.

What we remember is this: the Orioles played this exactly right. They didn't schlock up the occasion with phony announcements or scoreboard overkill. Mostly, they just unfurled a number on a wall:

2131.

And grown men cried for the next 20 minutes. Cried. Wept. Couldn't stop.

How did that happen, anyway? Why did it happen?

Here's why: it happened because baseball matters.

It matters to us in a way that no other sport matters.

There is no number in any other sport that could possibly be draped on the side of a warehouse and evoke the tears and passions that 2131 evoked. None.

For 24 hours, the number 2130 had hung on that wall. Everyone who saw it knew exactly what it meant:

Lou Gehrig: 2,130 games in a row, a record that could never be broken.

So to see that number change was all it took to unleash the earthquake in our souls that erupts when we realize we are witnessing something powerful and moving.

There is no sane reason that the rewriting of any line in any record book should be that moving. But this was a night that made it all so clear.

These aren't just numbers, not in this sport. They are numbers that tell stories. They are numbers that connect names and memories and generations.

Just the numbers alone can make you remember another night, deep in your past, at some other ballpark—maybe one that no longer stands.

They can make you remember what it felt like to watch Nolan Ryan throw a baseball, or Mike Schmidt swing a bat, or Rickey Henderson pump toward second base.

They can almost make you feel what your grandfather might have felt as he watched Stan Musial come to his town. Or Ted Williams. Or Lou Gehrig. They can bring back voices, freeze-frames, black-and-white images buried so securely in the back of your memory banks, you'd forgotten they were still rattling around inside you.

All sports have their memories, because memories are what sports are all about. But in baseball, we don't have to cue the marching band or the video machines to sledge-hammer anybody into remembering.

In baseball, we don't need anything more obvious or complicated than a number on a wall.

TRIVIALITY

Cal Ripken Jr. hit more home runs (345) while playing shortstop than anyone in history. Can you name the four other men who have hit at least 250 homers while playing short?

4

Why Baseball's History Matters, Scene 2

The place: ancient Tiger Stadium in Detroit. The date: September 28, 1999.

To the people who didn't get it, Tiger Stadium was just another rusting mass of steel and concrete by September of 1999, a decrepit structure made obsolete by peeling paint, obstructed views, and modern baseball economics.

But we know better. Those of us who get it know these places where we go to watch baseball games are not just buildings. They house much, much more than grass and dirt and half-eaten hot dogs.

They house our heroes and our heartaches. They house our passions and our memories. They house the seats where our fathers sat with their fathers. So after a while, they come to mean more to us than just about any place in the world.

Which means saying good-bye to them isn't easy, even when we know it's time.

By September 28, 1999, it was time for Tiger Stadium. Time for good-bye.

So on this day, the day of the 6,873rd and final regular season game at this historic place, 18-year-old Aaron Scheible led his 80-year-old grandfather, Ben Saperstein, to a pair of seats in the lower grandstand beyond first base. It was a special gift, from grandson to grandfather. Just like Tiger Stadium.

It had been 72 years since Ben Saperstein's first game in this ballpark: Tigers versus the '27 Yankees. He could still see that game in his mind's eye as vividly as he saw it then.

He pointed toward a spot in the left-field bleachers. That was where he and his big brother sat that day. Then he pointed again—toward the perfectly clipped grass in right field.

"And Babe," he said, "was right out there."

There used to be many parks in this land where a grandfather could utter those words to a grandson. With the passing of Tiger Stadium, however, there were only three—Fenway and Wrigley and Yankee Stadium.

Ty Cobb played baseball in these places. So did Walter Johnson. And Rogers Hornsby. And Jimmie Foxx. So you felt their presence when you walked through those gates.

"Every great player that ever played, just about, played in this stadium," former Tiger Darrell Evans told me on Tiger Stadium's final day. "So you always felt you'd better go out and not embarrass yourself, because you felt like those guys were sitting right next to you, saying, 'You'd better carry on that tradition.'"

And in baseball, that's exactly what these men do. They don't just play games. They pass on a great American tradition, from one generation to the next, to the next.

You don't notice that torch being passed. But then one day, that torch is flickering in front of your eyes, reminding you that what you just witnessed hadn't happened since April 23, 1936, when Goose Goslin did it.

Which is when you turn to your grandfather and ask: "Who was Goose Goslin?" And he knows everything about him worth knowing. Still.

Somehow, that explains why these places where baseball is played aren't mere stadiums. They're national historic landmarks.

They bring our memories back to life. They bring our grandfathers back to life. They connect these games and these players to the plot lines of our own lives.

Maybe that explains why we care so much. Why we care about these games. Why we care about these players. Why we care about these places where all they do is play baseball in front of our eyes.

But it absolutely explains why Aaron Scheible had no choice but to take his grandfather to Tiger Stadium on its final day in business. And Aaron Scheible knew exactly what he would say if anyone at school the next day asked him where he'd been.

TRIVIA ANSWER
Alex Rodriguez (344), Miguel Tejada (291), Ernie Banks (277), and Derek Jeter (251).

"I'll tell them," he said, "that I went to history class."

The Hall of Fame: Where Do We Go From Here?

The votes are in. The earth is still rumbling. Now let's try to digest the magnitude of what just happened—the shocking Hall of Fame election of 2013:

A man who hit 762 home runs wasn't elected to the Hall of Fame.

A pitcher who won seven Cy Young awards wasn't elected to the Hall of Fame.

A man who hit 609 home runs only got 12.5 percent of the vote.

A catcher who made 12 All-Star teams missed election by 98 votes.

Even a guy who got 3,060 hits found out on Election Day 2013 that he didn't do enough to be a first-ballot Hall of Famer.

It's enough to make you wonder: what kind of Hall of Fame are we building here?

In the wake of this stunning election, it's time for all of us to ponder that question. What is the Hall of Fame? What should it be? What is it supposed to be?

Do we really want to look up, 10 or 20 years from now, and find we've constructed a Hall of Fame that doesn't include:

- The all-time home run leader (Barry Bonds)?

- The pitcher who won the most Cy Youngs in history (Roger Clemens)?

- The man who broke Roger Maris' storied home run record (Mark McGwire)?

- The hitter who had more 60-homer seasons than any player ever (Sammy Sosa)?

- The greatest hitting catcher in history (Mike Piazza)?

- One of four hitters who ever lived with 3,000 hits and 500 home runs (Rafael Palmeiro)?

- And (aw, what the heck, might as well throw him in there) the all-time hit king (Peter Edward Rose)?

Let me ask you: what kind of Hall of Fame is that?

Do we really want a Hall of Fame that basically tries to pretend that none of those men ever played baseball? That none of that happened? Or that none of that should have happened?

Hey, here's a bulletin for you: it happened.

The '90s happened. The first few years of the 21st century happened. I saw it with my very own eyeballs. So did you.

It all happened, on the lush green fields of North America, as crowds roared and cash registers rung. It…all…happened.

And how did it happen? The sport let it happen. That's how.

Bud Selig let it happen. The union let it happen. The owners let it happen. The managers let it happen. The agents let it happen. The media let it happen. Front offices across the continent let it happen. And the players never stepped up to stop it from happening.

It…all…happened.

And no one in baseball has ever done anything, even after all these years, to make it un-happen, if you know what I mean. No records have ever been stripped. No championships have ever been stricken from anyone's permanent record. No numbers have been changed. No asterisks have ever been stamped in any record book.

It…all…happened.

So we need to have a long, serious national conversation, starting right now, about where those events fit into the contours of the Hall of Fame. I'm ready if you are.

Maybe we'll decide we want a Hall of Fame that renders all, or most, of that invisible. Maybe we'll decide we want a Hall of Fame that aspires to be a shrine, not just to greatness but to purity. I don't know how we get there, but maybe that's where this conversation will lead us.

But maybe we'll decide, once we think it all through, that's impossible. Maybe we'll recognize that what the Hall needs to be, in these complicated times, is a museum, and nothing more sainted or noble than that.

Maybe it needs to be a place that does what other great history museums do—tell the story of a time in history, for better and for worse, wherever it leads. Maybe that's not exactly what we would hope and dream a Hall of Fame should be. Maybe, though, that's what it has to be, because if we try traveling down that other road, we'll find nothing but forks and detours and roadblocks.

But once we have that conversation, at least we'll know how to vote and how to proceed and how to build a Hall of Fame for the 21st century.

If we decide it's a museum, then we need to put all of these men—the greatest players of their generation—in the Hall of Fame, and let the sport do what it should have done years ago: figure out some way to explain what happened back then.

There are many ways to do that. Put the good stuff *and* the bad stuff right there on the plaques. Erect informational signs that explain the context of that era—and every era in baseball history. Just be real and honest, and let the truth carry the weight of history in all its permutations.

But if that's not what we want, if we decide we want the Hall of Fame to be a holy place, where only the angels of baseball are allowed to reside, then we need to be prepared for what that means. For everything that means.

If it's a cathedral, not a museum, it means we're going to have to throw out Gaylord Perry. Sorry, Gaylord. And everyone who corked a bat or scuffed a ball or used an amphetamine. And anyone who was a notorious off-the-field scoundrel.

There's no place for them in this holy shrine. Is there? How can there be?

Then we'll also need to contemplate another powerful question: what happens if we elect a player one of these years and later find out that he, too, was a PED user?

Or here's a tougher question: what if we've already elected somebody like that?

I bet we have, to be honest. I know I'm not alone. When I had this conversation with one baseball official recently, he told me, with no hesitation, he thinks we probably have. Think what kind of mess it would cause if we ever find out who that is. Think of the ramifications.

If we decide, after our national conversation, we want the Hall to be a sanctuary, we would have no choice but to expel a player like that. Right? It's either holy or it's not. So if this is the route we settle upon, zero tolerance would be the only way to go.

On the other hand, if we decide this is a museum we're talking about, we could just rewrite his plaque. And let the truth do the talking.

I recognize that the Hall of Fame, as currently constituted, is both of these things. Part museum. Part shrine. I'm a fan of both wings. I think there's a place for both wings, one for historic events, moments, and artifacts, the other to shine the spotlight on the greatest players who ever wore a uniform.

But I'm also a voter. And when this year's ballot arrived, I was blown away by the impossibility of what I'm being asked to do.

I would love to be able to do what many of you are constantly asking us to do as voters: keep every "cheater" out of the Hall of Fame. Ladies and gentlemen, that can't be done. I apologize. But what you're asking is impossible. Literally.

What we know has been overwhelmed by the magnitude of all that we don't know. One player on this ballot (Palmeiro) tested positive and did his time. A second player (McGwire) admitted he took PEDs and said he wouldn't even vote for himself. And everyone else forces us to play the ultimate no-win guessing game.

Should I only single out players who showed up in Jose Canseco's book or on the BALCO witness list? Or should I be suspicious of anybody who ever grew a pimple? What's the standard of "proof" from an era where everyone just sat back and let history unfold? Could it possibly be any sketchier?

All I've ever wanted to be as a voter is consistent and fair. To every name on the ballot. Across the board. Well, there's only one way to do that, I think.

And that is to conclude, ultimately, that the Hall of Fame needs to live on as a museum. Where no one tries to apply a giant eraser to any period in history. Even this one.

Maybe you're with me. Maybe you're not. But we need to have that conversation. And we need to have it now.

And it shouldn't be just a conversation between media and fans. It should be a conversation that includes everyone. From Bud Selig to the folks who chisel the plaques in Cooperstown. And many thoughtful people in between.

If there's anything we've learned from the 2013 Hall of Fame election, it's that what we're doing now isn't working. You'd never know it from the balloting, but the '90s happened.

Now it's up to all of us to figure out what the Hall of Fame ought to do about it.

August, 2011

The Information Age

Once upon a time, it was all so simple. Pitchers pitched. Hitters hit. If the stars lined up, somebody with a glove caught what they hit. And that's how baseball games were decided.

Boy, how 1963 was that, huh?

But if you think that's how baseball games are decided nowadays, it's very possible you're still listening to music on a "record player." And running all over town trying to buy "film" for your camera. And looking up numbers in a "phone book."

Friends, we just don't live on that planet anymore.

And neither does the beautiful sport of baseball—no matter how unchanged it may look from afar on your old black-and-white TV "set."

Here, instead, is the planet we live on now:

It's a planet where Rays manager Joe Maddon flips open his iPad in a Starbucks, sips his morning cup of tea, and pores over the spray charts that dictate the funky shifts his team is about to unleash on David Ortiz that night.

It's a planet where Troy Tulowitzki can pedal away on his exercise bike while watching every pitch Tim Hudson has fired at him over the last five years.

It's a planet where it's now easier to find a video of every changeup Ricky Romero has ever thrown with two strikes and a runner on first than it is to find a light bulb at Home Depot.

It's a planet, in other words, that has been swallowed whole by technology, by data, by the sheer, massive, unstoppable onslaught of information.

And that Information Age hasn't just transformed baseball. It has practically revolutionized it—in less time than it takes Ronny Paulino to finish a home run trot.

"I think this is truly the second great renaissance in baseball," says Joe Maddon, a visionary kind of guy whose embrace of technology, info, and outside-the-box thinking has made him, for all intents and purposes, the Steve Jobs of managers.

The first great renaissance, Maddon says, arrived with Branch Rickey in the 1920s, '30s, and '40s, back when Rickey was pioneering the use of (gasp) farm systems and (shudder) statistics.

And the second great renaissance? That's been taking place, almost imperceptibly, over the last decade—but, to a greater degree, just over the last year or two or three. And looking back, it's not hard to figure out why.

Every once in a while in life, a bunch of powerful forces in the universe seem to converge on us at once. And all they do is change just about everything. Well, this is now, officially, one of those times. Think about it:

All of a sudden, you can watch every one of the 3 billion baseball games played this season—in your living room, on your tablet, even on your phone.

All of a sudden, while you were busy doing your laundry or drafting your fantasy team or something, the world was quietly being invaded by an army of sabermetric wizards, capable of computing Justin Verlander's road FIP against sub-.500 teams in games in which he throws more than 20 percent curveballs—and actually understanding the significance of that.

All of a sudden, thanks to those creative geniuses at Apple, the average big-league clubhouse now seems to house more iPads than batting gloves.

And all of a sudden, those clubhouses are being occupied by a new generation of technologically aware baseball citizens who are willing to use that stuff.

All of it.

Every second of every day.

So the impact of that renaissance is reverberating in more ways than most of us could possibly comprehend. But after working on this story for months, we've concluded there's one group of people in baseball that has felt that impact more than any other:

The hitters.

How? Well, we'd bet that if we polled all American baseball fans on why runs per game and batting average had dropped five seasons in a row between 2006 and 2011, 99 percent of them would answer "steroids"—or the lack thereof.

And you know what? They wouldn't be wrong. But there's another force at work that we now believe may have been nearly as powerful:

Information.

And even the hitters are starting to catch on. There was actually a time when they thought hitting came down to them against the pitcher. Now they're not so sure.

Nowadays, says that well-traveled batsmith, Jonny Gomes, "you can argue it's no longer mano a mano. It's no longer 'You Versus Him.'"

Really? So if it's not "You Versus Him" anymore, what the heck is it?

"You against the world," Gomes laughs. "That's how it seems, anyway."

Well, it seems that way for good reason, too—a reason we're about to spell out, as we examine The Information Age.

Here's the Pitch

In the beginning, you didn't need a PhD from M.I.T. to understand the art of pitch selection.

If you had a good fastball, you threw it. And if there was a big strong dude 60 feet away who could hit it, more power to him.

Boy, what a dumb concept that was.

Want to get a feel for what pitch selection involves nowadays? Listen to how Brian Jones, video coordinator for the Rockies, describes it. You won't believe we're even talking about the same sport.

Say you're a pitching coach or a catcher, and you've got a right-handed pitcher starting tonight against the Astros. You get out your iPad, tap your favorite app, and type out, say, "Carlos Lee." Here's how it would go from there:

"You have all these boxes you can change," Jones says. "Say you want to look at all right-handed pitchers versus Carlos Lee. It will pull up a strike zone and a guy standing there, and it will show you, like, every pitch. Then you can break it down by date. You can change the date range, and it will give you his stats, the pitches thrown, swing-and-miss percentage, everything you can think of, for those dates.

"Then," Jones goes on, "you could change it to where you say, 'I want to see all pitches low and away.' And it will change every piece of data [to] every pitch low and away. You can draw a custom area you want to pick on that strike zone, or out of the strike zone, and see all the pitches in those locations. Then, once you draw that, it shows you the data, all his stats and numbers, for that area you've selected, on that type of pitch.

"Then you can change it to runners in scoring position, ahead in the count, behind in the count, two strikes, seventh to ninth inning, anything you can think of. Any situation that you want to break down is readily available to see."

But you think it stops there? Ohhhhh, no. All those stats are synced to a video database of every one of those pitches.

So if you want to see how Carlos Lee reacted to every slider, low and away, that a right-hander had thrown him in a 1-2 count since 2006, that's now possible. You don't just have to read about it. Tap the screen on your iPad and watch it.

And if you don't think seeing all those pitches gives a pitcher a whole different sense of trust in a pitch than reading a scouting report or a computer printout, we can only respond: are you kidding?

"Now, you can watch for as long as you want, watching a guy swing and miss at a certain pitch," says Derek Lowe, who, at the time we spoke with him, was one of just five active starting pitchers left whose career began in 1997 or earlier. "So now, when you get ready to throw that pitch in a game, you have that mental image of watching a certain guy swing and miss at a slider 20 times. It gives you an added boost of confidence, like, hey, if I throw this guy this pitch, I *know* he can't hit it—because I just watched it for like 15 straight minutes on the video."

Down for the Count

In the beginning (or since 1889, at least), four balls equaled a walk. But three balls once equaled something else:

A fastball down the middle.

So for more than a century, hitters had faith that if they were patient, if they got ahead in the count, there was supposed to be a reward in it. They were supposed to get a hittable fastball out of the deal. And for all those years, they mostly did.

Boy, whatever happened to those days anyhow?

"Watch how many fastball counts where guys don't throw fastballs," says the Phillies' Ryan Howard. "I've had this conversation with a bunch of guys. I had it with Mark Teixeira like maybe a year or two ago, where we were just saying there's no such thing as a fastball count anymore."

OK, so that's not totally true. But the data conclusively shows fewer fastballs are being thrown in "fastball counts" than at any point in recorded pitch-tracking history.

We asked our friends at Inside Edge to study 1-0, 2-0, 2-1, 3-0, and 3-1 counts over a 10-year period. They found that the percentage of fastballs being thrown had been steadily shrinking for all of those counts, except 3-0.

And what's really fascinating is how much that rate has dropped just in the two years between 2009 and 2011. For example:

	2009	2011
ALL HITTERS' COUNTS	74.5 %	72.1 %
1-0	69.5%	67.3 %
2-0	82.1 %	79.7 %
2-1	69.1 %	66.79 %
3-1	85.8 %	83.5 %

OK, so that's still a lot of fastballs. But remember, a decline of 2 to 3 percent represents many, many pitches, just in those counts, over the course of a season. And even this data, says Inside Edge's Kenny Kendrena, is slightly misleading—because it includes "cutters" as fastballs, since Inside Edge only recently began classifying cut fastballs as a separate pitch type. So the actual percentage of true fastballs is far lower.

"You even get to a 3-2 count now, sometimes it's a crap shoot," Howard says. "You don't know what's coming."

Well, if Howard in particular has that feeling, the data shows us exactly why: by 2011, he was seeing fewer fastballs in "fastball counts" (55.0 percent) than any hitter in either league. And that percent had been plummeting precipitously, from 77.8 when he first reached the big leagues in September of 2004, to 64.7 percent in his Rookie of the Year season in 2005, to the 50s shortly thereafter. Some fun.

But if off-speed misery loves company, Howard should know he has plenty of it. Inside Edge told us eight different hitters were seeing fewer than 60 percent fastballs in "fastball counts" in 2011, among hitters with at least 100 pitches in those counts:

Howard	55.0
Prince Fielder	55.1
Matt Kemp	56.2
Alfonso Soriano	57.7
Jose Bautista	58.2
Laynce Nix	59.4
Brian McCann	59.4
David Ortiz	59.8

Three guys on that list—Fielder, Kemp, and Ortiz—had seen a major fluctuation in how they were approached just between 2010 and 2011. Fielder was seeing 65.1 percent fastballs in those spots in 2010. Kemp was getting 66.5 percent. Ortiz was at 68.9.

But welcome to the wonderful world of technology. As soon as the data shows that feeding those men fastballs in those spots can be hazardous to your ERA, the league adjusts—immediately. So when people start talking about the Age of the Pitcher, no wonder the first thing many hitters think is: *There's no such thing as a "fastball count" anymore.*

"Guys who have control are throwing those [off-speed] pitches for strikes in just about whatever count they want to throw it," Howard says. "So I think that definitely plays a huge part in it."

Hitting the Shift Key

In the beginning, Joe Maddon had his magic markers. And he had his charts. And that's how he helped the Angels position defenses back in the "olden" days, when he was still a bench coach in Anaheim.

Of course, those "olden" days were, like, a decade ago. But in retrospect, the info back then looks like ancient stone-tablet etchings compared with what he's using these days to devise defenses so innovative, they'd make John McGraw's brain explode.

"When we first began, it was very primitive," Maddon says. "All it really was, defensively, was a bunch of lines…where you kept track of where hitters hit the ball against you in the past, against your pitchers."

The amazing thing, though, was that, in those days, even aligning defenses like that felt practically scientific. But nowadays, there's not much difference between the way most baseball teams set defenses and the way Dick Lebeau does it in the Steelers' war room.

Thanks to companies like Baseball Info Solutions, all 30 teams know exactly where every hitter in baseball tends to hit the ball. So when you look out at the field and see third basemen practically playing up the middle, shortstops on the other side of second base, and second basemen set up on the outfield grass, 75 feet beyond the infield dirt, that's not guesswork, ladies and gentlemen.

That's the Information Age at work in modern baseball.

"Everybody wants to be aggressive," Maddon says. "They want aggressive pitchers. And they want aggressive offense. And they want aggressive base running. I want aggressive defense. I mean, if there's any kind of football tenet that I want to draw, I want us to be aggressive on defense, too, and force some issues there. And at the end of the day, when I talk to our guys, we preach: catch line drives.

"Now who are the better hitters? The better hitters are the guys who hit the ball hard. So if they hit the ball hard, you need to be closer to the spot where they hit the ball hard most often. And if they happen to mis-hit it, we're athletic enough to go catch it. So that's what this is all about—trying to get to the spot where the better hitters hit the ball hard most often."

It's no surprise, then, that, according to Baseball Info Solutions, no team in baseball applied more unorthodox shifts in 2011 than the Rays. But they're not alone. Over in the National League, the Brewers had already begun shifting on a handful of *right-handed* hitters. In a related development, their manager, Ron Roenicke, spent years coaching with Maddon in Anaheim.

"Joe and I used to talk about this a lot when we coached together," Roenicke says, "about how we're putting fielders in places where some guys never hit the ball. So it's about putting fielders in other places. There are times you're going to get burned. But if you look at it over the course of the year, how many hits you might save, that's what you consider before you do it."

Hang on, though. There's more to this than that. The data on the computer, and the video that goes with it, have gotten so precise that teams also know now which pitch is most likely to get a hitter to hit a ball to a certain spot. Here's how easy that is:

"You look at the spray chart on the computer screen and draw a square with your mouse on that area [of the field] you want to see," says Brian Jones. "And whatever balls went through that square, I can see what types of pitchers those were…It's like a virtual video spray chart. So your infielders and your pitchers, everyone's in sync."

Now imagine being a hitter, marching up there in a critical spot. He isn't just dealing with special defenses aligned only for him. He's also coping with pitch selection designed to work specifically with those defenses. It's incredible anybody ever gets a hit.

"It's like if you're playing football and you're playing Army," Jones says. "You're not going to run five defensive backs out there if they're going to run the option on you all game. It's similar to that. Why am I going to put four safeties on the left side if there are only going to be two receivers? The answer is: you don't."

An Apple a Day

In the beginning, there were tapes. Big, clunky VHS tapes that had to be loaded into bigger, clunkier VCRs. And that's how players watched video once upon a time.

Eventually, a few of the more advanced teams started editing those tapes to produce custom DVDs for a few technologically savvy players. And as the years rolled along, more and more players started lugging around laptops so they could crank up that video from airplane seats and hotel rooms.

Then came the iPod, an invention that made it possible for players to watch every episode of *Lost* and every pitch against the Blue Jays with just about the same ease. But the screens were smaller than Joe West's strike zone.

And loading that video onto each iPod presented major, time-consuming technological challenges. So even the iPod had its limits.

So for years now, teams have been using video in some form or other. But it was the year 2010—drum roll, please—that life in the video room, as we used to know it, changed forever.

All because of the iPad.

"Now," says longtime reliever Jason Isringhausen, "guys are carrying all the information in the palm of their hand. It used to be on tapes this big."

He spreads his hands about three feet apart. And we both know those tapes weren't that big (although the VCRs were). But you get the idea.

Thanks to the iPad, "you don't ever see guys reading magazines anymore," says Brian Jones. "It's more guys on their iPads. It's become part of the baseball uniform almost."

When you look around a baseball clubhouse these days, everybody is fiddling with an iPad. We'll never know for sure how many of them are breaking down video and how many of them are playing Angry Birds. But the iPad hasn't just given them all a new toy. It's also a symbol—of the mind-set of the modern player.

"The game has gotten younger," Jones says. "So the pitchers now grew up with more technology in their life. Before, guys didn't know how to use it that much. And you've still got coaches who can't even check their email without help.

"Now we've got 22-year-old kids who have barely even known a life without iPods. They probably barely even know what a CD is. So their adaptation to technology, and not being scared of it, has allowed them to use this information more freely and easily."

At the same time, the technological revolution has brought us apps and innovations that make it possible to load astounding amounts of video onto one iPad, link it to massive quantities of useful data, sort it a trillion different ways, and allow these guys to find just about anything they need—with one tap of their screen.

So Derek Lowe tells a story about visiting the weight room on a trip to Colorado—and finding Troy Tulowitzki watching a video on his iPad while he was working out.

And Phillies catcher Brian Schneider tells a tale about leaning back in bed the night before he catches, making a quick run-through of the next day's lineup, and letting his brain sift through it all overnight.

And Joe Maddon reports he wakes up every morning, heads for Starbucks, opens his iPad, finds an email packed with everything he needs to know to reinvent that night's strategizing, and starts plotting out his game plan between sips of tea.

"It's just come so far," Jones says. "Back when we were [loading video] on the iPod, we'd say, 'Man, it would be nice if this was just a little bigger.' Now the iPad has just kind of changed everything. We don't have to have these guys come into our video room, to look at the computers. The iPad is with them wherever they go. You see guys in the elevator at the hotel, and they're carrying nothing but their iPads. It's kind of become the new wallet."

Time to Burn "The Book"

In the beginning, we're pretty sure, there was still information. It just got absorbed—and passed along—pretty much the same way the cave men did it. Via eyeballs. And mouths. How could that possibly have gotten anybody anywhere?

"When I first started," says Derek Lowe, "it was kind of your own eyes. You had to talk more to the guy who pitched before you or the catcher, or try to use that type of knowledge. I think you had to watch the game more. Now, it's just endless. And sometimes, there's so much [info] available now that if you don't use it wisely, I think it can become a negative."

Well, he's right about that—to a point. If you don't know what you're looking for, or you don't pay attention, the Information Age can't possibly work for you, except by accident.

But in the big picture, all those skeptics who think the effect of all this information on the modern game is overblown need to seriously adjust their rabbit ears.

If used intelligently, this is info that works. Period.

If you put enough fielders in spots where hitters most often hit the ball, more balls get caught. And if you throw enough quality pitches, in unpredictable sequences, in places where those same hitters have the least success, fewer balls get hit hard.

So mull this over again. If used intelligently, is there any argument that the way this info is being applied "can become a negative?"

Let's go back to Ryan Howard. In 2006, he batted .313/.425/.659/1.084. But as the data flooded in—showing which pitches he hits, which pitches he scuffles against, and where he repeatedly hits the ball—guess what happened?

By 2011, he was seeing fewer fastballs than any hitter in the game. He also was seeing fewer fastballs in "fastball counts" than any hitter in the game. And only a half-dozen players in the sport were forced to hit against as many shifts as he sees.

So what effect has all that had on him? His 2011 numbers, before he blew out his Achilles: .253/.346/.488/.835. That in itself tells a big part of the story. But there's more. His batting average on ground balls and short line drives in 2010–11 was just .197 against The Shift, but .278 when he saw no shift. And one year, when the Phillies kept track for a whole season, they computed that he lost 35 to 40 legitimate hits because of The Shift alone.

So what's the evidence this information doesn't work again?

Makes you wonder why more teams don't devise defenses the way the Rays do. They employ so many unique shifts on so many hitters that 120 more balls in play were hit into one of their shifts over the 2010–11 seasons than any other team in baseball, according to Baseball Info Solutions.

Think it's some kind of fluke that they were also "saving" many more runs than any other team in baseball? They finished with 85 runs saved in 2011, Baseball Info Solutions reports. The next-closest team, the Diamondbacks, were at 54.

So why aren't more teams approaching defense the way the Rays approach it? Because some of them are still stuck in a time warp. That's why.

"You have to be willing to use the information," Maddon says. "There's active and passive information. I know there are other teams that are getting a lot of good stuff. But then, are you able to utilize it during a game? Are you willing to utilize it during a game, or even prior to the game?

"I think there are so many old-school tendencies or advocates that are unwilling to go in this direction that at the end of the day, I don't even think they know why they're really unwilling to do this...Quite frankly I don't know why every team wouldn't want to do it, because the information's there.

"I guess," he says, "it just depends on organizational philosophy. Are you comfortable with the haphazard, 'I-think-this-is-going-to-work' approach, or the 'this-is-what-happened-in-1987-and-it-worked-then' approach? If you are, that's fine."

But if you are, you're a member of a species that's on the verge of becoming as extinct as the Whooping Crane. And if you're still strictly managing by The Book, because that's how Connie Mack did it, we now know conclusively you're using the wrong book.

"I think The Book is something that should be read and can be read," Maddon says, "but not to be taken literally to the point that it had been for so many years. I mean, after all, The Book was handed down pretty much word-of-mouth...But as with most things that are handed down word-of-mouth, a lot of things are normally lost in the translation. And furthermore, when that word of mouth was created, whatever year that was, all this stuff was not available."

But it's available now, all right—eminently available—to every team in the game. And more of them are using it extensively than at any point in baseball time.

The teams using it best understand there are still human beings involved here. So "you can't be a slave to the data," says Reds pitching coach Bryan Price. And "you can't overdo it," he says. And above all, he knows, you're still at the mercy of how players use what they've learned. A bad pitch is still a bad pitch—and the iPad didn't throw it.

"But you can live with a good plan that's not executed," Price says. "It's a lot harder to have a bad plan, or no plan. And one thing about all the information that's out there now: There's no way anyone is going out there with no plan."

And that, friends, is disastrous news for the hitters.

There are always going to be great hitters who rise above all those devious plots to stop them. There are always going to be athletes so talented that there's no safe way to pitch them or defend them.

But for the rest of the species, the Information Age is the worst thing to happen to hitters since steroid testing.

"If a pitcher can execute what he's trying to do with a hitter," says Brian Jones, "and he has all this information about him, of where he struggles—broken down on paper and on video—I feel sorry for the hitter sometimes.

"If your strength matches their weakness and you can execute, the hitter virtually has no chance."

And unfortunately for hitters everywhere, he has The Information to prove it.

The Age of the Pitcher

Once, there was a time when a 73-homer man roamed this earth.

And seven different teams scored 900 runs—in the same season.

And two pitchers led their league in Earned Run Average with ERAs north of 3.00—for the first time in modern history.

Boy, how long ago does all that seem, huh? The game of baseball is so different now, it feels like those days—the Age of Offensive Insanity—happened, what, 75 years ago?

But we're not talking about life in the 1930s, friends. We're talking about real-life occurrences in this sport just since the year 2000.

So how has this sport changed since then? Heh-heh-heh-heh. You really want to know? You really want to know why we now look at this era as The Age of the Pitcher? All right, let's spell it out for you:

- Want to guess how many fewer runs were scored in the 2012 season than were scored in the 2000 season? How about nearly 4,000. Right. We said four thousand runs.

- Want to guess how many fewer home runs were hit in 2012 than were hit in 2000? How about almost 800. Yessir, eight hundred.

- Back in that 2000 season, there were 571 times when a team scored at least 10 runs in a game. By 2012, that number had dropped to a mere 280—a plummet of about 51 percent.

- And as recently as 2011, Matt Kemp led the National League in home runs with 39. Back in 2001, you might recall, Barry Bonds also hit 39 home runs—before the All-Star break.

So have we established yet that the art of hitting ain't what it used to be? We're pretty sure we have—and we don't even need to wait for a verdict from the Roger Clemens jury.

But that just tells us what *has* happened. What we set out to do, during two months of reporting on this piece, was to figure out how and why it happened. How exactly did this turn into the Age of the Pitcher? And can we be sure this is really the Age of the Pitcher, and not merely the Age of No Offense? It's time to examine all of that.

The Test Pattern

OK, let's get this issue out of the way right off the top. If there's anything we've learned in recent years, it's that it isn't only good pitching that shuts down good hitting.

It's also the power of the test tube.

It was in 2005 that punishments for a positive Performance Enhancing Drug test finally kicked in, with 10-day suspensions for a first offense. In 2006, those suspensions increased to 50 games. That was also the year baseball started testing for amphetamines. A year after that, in 2007, Bud Selig told George Mitchell to start digging away, to compile the Mitchell Report. Well, guess what happened?

Hitting hasn't been the same since. What a coincidence.

Run totals have dropped in every season from 2006 through 2011. Home runs have dropped in every season but one (2009) in that span. And we've seen a massive plummet in homers of 450 feet or more, from 144 in 2006 to just 93 in 2012. Is anyone surprised by any of this?

End of Steroid Era = End of Age of Offensive Insanity. Well, whaddaya know?

It was tough finding anyone inside the industry who wanted to say, right out loud and on the record, that subtracting steroids from the fabric of the sport is the overriding reason everything has changed in the last five or six years. But off the record, almost nobody tries to pretend otherwise.

At one point, we were talking to a major league manager for this story.

We ran several powerful theories by him on why pitching now rules the sport. He agreed with all of them. But finally, he couldn't help himself.

"What about steroids?" he interrupted. "You're not gonna ask me about them?"

Heck, did we even have to? But it isn't just steroid testing that has transformed baseball. Without amphetamines, position players these days are wondering, by the Fourth of July, whether they're going to have the strength to make it through the season.

"You can definitely see it in the second half," says one NL executive. "These guys are cooked. They're OK through June. But then the weather starts to get hot, they've played 80 to 90 games, and then the grind, the travel, the schedule starts to get to them."

But as players often point out, it wasn't only the hitters who were juicing or popping greenies. Just check out how many pitchers have been suspended for PED use since 2005. Clearly, there's more going on here than just chemistry. So read on.

Fun with the Gun

We hear this from hitters all the time: pitchers throw harder now. Much harder. And not just some of them. Practically all of them—other than maybe R.A. Dickey.

So we set out to determine: is that true?

We started by consulting with our friends from Inside Edge, who have charted virtually every pitch in the big leagues since 2005. They verified that average fastball velocity has been rising steadily, from 90.2 miles per hour in 2005 to 91.2 mph by 2012. And that's a more eye-opening number than it might appear on the surface—considering that more than 600 men took the mound in a major league game during the 2011 season.

We also looked at FanGraphs' rankings of all pitchers' average fastball velocities to see if the number of guys who chuck it up there at 95 mph or above has been on the rise. Take a look at this trend among pitchers who worked at least 30 innings in a season:

PITCHERS WITH AVG. FB VELOCITY OF 95+	
2007	11
2008	16
2009	24
2010	29
2011	35

Think about that for a moment. Can that really be true—that the number of smokeballers blowing 95 mph and up *tripled* in five years? Even other pitchers have a hard time comprehending that phenomenon.

"I've never seen as many hard throwers on every single team as I do now," says Derek Lowe. "It seems like every team has three or four guys coming out of that bullpen throwing 95 miles an hour."

But this word of caution: we can't be totally sure if those numbers are accurate. They might tell us more about how we measure velocity now than about the pitchers we're measuring. So we went about this another way: we asked scouting directors what they see when they show up at high school and college games.

"When I first started doing this 25 years ago, if you saw a kid touch 90 [mph] at 17 years old, you were like, 'Oh my god,'" says the Indians' vice president of scouting operations, John Mirabelli. "That guy became an automatic prospect. Now, just about every guy [on a scouting director's radar] throws 90—and most of them throw 92…You never saw amateur guys throwing in the upper 90s. Now you see it all the time. It's unbelievable."

Other scouting directors spun the same tales, over and over. And that tells us something: this is not a mirage.

So where is that velocity coming from? The theories go like this:

1. More long-tossing to build up arm strength.

2. More and more kids seeking out personal pitching coaches, most of whom once played professional baseball, who are passing along advancements in throwing programs and better mechanics.

3. An explosion in the use of personal trainers, even by teenagers.

4. Less abuse of young arms by coaches, thanks to new rules, pitch counts, and workload limits.

And then there's this: kids are now obsessed with velocity, because it's all we ever seem to talk about: How hard Justin Verlander throws…how hard Aroldis Chapman heaves it…how hard *every* pitch in a big-league game travels. It's right there, in the corner of every flat screen in America—and anywhere else kids look, for that matter.

"It's fun to throw hard," says Eddie Bane, the Angels' former scouting director. "Every minor league ballpark you go to has a radar gun. If you throw hard, it's a statement. It's the one thing no one can take away from you—how hard the gun says you throw. Kids read about that stuff, and they grow up wanting to throw hard."

Well, whatever it is that's going on, it's going on everywhere from Yankee Stadium to high school fields in North Dakota. And the bottom line is this: it's a big, big reason it's now harder to hit than ever.

Cutters, Splits, and Gyroballs

But there's another fascinating trend at work among men who pitch for a living: They throw their fastballs harder than ever…but they also throw their fastball less often than ever.

Or less often than at any time since Inside Edge began recording this data, anyway.

In 2005, major league pitchers threw their fastball 63.8 percent of the time. But by midway through the 2012 season, only 61.4 percent of all pitches thrown were fastballs. And don't be fooled by a drop of "only" 2.4 percent. That's a big difference. It comes to more than 6,000 fewer fastballs that hitters now see over the course of a season. Yep, *six thousand*.

So no wonder hitters think that pitchers are throwing more different pitches than ever. Those pitchers now have 6,000 more opportunities a year to mix in every off-speed pitch in their repertoire.

"It used to be," says Phillies catcher Brian Schneider, "that you'd say, 'What's this guy [throw]?' And it would be like, 'fastball-curveball, fastball-slider, fastball-change.' Now you see cutters all over the place. You see the two-seam comebacker.

It might be inside to a lefty and back-door to a righty. So you've got pitchers throwing cutters to both sides of the plate, throwing splits to both sides. It just seems like everyone you face has all these pitches. It never used to be like that."

There isn't enough data that goes back more than a couple of years to prove that, in fact, pitchers do throw more different pitches than they used to. But we do know this: they utilize the tools they do have in their tool box in more innovative ways than at any time in most people's memories.

"I just think pitchers are equipped more," says the pitching coach for Schneider's own staff in Philadelphia, Rich Dubee. "They do different stuff with the pitches they have…I think it's because the strike zone shrunk. You didn't have the high strike. You didn't have the width [off the corners] of the plate. And I think because of that guys became more creative."

So pitchers now throw their changeups to right-handed *and* left-handed hitters instead of just one side or the other. They throw a potpourri of breaking balls to every quadrant of the strike zone. They've gotten "more educated," says Marlins catcher John Buck, "about how they hold the baseball and what that grip can make the baseball do."

And the upshot is, the hitter has less and less idea of what's coming. In any count. No matter who's on the mound. Every pitcher on a staff now features an almost unprecedented variety of ways to go at them—"from the front of your staff," says Buck, "to the back of your staff."

There appears to be a definite rise in sidearming bullpen specialists—both left-handed and, in the last couple of years, right-handed. That's a species Red Sox hitting coach Dave Magadan calls "the cross-fire guys—the guys who step here [exaggerated step toward foul line] and then throw over here [steps back and fires sidearm across his body]." Never fun to hit against.

Use of the sweeping, swing-and-miss curveball is also way up—from 8.0 percent in 2005 to 9.8 percent in 2012. And Inside Edge has verified a definite upswing in the pitch that hitters complain about most—the cutter. Just since 2009, when Inside Edge first started tracking cut fastballs, they've grown from 2.8 percent of all pitches thrown to 3.8 percent. That means more than 10,000 cutters are now being delivered every year.

"It seems like everybody throws a cutter now," says veteran utility man Adam Kennedy. "And the pitchers who can [throw] that same pitch, off the same plane [as their fastball], they're the ones that can really excel with that. It's very hard to read when it comes out of the hand. And the more pitches that come out of the hand at the same plane that do different things, obviously, that's where it gets really difficult."

Information, Please

Incredibly, we haven't even touched yet on the single most revolutionary change in the entire sport over the last few years. It isn't testing. It isn't the cutter. It isn't even that technological gift from the heavens that lets us watch live baseball games on our phones. Nope, it's something way more powerful than all of that.

It's the Information Age. And it's wreaking havoc with the lives, the batting averages, and the psyches of hitters everywhere.

We've already written a detailed look at the explosion of information in modern baseball and how it's changed the game. So if you want to bask in the full panorama of that phenomenon, you can find that right here in this very book. See how we aim to please around here? But we can sum up that opus this way:

The hitters are doomed.

Why? Because, before they even step into the batter's box, the pitcher they're facing, the catcher calling pitches, and the coaches who have sifted through the onslaught of information know *everything* about them:

Exactly where their holes are…exactly which pitches they swing and miss at…exactly where they tend to hit the ball…and exactly how to make their lives miserable.

And now, the scouts, stats wizards, and coaches don't even have to hold a meeting anymore to relay all that info. It's all been plugged, nearly instantly, into the pitchers' and catchers' iPads. So they've seen, with their own eyes, exactly what's happened the last 100 times somebody threw a two-strike cutter to, say, Alfonso Soriano. Scary.

In other words, the selection of pitches that pitchers employ to attack hitters these days is no longer guesswork. It's science. And it's lethal.

"Just like Peyton Manning goes to the line of scrimmage, reads the defense, and calls the right play, you have that same interaction between the pitcher and the hitter," says Padres GM Josh Byrnes, one of the first people in baseball to use video scouting, back when he worked for the Indians in the mid-1990s.

"It's the one part of the game where you have total control," Byrnes says. You control where you want to throw every pitch of the game. If you have a good plan, and you have a pitcher who can execute the plan, it works."

But wait. You have to be thinking: Don't the hitters have the same kind of info on all the pitchers they face? And the answer is: Of course, they do. But…

"If you're a pitcher, you see an immediate result," says Magadan. "You know a guy's got a hole. So you hit that spot, you expose the hole, and you get an out. But if you're a hitter and you know the hole, you can get all the information you want. But it takes hours and hours of working on it, and hitting off the tee, and doing soft-toss, and gradually working your way to where either you lay off the pitch or you find out how to hit it. And if it's a pitch in the strike zone, you'd better find out how to hit it, or you're going to have a short career. So to me, the pitcher has a big advantage there."

But even if that pitcher gets behind and lays one in there, he still has the upper hand—because the defense will probably be deployed in some new-fangled, data-driven shift that stations a man with a glove right where the hitter is most likely to hit the ball.

And if all that doesn't cause every hitter alive to call his therapist, how about this: some of these shifts have more to do with mind games than baseball strategy.

"We have percentages that we work by regarding shifting," says Rays shift-maestro/manager Joe Maddon. "But then, sometimes, we'll just do it because I want to make the hitter think of something else. You almost want to try to force the way they think by what you do. And whenever you [mess] with someone else's athletic mind, a lot of the time that can play on your side. So all this stuff is calculated."

Oh, it's calculated, all right. It's all calculated into baseball's grand, modern-day conspiracy—against the hitters.

Is it the Pitching or the Hitting?

So now that we've explored the many, many levels behind the rise of the pitcher, we still haven't answered the biggest question of all:

Is this the Age of the Pitcher—or simply the Age of No Offense?

Well, we've thought about this for a long time. We've examined the numbers. We've talked about it with a million people. And, with all due respect to the pitching population of this great land, we think this is more about the decline of the poor, overmatched, PED-free hitter than it is about the most dominating pitching era since the '60s.

Have you checked the stat page lately? The Mariners hit .234 in 2012—the third-worst team average by an AL team in the DH era (and the second-worst, behind only the 2011 Mariners, if you don't count strike years).

Seven teams had an on-base percentage of .310 or lower in 2012—which is one more than the number that did that in the 11 seasons from 1999 to 2009 put together.

And three different lineups had team batting averages of .238 or lower—as many as in the previous 19 seasons *combined*.

"Look at the lineups you see now," says former Blue Jays GM J.P. Ricciardi, currently a special assistant to Mets GM Sandy Alderson. "Look at the National League lineups. Is there any lineup anymore that makes you say, 'Oh my god?'"

"It's hard to find offense," says Byrnes. "We just went through a draft, and let me tell you: it's hard to find guys you know can hit."

We've already laid out what's happened to hitters in the big leagues. But why is it even so hard to find young hitters—the brilliance of Bryce Harper and Mike Trout notwithstanding? Excellent question.

"It's just like society," says the Phillies' assistant GM for amateur scouting, Marti Wolever. "This is a game of failure, and that plays on the frustration level of kids. It takes a lot of time and work to perfect a swing. And I don't know if a lot of kids want to take the time to do that in the society we live in."

But these days, from all the evidence we've assembled, it appears that even many of the guys who can hit—or, at least, used to be able to hit—are now playing right into the pitchers' hands.

Both Mattingly and his general manager, Ned Colletti, have virtually the same theory: the game has changed—but the hitters haven't.

Even as the home run rate spirals ever downward, Mattingly sees hitters who hit as if they hadn't noticed. They coil. They guess. And they let it fly—as if routine fly balls were still traveling 440 feet. And all they get out of it is a lot of outs—and strikeouts.

"Guys have gotten away from the good solid hitting mechanics of the past," the Dodgers manager says. "It used to be that if you struck out 100 times, it was a big deal. Now if it's 'just' 100, you're kind of a low strikeout guy. That tells me mechanics are getting worse."

"How many times," asks Colletti, "do you see a key situation in a game, and a reliever comes in, and the first pitch is a changeup, and the hitter is way out in front of it, because all he's thinking is, *I'm going to get a fastball. How hard can I hit it?* Guys pitch different in this era. Pitchers think different in this era. But it's almost like the hitter's still thinking like it's the old era. He's swinging from a different era than the pitcher's mind-set."

Excellent theories—and the data proves that both of them are dead on. Maybe most offensive numbers are dropping, but not strikeouts. In 2012, believe it or not, there were nearly 6,000 more of them than in 2005. Right, *six thousand.*

And the numbers clearly show that while the percentage of fastballs thrown is declining—as are fastballs thrown in what used to be "fastball counts"—hitters are swinging and missing at the fastballs they do see at a higher rate than ever.

So the hitters aren't just losing the war of numbers these days. They're getting massively outmaneuvered in the never-ending baseball chess match. And they know it. They feel it. Many of them aren't even sure what to do about it.

"I just think the game of pitching has evolved more than the game of hitting," says Brian Schneider. "I mean, how much more can the game of hitting evolve? Pitchers can add different pitches. But as a hitter, you can't add different swings."

"I would like to think that, just like in life, it's a circle, and we'll figure out something," says Adam Kennedy. "Maybe they'll run out of quality arms for a while. I don't know. It makes for a lot of sleepless nights, rolling around restless. But it's just part of the fun. It makes that bloop hit just that much more special."

You'd think, listening to that kind of talk, that the hitters are resigned to their fate. But up in the front office, the folks trying to put together teams still ask: why?

"You know, guys can still hit," says Colletti. "It's not like 1968, when Carl Yastrzemski was winning the batting title, hitting .301. We've still got guys hitting in the .350s. So it can be done. It's all about how you approach your at-bat. If you're not a home run hitter, don't try to be."

"For this to change," Don Mattingly concurs, "the hitters are just going to have to get better. The pitcher always has the advantage. He knows where he's going to throw it. And the defense is going to be better than before, because of all the shifts they play. So you're going to have to be better to hit .330 or .340 than you were 10 years ago."

That means the hitters are going to have to be as prepared as the pitchers and catchers they face. It means learning how to foil the shifts by going the other way. It means understanding there's no such thing as a "fastball count" anymore. It means checking their own data, to learn their holes, and putting in the work it takes to close them.

And it means understanding that the Steroid Era is over—and those 4,000 runs and 800 home runs that have disappeared since 2000 aren't coming back.

That's the world we live in now. It ebbs. It flows. It evolves. It always has. It always will. For a decade, it flowed in the direction of the monster mashers at home plate. It's now ebbed way back in the other direction, to the men who throw the pitches.

But does that mean we're stuck forever in the Age of the Pitcher? We're not so sure. And we're not alone.

"I don't know if it's the Age of the Pitcher. I just think it's the Age of Baseball," says Marti Wolever. "It's the age of where the game used to be. I think we've come full circle. We stepped outside that circle for a long time, in a lot of ways. But it wasn't reality.

"So now," he says, "we're back to reality. And that's a good thing."

The Stuff Winners Are Made Of

AUTHOR'S NOTE: I've always been fascinated by the qualities that separate champions from everyone else, winners from everyone else, superstars from everyone else. On the eve of the 2010 baseball season, my never-ending quest to define those qualities inspired me to write this column, about a group of men who've got "it"—and what makes them tick.

He's a man defined by the rings he's won in October. But the quality that *really* separates Derek Jeter from the masses is the unstoppable force that drives him from April to September.

We know it as energy. But it's more. Or focus. But it's more. Relentless concentration. But it's more. What Derek Jeter really has is an ignition with no "off" switch.

It's there in his first at-bat on opening day. It's there in the ninth inning of Game 162. And it's always pumping—every day, every inning, every pitch in between.

It's the stuff winners are made of. Some men have it. Many don't. Some teams get it. Many don't. And as we stand at the precipice of another baseball season, we can guarantee you this:

It *will* show up over the endless baseball marathon ahead. It *will* in time separate the teams that win from the teams that don't. In a season where you can make a case for why 22 teams can make the playoffs, it *will* be baseball's great divider once again.

If you can't play baseball with never-ending energy and focus every day of this long, relentless, exhausting season, you *will* be exposed. Happens every year. And it *will* again in 2010. And in all those seasons to come.

"When people ask me what separates the good players from the great players, that's it," says the Yankees' Andy Pettitte, a man who has played with six MVPs, six Cy Youngs, and five World Series MVPs. "And that's what makes this team so good. I can't believe the intensity our position players bring to the ballpark every day."

He ticks off the names of the legendary, turbo-driven Yankees he has played with, from Paul O'Neill to Jorge Posada, from Tino Martinez to (yes) Alex Rodriguez. But after listing all those names, Pettitte says:

"Derek is the best. I can honestly say I've never seen him give away an at-bat. Never. Not any."

We have words for the quality he's talking about: *Intensity. Hustle. Energy. Passion.* But none of those words quite define what this is about.

Anybody can crank it up for a day. But baseball is a game you play *every* day. So to play with energy every day, to maintain concentration every inning, to hustle on every play requires a level of excellence, commitment, and competitive inferno that most human beings can't even comprehend, let alone reach.

Derek Jeter isn't the only player in baseball who rises to that level, of course. He's just the poster boy. So to try to paint this picture, we spoke with three players who exude the kind of hyper-energy we're talking about—Jeter, Chase Utley, and Johnny Damon—as well as two managers who have long done their best to demand it—Jim Leyland and Charlie Manuel.

They all go about it in different ways. But they all have this particular "it"—the stuff that winners are made of. So listen to them talk about what that "it" factor is, and you'll understand what this phenomenon is all about.

"Over the course of 162 games, it's difficult to have that energy every single day," says Utley. "But if you have it, you can create something. If nothing's there, you can still create something with that energy."

"It's a mind-set," says Jeter. "You know what I mean? I'm not one who believes you can turn on and off a mind-set. Either you have that mind-set or you don't have that mind-set. That's a difficult thing with this long season. If you lose focus, you're in trouble."

"You'd better have it, but it's a tough thing to do," says Damon. "I just know the first time you come to the ballpark without it, you can get embarrassed. And you can wind up, as my old coaches used to say, with egg on your face. But that's why this game's not for everyone. The average guy goes out and tries to play in a softball league for one day and he's sore. We have to try to be ready 162 games a year. Plus spring training is about 20 more. And if you make the playoffs, that can be another 19. So you'd better have that energy."

All three of those men love the big game and live for the defining moments in every season. But what divides them from the mere mortals is that they feed off every little moment in between—in their own, totally distinctive ways.

Jeter is the king of cool. Utley is the opposite—so intense his teammates are sometimes afraid to speak to him when he locks into his zone. And then there's Damon—a fellow who comes to the park every day with a smile on his face, wondering exactly how much fun he can have trying to figure out how to win today.

"To some guys it's baseball, and to other guys it's a job," says Leyland. "That doesn't mean the guys who think it's a job aren't good at it. But that's what it seems like…To some guys it's like playing Little League, and that's what Johnny Damon reminds me of. He's like the Little League kid who can't wait to get there, has their hat turned sideways and they're going for ice cream afterward, no cares in the world and can't wait to play the next Little League game."

But Damon says he was taught early on—by his first big-league role models in Kansas City, Greg Gagne and Gary Gaetti—that there's more to baseball than just having fun, that you never mail in an at-bat, ever.

Then he "learned how to win," he says, when he got to Oakland and was mentored by Jason Giambi on how to dig in and grind out those big at-bats. And now he does his best to spread those lessons—the daily doses of fun, the importance of every game, the art of the great at-bat—wherever he goes.

"He's a winner," says his GM in Detroit, Dave Dombrowski. "He's been great for us. Tremendous. I always knew he was a good player. But I didn't realize the other stuff he brings to the table."

Utley, meanwhile, brings much of that same stuff. But baseball is no yuk-fest to Chase Utley. The Phillies second baseman is consumed by his work, immersed in every second of every game like just about no one you've ever run across.

"I've been in baseball 42 years, and I've seen a lot of intense players," says Phillies coach Pete Mackanin. "But without question, he's No. 1…You know, Chase is a friendly guy, but I'll put it this way. During a game, I don't bother him. He's got something on his mind, and he's totally focused. I don't know if I could have played if I was *that* focused."

You wouldn't expect a man who has spent 42 years in professional base-ball—as a player, coach, and manager—to talk about a fellow baseball creature with that sort of how-does-he-*do*-this awe. But Utley is so driven, so intense, so obsessed with excellence, he's a constant topic of exactly this type of con-versation within his own sport.

Eventually, even he became aware of how other people talk about him. But that has only reinforced his passion for how he goes about it.

"Some of the compliments I've gotten over the years have kind of stuck with me," he says. "Like, 'I enjoy watching you play,' or, 'Don't change the way you play.' Things like that, you don't forget. [His late, great coach] John Vukovich used to tell me that. Other coaches on other teams have given me those kinds of compliments. You're not looking for those compliments. You don't expect them. But when they happen, you appreciate it."

Jeter—another source of nonstop conversation in the same circles—had a similar experience about a decade ago, with a gentleman by the name of Hank Aaron. It still blows The Captain away.

"It was in Boston, at the All-Star Game in '99," Jeter says. "We had all the players out there on the field, huddling around Ted Williams. And I got a tap on my shoulder. It was Hank Aaron. I'd never met him before. He said, 'You're the guy I've been looking for. I've been wanting to meet you.' I said, '*You've* been wanting to meet *me*?' He said, 'I really enjoy the way you play the game.' And coming from him, those are the things you remember forever."

So if old-school baseball men of that stature are seeking out the likes of Jeter and Utley, just to say they notice there's something, well, different about the way their bonfires burn, you know this isn't something we're dreaming up just to get us through another work day. This is a real, tangible quality that places the truly special winners and leaders in a category all their own.

Jeter still believes it's a quality that was instilled in him by his father, Charles, a social worker who competed with him as a kid in anything and everything—and "never let me win."

"I think those are lessons that you learn, that life can be difficult at times," Derek Jeter says. "So you've got to have that mind-set, to want something. You have to work for it, and it's not going to come easy. I enjoy competing—at anything. And I want to win. You've got to enjoy competing. If you don't enjoy it, then I think it's very difficult to focus in on every game."

But Jeter, Utley, and Damon are only interested in talking about their own mind-set for so long, because they also understand their season's work isn't about them. It's not about the numbers *they* put up. It's about the number their *team* puts up—in the old "wins" column.

"It's not just me," Utley says. "It's our team. Our team plays with a lot of energy…We always bring that intensity level that can push us over the top at times when we're not at the top of our game."

When people talk about teams "learning how to win," learning this art seems like a big part of it—the art of maxing out the energy meter every single day. But Utley looks around at the personalities in his clubhouse and wonders if that's how it worked with his team.

"I'm not sure if you learn that," Utley went on. "I think the type of guys we have here play that way. And when other guys come into this organization, and they see guys playing hard every day, it sets that tone, that here we play the game the right way."

But the truth is, no team can have everybody playing that way every minute of every day of the longest season in sports. It isn't humanly possible. So what happens when teams slide off those tracks? That's when their leaders—and managers—have to grab the steering wheel.

Jeter and Utley may not be the loudest voices in their ballparks. But when they're asked if they'll say something if they see a teammate playing with his head somewhere else, they both snap back with a thunderous "Yes."

"People say I'm not vocal. How would *you* know?" Jeter says, pointedly. "One thing I don't do is do it through the media."

"If something has to be addressed, I have no problem addressing it," Utley echoes. "It might not be pretty. But I think, because of the way I play, guys respect my two cents."

Sometimes, though, these issues become too big for a player—any player—to address. And that's why managers get paid the big bucks.

Let's jump in the Way-back Machine and head for April of 2006. It's a getaway day for the Detroit Tigers that turns into an unsightly 10–2 loss to Cleveland. Afterward, the new manager, Jim Leyland, stomps into the clubhouse to tell his team it "stunk," that it had essentially cruise-controlled its way to this loss, and that if this is going to be the effort level, he'll be happy to go get new players with a different effort level. Then he invites the media into his office and tells the world the same thing:

"We stunk, and that's not good enough," he rants. "This stuff has been going on here before, and it's not going to happen here. We had a chance to take a series. I'm not talking about anyone in particular. I'm talking about the team, myself, the coaches, and everybody else included. It's my responsibility to have the team ready to play today, and they weren't ready to play. They were ready to get on the plane and go to Oakland. If they won it was OK, and if they lost it was OK. That's not good enough."

As famous 21st-century managerial tirades go, this one might be No. 1. But Jim Leyland didn't launch into it to make the Sound Bite Hall of Fame. He had a bar to raise—for a team that had *averaged* 100 losses a season over the previous five years.

"You have to remember this was a talented team that had floundered around, and they really didn't believe in themselves," Leyland says, as he looks back on that day. "They didn't realize how good they were. I saw some things in the last few innings of that game that day, and it just hit me wrong, and I said what I felt. I mean, it could have blown up in my face, but that's what I believed. Now, I'm not saying I had anything to do with anything. But fortunately, after that, they started going out and grinding out nine innings every day."

Yeah, he probably didn't have anything to do with the fact that his team climbed off that airplane and won 12 of its next 15 and 28 of its next 36, then kept rolling all the way to the World Series. Yeah, that was probably just a coincidence.

Right. Sure it was.

"He was smart," says then-Tigers reliever Chad Durbin, "because he didn't just allow it to stay in the clubhouse. There are certain things you do and don't tell the media. But in this case, he let them know what he was thinking, because then it became bigger than just a speech that ends in five minutes and you're done. It became newsworthy, and that made it more relevant to everybody."

The message the manager sent that day—that it's not acceptable to play a game where if you win it's OK and if you lose it's OK—"made them aware of the expectations," Leyland says. But just because we know now that it worked doesn't mean he knew it would work at the time.

"It's a button you have to push at the right time," he says. "It's a real dangerous button, because if you push it at the wrong time it can be disastrous."

All managers have their fingers on that button every minute of every day. What often defines the best managers is their innate ability to sense precisely when to push it.

The manager of the 2008 and 2009 National League champions also turned out to be a man who has mastered that sense. Charlie Manuel may seem like a player-friendly softie from the outside. But his bench coach, Mackanin, says: "You know that quote, 'Don't mistake kindness for weakness?' That's Charlie."

Manuel has yanked his MVP shortstop (Jimmy Rollins) out of a game for not hustling. He has taken on his opening day starter (Brett Myers) in the dugout, with the TV cameras pointing. He has summoned more players to his office for a "chat" than anyone will ever know. And his team meetings, while rare, are legendary for their "this-is-not-the-way-we-play" lectures.

Charlie Manuel loves his team and loves his players. But "every team has guys," he says, "who you've gotta watch, because they like the attention, and all of a sudden, the game starts to become more about them than the team and winning the game. Well, the game is the No. 1 priority…But guys will forget sometimes. They'll get caught up in who they are. And that's not good."

But it isn't so much runaway egos that Manuel is most on the lookout for.

It's signs that his team has started to get a little too comfortable. And that's when it becomes time for him to push that button, and launch into his favorite topic—getting his troops back to "playing the game the way we always have."

"I've said things to our team about energy," Manuel says. "Sometimes I'll say, 'Look in the other team's dugout. Right there is what we had. That's what we've got when we're playing good. That's what we want to keep. And look, they've got it and we don't have it right now.' You have to remind them. If you're a manager, you'd better be talking about those things."

He has always picked his spots to send those messages. But the men in his clubhouse say he's had an incredible knack for finding the right time, saying it the right way, and getting his team's trajectory back on course. It's all, Utley says, part of the "hidden genius" of Charlie Manuel.

We spend a lot of time in our lives talking about what makes teams win. Funny how little time we spend talking about this part of the equation. Explain to us sometime why we talk less about what makes winners tick than we do about money. As big a factor as those dollar bills can be on some levels, they're overrated on so many other levels.

"People always mention money," says Jeter. "We've been spending money for years. Lots of [teams] spend money and don't win. Money gives you the opportunity to win. But it doesn't mean you're going to win the World Series. You have to have that mind-set in order to win."

Oh, money can buy you CC Sabathia. We understand that. But you know what it can't buy? It can't buy you the flame that ripples through Derek Jeter's brain every night of every season. It can't buy you the look in Chase Utley's eye, every at-bat of every season. It can't buy you the voice in a manager's head that tells him when it's time to push That Button.

There are forces in the baseball universe that are way more elusive—and way more important—than money. It's the stuff winners are truly made of. And if you don't recognize what that stuff is by now, we guarantee you'll recognize it by October—because the eight teams still playing by then will never survive the treacherous journey down Highway 162 without it.

The Best Records in Baseball

(Now that Barry Has Ruined the Home Run Records)

AUTHOR'S NOTE: Back in 2006, as Barry Bonds was bearing down on one of the most romantic numbers in sports, 714 (i.e., the number of home runs George Herman "Bambino" Ruth hit), I noticed something. The whole world seemed to be venting about it, not romanticizing about it. And that, to me, was such a sad development for the sport of baseball, it inspired this piece, about the best records that hadn't been obliterated by the PED era. One thing you should know: since it isn't 2006 anymore, I updated all the numbers in this piece, to help it resonate today the way it did back then.

If the biggest name in baseball can hit his 714th home run and nobody outside the 415 area code even claps, that should tell us something.

And not just about the man hitting the home run.

It should tell us something about what has become of the mighty home run itself.

When Barry Bonds and his cohorts in the Asterisk Generation can perform radical surgery to remove all the romance from one of the most romantic numbers in any sport—714—it's time to reevaluate.

It's time to reevaluate the home run and what it means in our culture.

And it's time, especially, to reevaluate what we've always looked on as our favorite records in the record book.

If numbers like 714 are going to cease to mean anything, then what do any home run records mean? And if the home run records are no longer the coolest, most celebrated records in baseball, then what replaces them?

So we asked that question to a bunch of baseball people—players, ex-players, executives, historians, writers, and great statistical minds:

"If we take all home run records out of the argument, what are the 10 best records in baseball?" *That's* the question.

But by "best," we don't mean: which ones are the hardest to break?

Look, even Fernando Tatis (two grand slams in one inning) has an *unbreakable* record. But it's not a record anybody cares about.

What we're looking for are the records people care about most. We're looking for the records that would create the most buzz if someone were closing in on them.

We want electricity. We want poetry. We want (here's that word again) *romance*. We don't just want John Kruk to be talking about these feats. We want Katie Couric to be talking about them. We'd even settle for Kelly Ripa.

That won't be possible with all 10 of these. Katie and Kelly should know that up front. But that's the goal.

We also need to warn you: as we went along in this debate, we found out it's time to reevaluate one more thing—what constitutes a "modern" record.

Nap Lajoie hit .426 in 1901. Jack Chesbro won 41 games in 1904. But do those records have any relevance to "modern" baseball? Be serious.

So for the purposes of this piece, we're going to consider .400 and 30 wins to be de facto records, even though they're not records you'll currently find in any record book. Hey, it's our book. So we're invoking the old author's-privilege card. Got a problem with that? See you in court. But until then, here they come.

The 10 Best Records in Baseball

Joe DiMaggio's Hitting Streak (56 Games)

How Long It's Stood: Since 1941

Closest Call Since: 44 games, Pete Rose, in 1978

This is it—the record that has it all. Held by one of the most worshipped players of all time. And so time-tested that only one guy (Rose) has gotten within two weeks of breaking it. Yet it still doesn't feel untouchable.

It's also 100 percent controversy-free (even though esteemed historian Pete Palmer says, correctly, that hitting streaks in general are "highly overrated.") And for sheer buzz factor, it's off the charts, because "it's something that builds, day after day after day," said ESPN's own streakmeister, Orel Hershiser. "Look at Jimmy Rollins (who hit in 38 in a row) and what he just went through. That daily buzz is pretty cool."

In a poll where just about nobody agreed on anything, this was a runaway winner. So it's official. This is now the standard by which all records should be judged.

400 Batting Average

How Long It's Stood: Since Ted Williams hit .406 in 1941, 65 years ago

Closest Call Since: .394, by Tony Gwynn, in the 1994 strike season

OK, we know what you're thinking: this isn't a record. Well, it's true. It isn't, technically. So we plead guilty. But let's consider the "actual" records.

Hugh Duffy hit .438 in 1894. That's the all-time record. Lajoie batted .422 in 1901. That's the "modern" record. Rogers Hornsby hit .424 in 1924. That's the live-ball record. And nobody has gotten to .400 since Williams, who did it in Franklin D. Roosevelt's third term.

Has anything in baseball changed since then? Not much—except for light bulbs, six expansions, globalization, and the invention of closers, televisions, computers, and a little contraption called airplanes. In other words, everything has changed, except the shape of the ball.

So admit it. Don't we need to reshape the definition of "modern" records? Of course we do. And as we ponder how to do that, we've been convinced by our panelists that under any definition of what constitutes "modern" baseball, a .400 average represents some kind of record, even though technically, it's only a magic number.

But it's that magic we're looking for in the first place. And the buzz over a pursuit of .400 would blow away the pursuit of just about any record. If somebody wants to take a run at Ted and .406, even better.

"I think that the chase for .400 would out-buzz everything else on your list," said ESPN's Keith Law, at a time when he was a Blue Jays executive. "It's a day-in, day-out thing, and its only conclusion is the end of the season [not a single 0-fer], so it can stay in the news long enough to build interest. I would love for someone to chase it, because it would bring a lot of positive press to the game."

If you want to get technical on us, we could live with listing .406 as The Record, or even .394. But in reality, it's that number, .400, that would start a million hearts thumping. So for now, we'll lay that one out there and figure out the details later.

Pete Rose's 4,256 Hits

How Long It's Stood: Since 1986

Closest Call Since: Paul Molitor got to 3,319 (937 away) before retiring after the 1998 season

When we measure the potential buzz around any record, it isn't always generated by the number itself. Sometimes, the X factor is just who holds the record.

Well, the guy who holds this record is the all-time human lightning rod. So if anyone ever does take a run at Rose, the story angles will be flying at you from every direction—east, west, south, and Mars.

"This would be a huge deal," said Hershiser, "just because it's Pete…You'd have everything about Pete being brought back up and tons of stories being brought back up. You'd have two lives dissected instead of one."

30 Wins

How Long It's Stood: Since Denny McLain won 31 in 1968

Closest Calls Since: 27, by Steve Carlton in 1972 and Bob Welch in 1990

Welcome back to the same debate we faced with .400. Want to call McLain's 31 the new "modern" record? Fine. Want to go with 27? Cool.

But we live in a world that loves its round numbers. And 30 is another one of those numbers that would rev up pulse rates all over America if any pitcher ever got to August 1 with 20 wins.

Then again, no pitcher has done that since Wilbur Wood in 1973. And only three pitchers since the 1980s (Pedro Martinez in 1999, David Wells in 2000, and Ubaldo Jimenez in 2010) have won 15 by the All-Star break, either.

So in a sport in which no non-knuckleballer has made 40 starts in years (since Jim Clancy, 1982), 30 wins might not be much more reachable than Jack Chesbro's 41.

"But if anybody ever did it, there'd be an unbelievable buzz," said Indians assistant GM Chris Antonetti, "because he'd have to do it in 36 starts. So what would his record be—30–1, with five no-decisions?"

Cal Ripken's Iron Man Streak (2,632 Games in a Row)

How Long It's Stood: Since Ripken pulled the plug on September 20, 1998

Closest Call Since: 1,152, by Miguel Tejada (almost 10 years too short), or 1,768 (a mere five or six years shy) if you count Hideki Matsui's multi-continent streak (the last 518 as a Yankee)

Think this record will hold up for 56 years, like Lou Gehrig's did? Heck, it might survive for 356. And the longer it stands, the higher it could elevate on this list.

On the other hand, it's also possible our view of this record is colored by the emotions of Ripken's magical night. Next time, though, you won't have Gehrig's legacy to stoke the flame. And next time, (we hope) you won't have the pain of an eight-month strike to ease. And next time, what are the odds that someone can merely unfurl a number on a wall—and people will cry for the next 20 minutes?

So we may just be overrating the buzz quotient for this feat. But maybe not. Pete Palmer called this "probably the most difficult" modern career record to break. And the true appeal of it, said longtime baseball exec Dan Evans, is that it's really about "showing up to go to work—something everyone can identify with."

Orel Hershiser's 59 Straight Shutout Innings

How Long It's Stood: Since 1988

Closest Call Since: 42, by Arizona's Brandon Webb, in 2007

The ever-modest Hershiser wouldn't vote for his own streak. But so many of our other panelists did, we easily could have bumped this even higher on the list.

Many streaks are overrated, but this one is actually underrated. In fact, the always-incisive Rob Tracy, of the Elias Sports Bureau, called it "the most underrated occurrence of all time."

Almost nothing manufactures buzz like a cool streak, and we are giving extra points for buzz. And in an era when almost nobody averages seven innings a start, we're talking about a record that might take a starter nine consecutive shutout outings to break. So think about the insanity as that wave of zeroes reached six and seven and eight starts.

"Or if the guy who was chasing it turned out to be a reliever, like a Mariano Rivera, it would be almost like a DiMaggio-type streak," Hershiser said, "because it would mostly be an inning a game, a game at a time, over a couple of months."

So we admit it. We love this record.

Hack Wilson's 191 RBIs

How Long It's Stood: Since 1930

Closest Call Since: 184, by Lou Gehrig in 1931, the year after Wilson did it

Closest Call in the Last Half-Century: 165, by Manny Ramirez in 1999

The amazing thing about this record, said Pete Palmer, is that Rogers Hornsby would have been hitting in front of Wilson in 1930 had he not gotten hurt and missed most of the year. "I wonder how many he would have had with Hornsby on base before him?" Palmer mused.

Regardless, this record has gone so unchallenged for so long, it's hard to say what kind of hysteria might erupt if Albert Pujols were 10 RBIs away with the days peeling off the September calendar—even in an age where RBIs aren't what they used to be.

When Juan Gonzalez became the second player in history (with Hank Greenberg) to knock in 100 runs before the All-Star break, in 1998, he was a major topic of midseason conversation. But he was also a sideshow to the much more electric home run madness that summer.

With no distractions and the right masher chasing this record next time around (assuming there is a next time), we'd predict a much more raucous scene.

Bob Gibson's 1.12 ERA

How Long It's Stood: Since 1968

Closest Call Since: 1.53, by Dwight Gooden, in 1985

The heck with home runs. Here's a record that needs an asterisk. Gibson rolled up this record in the last season before A) the lowering of the mound, B) the shrinking of the strike zone, C) the second wave of expansion, and D) division play.

We also shouldn't forget that he compiled that 1.12 ERA in a season when six other starters had ERAs below 2.00 and the *average* pitcher had an ERA under 3.00.

In fact, reports Pete Palmer, if you "normalize" ERAs by comparing them to the league average, Greg Maddux's 1994 season was better than Gibson's, and Pedro Martinez has had two seasons (1999 and 2000) that were better.

But there's still a place for pure numbers in this game. And Gibson has an aura that keeps this record on the exalted list.

Beyond that, it's incredible to contemplate a season in which a pitcher made 13 starts in which he allowed zero runs and 11 more in which he gave up one run. And then there's our final criterion, the number itself—1.12.

If people can hear a raw number and know exactly what it refers to, it's not just another record. This one sure qualifies. So if anyone ever does make a run at it, we'd all pay attention—even though, as Antonetti quipped, "you'd have to keep your calculator out."

Rickey Henderson's 130 Stolen Bases

How Long It's Stood: Since 1982

Closest Call Since: 110, by Vince Coleman, in 1985

As long as Rickey was still out there doing his thing for the world-famous San Diego Surf Dawgs (of the independent Golden League), it was hard to fathom that this record had been around as long as it actually has.

But it's getting harder than ever to envision somebody making a charge at this, barring a major philosophical shift in how the game is played.

Since Henderson set this record, half that many steals would have been enough to lead one league or the other 36 times in the 31 seasons between 1983 and 2013. And nobody has been within (gulp) 50 of breaking this thing since 1988. So if someone ever did challenge it, he'd be one of the most magnetic players ever, chasing a Hall of Famer and cult hero.

"I like this," said Keith Law, "because it's built around an exciting event, and another season-long chase. You want something that makes people get up in the morning or get to the office and say, 'Did Smith do X last night?' You want something that makes the mainstream newscasts."

Nolan Ryan's 383-Strikeout Season

How Long It's Held Up: Since 1973

Closest Call Since: 372, by Randy Johnson, in 2001

We'd better confess: Ryan's 5,714 career strikeouts actually got more votes than his greatest season. And so did his seven no-hitters. But we're exercising a little writer's privilege here—and overruling our own voters.

Why? Because who the heck is ever going to approach 5,700 strikeouts? Roger Clemens was a power pitcher for 24 seasons, and he still finished more than 1,000 Ks short.

And seven no-hitters is an event that wouldn't generate any buzz even if somebody came along to throw six—because you'd never have any sense of anticipation that the seventh was on the horizon.

But a single-season record chase comes with built-in drama—because it's a race against the calendar, a duel between one great player and the countdown to the end of the season.

"So the part of this that would be the most fun," Hershiser said, "is the part where people sit around and ask each other: 'How many did he strike out last night? How many more does he need? Let's see. He got 12, so he's 50 away. He's got three starts to go. How many does he need to average?' That's where it gets cool."

But don't start that countdown yet. To break this record in a 36-start season, you would need a pitcher who averages 11 strikeouts a game. To break it in a 250-inning season, you would need a starting pitcher who averages 14 whiffs per nine innings.

So the buzz would be no problem, laughed Hershiser, because "the guy who breaks it would be a guy who generates that buzz his whole life."

Just for Fun: Other Records That Got Votes

Johnny Vander Meer's back-to-back no-hitters
Ryan's seven no-hitters
Ryan's 5,714 career strikeouts
Cy Young's 511 wins
Ichiro's 262 hits
The Cubs' and Mariners' 116-win seasons
Earl Webb's 67 doubles
The 20-strikeout games (Roger Clemens, Kerry Wood, Randy Johnson)
Ty Cobb's .367 career batting average
Rube Marquard's 19 wins in a row
The 1916 Giants' 26-game winning streak
Connie Mack's 50 years managing the same team
The Yankees' 27 World Series championships

Chapter 2

It Happens Every Spring

March, 2008

The End of Al Lang

St. Petersburg, Florida—On March 28, 2008, at the historic corner of Bayshore Drive and First Avenue South, the Reds and Rays trotted out to play a baseball game.

Except this one wasn't just any baseball game.

This one was good-bye.

Good-bye to a place known as Al Lang Field, even though—thanks to the dubious corporate forces that overpower our lives these days—that wasn't even its name at the end.

Good-bye to a place that, for some reason, inspired about a million fewer tears, and a billion fewer verses of poetry, in the spring of 2008, than Dodgertown, even though the history of this site is even deeper, even longer, even richer.

Good-bye to a place that hosted more spring training games—more than 2,000 of them—than any site on the American baseball landscape.

Lou Gehrig trained here. Stan Musial trained here. Grover Cleveland Alexander and Tom Seaver trained here.

Joe DiMaggio got four hits in his first spring training game as a Yankee here. Don Zimmer hit the first Grapefruit League triple in the history of the Mets here.

Babe Ruth once launched home runs here that traveled across First Avenue into the balconies of the now-defunct West Coast Inn.

Mickey Mantle once smoked a mammoth, game-winning, opposite-field home run here that high-hopped off the asphalt beyond the left-field fence and plunked into the turquoise waters of Tampa Bay.

The Cardinals trained here for 60 years. The Yankees trained here for 36 years. The Mets trained here for the first 26 years of their existence. The Braves, Orioles, Giants, and Rays can also say they called this home, at least for an idyllic month and a half. For nearly 70 years, it was the home for two teams every spring.

So simply to call this place a ballpark doesn't seem to do it justice.

"It's like a museum to me," said legendary Cardinals instructor George Kissell, the man who has undoubtedly been a part of more baseball games at Al Lang, over the last half-century or so, than any living American. "It's a museum of baseball."

The museum opened on March 6, 1922, when Billy Southworth, Mule Watson, and the Boston Braves held their first workout at what was then known as Waterfront Park. The gallery hasn't quite been open continuously since then—thanks to a couple of ballpark renovations here, a couple of lost war years there. But pretty close.

So we're talking more than eight decades of baseball, eight decades of lore, eight decades of memories.

Until now.

Now, we're just talking good-bye.

Good-bye to the most picturesque setting ever to house any spring training ballpark—just across the street from a harbor dotted with sailboats, along the St. Petersburg pier.

"As a player there, you'd come out of the game early and go right over there and fish," said Billy Hatcher, who spent many a spring visiting Al Lang as a player, then spent eight more as a coach for Tampa Bay. "They've got snooker in there, redfish—right off those docks. You could play, you could fish, and never even have to leave."

But you didn't need a fishing pole to bask in the beauty of that waterfront. You couldn't beat the water vistas from any seat down the first-base line, or from the sun-splashed right-field berm, which often seemed more packed with occupants than the stands.

Speaking of sun-splashed, no discussion of Al Lang Field would be complete without some mention of that big orange ball in the Florida sky. Because this park has to rank at the top of any list of suntanning (or sunburning) capitals of the world. Right behind, say, Ecuador.

"I know they say the sun is 93 million miles away from earth," quipped veteran scout Bob Johnson. "The only exception is Al Lang. It's four miles away from Al Lang."

Oh, the ballpark itself is no candidate for *Architectural Digest*. We'll concede that. No brick. No ivy. No earth tones. No manufactured charms. Just a simple concrete shell with 6,439 seats. But the setting, the harbor, and the palm trees beyond the outfield fence salvage the ambiance. And the history that has unfolded here oozes out of every blade of grass.

"I've seen a lot of great players come through here," said Rays coach Don Zimmer, who had been coming through, and to, Al Lang for most of the past 50 years himself. "Musial. Enos Slaughter. Mantle. Maris. Yogi. I could go on and on."

In fact, he did go on and on, like every longtime baseball man we asked about Al Lang Field. We asked the questions. They'd get a look in their eye. Then the stories would pour out of them, one after another, like a Ken Burns miniseries come to life.

"First game I ever played here," said Zimmer, "I went to field a ground ball. And it came up and hit me right here. [He paused to jab a finger into the top of his head.] I had a knot in my head as big as a baseball. I still remember Buzzie Bavasi saying, 'Son'—he always called me 'son'—'Son, go on home. You're gonna kill me.'"

Hey, Ron Gardenhire could relate to that: "You know how many balls I missed in that park?" laughed the Twins manager, and former Mets infielder. "I was even telling the boys, 'Boys, I made some quality errors on that field.'"

But Gardenhire's most enduring memory is of a ball he didn't catch or hit. The immortal Dave Kingman pounded that one—and splattered it off the building that is now the Mahaffey Theater, located more than 100 feet beyond the left-field fence.

"He hit that ball, and it went over the light tower and short-hopped the building," Gardenhire said. "I still remember him hitting that ball and me going, 'Oh my god.' It went so high that we went, 'No way.' Then it went over the lights, and we see it go like this [pointing that-away]. Then it bounces up and hits the frigging wall and goes like that [pointing this-away] and comes back toward us. And we're like, 'It hit the frigging building, boys. No way. You can't do that.'"

Ah, but Kong Kingman did it, all right. And it sure wasn't the only memorable home run in Al Lang history.

Ruth, Mantle, DiMaggio, Musial, and Cal Ripken all whomped storied blasts on this site. But the home run that former Cardinal Andy Van Slyke can't get out of his brain was hit by a fabled minor league masher named Mike Calise.

"Mike Calise hit a ball that was the hardest, longest line drive ever hit by mankind," said Van Slyke. "There's a spot a foot from the very top of the right corner of the green hitting background. And he hit that ball so hard, it stuck there, in between the rails. I think they're three inches apart, and the ball was four inches. And it stuck. Most amazing thing I've ever seen. That's beyond physics. That's like *The Matrix* stuff."

But most of those Al Lang home runs? They were the stuff of pure baseball.

"I played a spring training game there one day, and I hit two home runs off Bob Gibson," said Phillies manager Charlie Manuel. "Only two hits he gave up, too. And he pitched nine innings that day. When the game was over, Gibson was out there doing his sprints. And he looked right at me and said, 'You know, young fellow'—I'll never forget him calling me 'young fellow'—'if you got those hits off me during the season, I'd have hit you.' So I guess I got lucky."

Yeah, but not everybody was so lucky.

In Tommie Agee's first spring game as a Met in 1968, a Gibson fastball got away (cough, cough), clanked off Agee's noggin, and landed him in the hospital. And Braves special assistant Jim Fregosi vividly recalls the similar adventures of his new Mets teammate, John Milner, in his first spring meeting with Gibson a few years later.

"First time up against Gibson, he hit a double to left-center," Fregosi said. "Next time, he hit a double to right-center. Next time, Gibson drilled him. And after that, he always had the Gibson Blues. It was like Gibson's way of saying, 'Hey, welcome, kid.'"

Heh-heh. Welcome indeed. Spring training baseball may be the mellowest spectacle in sports. But those Bob Gibson HBPs remind us that the mellowness can disappear at any given moment, on any given pitch.

In the spring of 1987, for instance, the Mets and Red Sox found themselves meeting at Al Lang for the first time since the '86 World Series. And for the Red Sox, the memories of Darryl Strawberry's slightly too hot-doggish October trot around the bases, after a Series homer they couldn't forget, hadn't exactly faded.

"So in the second inning," former Red Sox GM Lou Gorman remembered, "Al Nipper was pitching. And Strawberry had homered off Nipper in the World Series. So the very first pitch nearly hit him in the head. Second pitch nearly hit him in the side. And the third pitch hit him. Strawberry dropped the bat, charged the mound, and a big fight broke out. About five, six guys got thrown out. This was like the third game of spring training.

"I'll never forget that afternoon. I don't think I've ever seen a fight like that in spring training—ever."

Just goes to prove, though, that if it could happen in a baseball game, it undoubtedly happened at Al Lang Field, at least once or twice.

Like the 17-inning spring training game the Yankees and Red Sox played in 1948, for example. We can guarantee you'll never see one of those again.

It's believed to be the longest major league spring training game ever played. And that's kind of fitting, too, since the longest continuous professional baseball game in history was also played at Al Lang—a 29-inning Florida State League classic in 1966.

"Great game," said Billy DeMars, who managed against Sparky Anderson that night. "You know, there was one fan who watched the first nine innings. Then he went out and went bowling. Then later, he's on his way home and saw the lights on. So he figured, what the heck. Came back in and saw the rest of the game."

There are enough stories like that to fill an encyclopedia. But some of the tales are different. You can't diagram them on a scorecard, because they're not really baseball stories. They're life stories.

They're tales like the one told by Tampa Bay manager Joe Maddon. He was playing for Lafayette College in 1973. His team was in Tampa for a college baseball tournament. He knew that somewhere up one of these roads, his favorite team, the Cardinals, played their spring training games. So he snuck out of the dorm and hitchhiked to Al Lang Field, all by himself.

"And I walked through the portal over there," Maddon said, pointing down the first-base line, "and it was absolutely magical. I was 19 years old, and I thought, *This is heaven on earth.*

"Those are the kind of feelings you can never re-create because they're once-in-a-lifetime moments that will always stay with you. I swear to God, I can see it in my mind's eye right now…So when I got here [as manager] in 2006, I walked out here and that was the first thing I looked at—that portal out there. And you think about how far this has come for me, and it's very emotional.

"Reflect on when you were in college and those moments when you think, *What am I going to be doing 20, 30 years from now?* And then you get in a position where you can look from the other way up, up from the field to that place in the stands. And that's quite exciting."

In a way, it's the stories like these that resonate the deepest. After all, you can't find anything that happened in this place recorded in any baseball encyclopedia. The stats don't count. The box scores fade away. But they're not the true legacy of Al Lang Field.

This was a place where everything that happened—spring training, Florida State League, Florida Instructional League—was all leading somewhere else. For eight decades, this was where baseball players came to get ready—and to get better—for more meaningful times ahead.

"Al Lang was sort of like a sperm bank for major league baseball," said Van Slyke. "It was a breeding ground for a lot of good players.

"Put it this way. There's no other field in the history of the game that produced as many stars as Al Lang. So I think they need to take out a cubic foot of dirt, take it to Cooperstown, and say, 'This is the dirt that produced more major leaguers than any other field in the history of the game.'"

Oh, and Andy Van Slyke had one other inspired suggestion—except, unfortunately, it's too late now.

"The biggest mistake baseball made," he said, "is not naming that field after George Kissell, because George Kissell had more influence on that field than any other human being, because of all the instruction he provided to all the players who ever played there."

George Kissell is one of those names that just about no one outside baseball seems to know—but everyone inside the baseball universe worships. He was the brains, the soul, the energizer behind the Cardinals' player-development system from the late 1950s until as recently as 2004.

He taught a converted catcher named Joe Torre how to play third base. He taught Lou Brock how to slide. He took a minor league infielder named Earl Weaver under his wing and taught him many of the intricacies that made the Earl famous.

And George Kissell's home office, for almost all those years, was Al Lang Field. It was where he held court in spring training. It was where he ran the Instructional League. It was right up the road from where he lived. So much of this place is inside him, and so much of him is inside this place, that Zimmer says, "When I think of Al Lang Field, I think of George Kissell. There's a real legend."

But finally it was George Kissell's time to say good-bye, too. He was 88 years old, and he was losing a friend. Needless to say, he wasn't real happy about it.

"I never thought baseball would ever leave there," Kissell said. "I thought there would always be baseball there."

Every once in a while, he said, he would still drive by the ballpark when it was empty. Yet he could still hear a very loud sound.

"I can hear the hooting and hollering going on when a guy got a base hit in spring training," he said. "Ninth inning. You've got a rally going. And gul' darn, they'd be hooting and hollering. I can still hear that."

Luckily, he could hear it in his head, not in his ears, because now, the only sound any of us will be able to hear with our ears is the sound of silence.

"I drive by it sometimes, and I can't imagine it not being there," Kissell said, his words dripping with hurt. "I just can't imagine it, 'cause I had a lot of fun in that place."

And it wasn't just him. This was a special place on the sporting earth. A place that connected the dots between so many generations of baseball. A place that linked Babe Ruth and Evan Longoria, Miller Huggins and Joe Maddon, fans wearing top hats to fans wearing tank tops.

A place that helped us say hello to another baseball season, spring after spring, for 86 years. But not anymore. Now, when we gaze at the corner of Bayfront and First Avenue South, we'll be saying something else.

This one, we're afraid, is good-bye.

Josh Hamilton Is Back

AUTHOR'S NOTE: My favorite Josh Hamilton story of all time didn't happen on the night he sent four home runs flying through the Baltimore ozone, or the night he lit up Yankee Stadium in a spine-tingling Home Run Derby. It actually happened during spring training in 2007, when it started to become clear that there was still something incredible inside this man who had done everything he could to obliterate a once-beautiful career. It happened in a Dairy Queen. And you'll find it in this piece, which we present virtually untouched, just to preserve the joy of discovery that was bursting out all over Florida at the time.

SARASOTA, FLORIDA—Sometimes, the stories we tell aren't really baseball stories.

Sometimes, they're just the stories of human beings—people who rise, who fall, who sadden us, who inspire us. We only use baseball as a reason to tell those tales.

So we know that if it weren't for baseball, there might be no reason to tell the story of Josh Hamilton right now. But thankfully, baseball has given us that excuse.

Thankfully, one of the great human stories in America is suddenly unfolding in front of us, on these baseball fields beneath the Florida palm trees.

For too long, Josh Hamilton was the talk of baseball for all the wrong reasons. Now he's the talk of baseball for all the right reasons.

He has climbed out of a real-life horror film and back into the uniform of the Cincinnati Reds. And if he keeps playing the way he is playing, he is going to make the Cincinnati Reds, as just your standard five-tool reserve outfielder.

He is 25 years old now. It's nearly eight years since the Devil Rays made him the first pick in the 1999 draft. There is a three-year black hole missing out of his career. And the stuff he is doing this spring, he has no business doing. But he is doing it anyway.

A week into spring training, he's batting .476 (10-for-21). He has mashed a 500-foot home run. And there isn't a National Leaguer in the state of Florida with more hits than he has (10).

So already, says teammate Ryan Freel, "he's a great story."

And he is. But not just a baseball story.

"Getting back here, it means a lot, baseball-wise," says Josh Hamilton. "But also, it's going to mean a lot when I get to tell my story to people."

He is telling that story pretty much every day now, to anyone who asks. And those of us who type for a living are all too happy to help him tell it.

It is the classic saga of the all-American boy whose life unexpectedly careens down life's darkest alley—but then, remarkably, zig-zags back in the other direction. And now here this guy is, on the cusp of doing something few humans get the chance to do:

Grabbing hold of an unspeakably tragic script and crafting a much different ending. But not on any keyboard.

In real life.

He is a walking Hollywood stand-up-and-cheer production. He is teaching us all a lesson about why it is we give second chances in life. And he is basking in it all.

Asked what he is savoring most about this spring of rebirth, Josh Hamilton's face takes on a look we don't get to see much—the look of a man who knows he is living a dream he thought he'd let slip away.

"Just getting back on the field," he says. "Sunshine. Uniform on. All of it. It's so good."

So good. Too good. Too good to feel real, even. Every day seems to bring a whole new reason to ask: is this really happening?

Imagine this scene, for instance:

Imagine our hero, driving home from a spring training baseball game, his wife by his side, a smile on his face…and his major league baseball uniform still on his back.

"I wore my uniform home from the game the other day," he admits. "I rode home with my wife from the Twins game and stopped at Dairy Queen, with my uniform on. And when I got home and took it off, I just looked at it."

Looked at it?

"Yeah," he says. "To take in the moment."

At the Dairy Queen, he reports, "I had the biggest burger I could get. It reminded me of being in a Legion baseball game. Or high school. It's just that feeling of, it's a game. And just having fun with it."

Who would have thought a couple of years ago that this guy had many—or any—fun days left in anybody's baseball uniform?

Somehow, he had descended into a drug abyss from which there appeared to be no escape. He'd been suspended by baseball indefinitely, for violating the terms of his treatment program. His wife had left him. He had an infant daughter he'd barely laid eyes on. He'd pushed away all the friends who had reached out to help him.

And then he turned up on his grandmother's doorstep in September, 2005. He'd lost 50 pounds. He had nowhere else to turn. She took him in and fed him, and all seemed right in his world, finally. But it wasn't. A couple of weeks later, she looked into his eyes, knew he was high, and confronted him.

"She told me she couldn't take it anymore, that I was hurting the people I love," Hamilton says. "My grandmother seeing me like that—that was the turning point."

That date was October 5, 2005. It is burned into Josh Hamilton's brain, because of what it signifies. It was the day his life took the U-turn that led him back to this special place.

There were many checkpoints along the journey back, many profound religious experiences, many people who helped, many people who cared. You'll see them all in the movie some day.

But the forces that led him to this team, in this spring, at this point in his life are so powerful, so cinematic, so packed with elements of fate and coincidence that even his teammates get chills talking about them.

"I told him, 'There's a reason why you're here. All this stuff happened for a reason,'" Freel says. "And he believes that."

Technically, Hamilton is in this Reds spring training camp because they maneuvered to obtain him in the Rule 5 draft of unprotected minor leaguers. But there is more going on here than the technicalities.

What were the odds that Josh Hamilton would wind up playing for a team whose manager, Jerry Narron, has known him since he was a teenager?

What were the odds that Narron's brother, Johnny, actually coached Hamilton in a summer draft-showcase setting a decade ago—and had a son who had grown up with (and played baseball and basketball with) Hamilton, since he was (gulp) nine years old?

And what were the odds that Reds GM Wayne Krivsky would work out a deal with the Cubs for the No. 3 pick in that Rule 5 draft before he even knew there was this connection between his manager's family and his future draft pick's family?

"The amazing thing to me," says the manager, "just by the grace of God about how all this worked out, is, the night before the Rule 5 draft, Wayne wanted to run it by me about drafting somebody with a past. Wayne said his name, and my jaw just dropped—because Wayne had no idea I even knew him."

In fact, Narron—as caring a man as you'll find in anyone's dugout—had been beating himself up for years, just because he'd never reached out to Hamilton during those darkest days. So Narron told his GM, "If anybody can get this thing done, we can get this thing done together."

For added support, the Reds then hired Narron's brother as their new video/administrative coach. And they're committed, says Johnny Narron, "to be there for Josh, for whatever he needs…on and off the field."

But so far, it has all worked out so poetically, it feels more like a fairy tale than the poignant comeback drama of a troubled young man.

This guy missed three full seasons (2003–05), remember—and got just 50 at-bats, in a short-season league, in 2006. So how many players could lose that huge a chunk of their career and still look like one of the most talented players on the field?

"I compare it to the guys who went off to World War II, missed two or three years, and then came back and were able to play," says Jerry Narron. "For somebody with average ability, it would be impossible. But Josh has got much more than just average talent."

Oh, he had his doubts it was all still in there. But "at the same time," Hamilton says, "that just lets you know that it's a God thing, because to be out of baseball that long and to come back, and to still have the ability I have, it's just one of those things that lets me know that this is what I'm supposed to do."

And maybe it is. Another one of his new teammates, Jeff Conine, watched all this with a sense of awe.

"I know if I took three years off," Conine says, "I wouldn't be able to make contact with the ball, let alone hit balls 500 feet."

It won't always come this easy, obviously. Josh Hamilton knows that. We know that. The pitchers will get serious. The breaking balls will get sharper. The word will get out. That batting average won't be pushing .500 for long. His playing time will shrink. The temptations that swayed him once will always be there.

But spring is supposed to be a time for feel-good stories. And no one in baseball has made more people feel good in this spring than Josh Hamilton.

His wife, Katie, and his two daughters sit there in the stands every day—watching, cheering, praying. Every day, the calls, the emails, the text messages roll in from all the people rooting for him. And Josh Hamilton does his best to take it all in.

Asked if there has been one moment this spring when it hit him that this was really happening, he replies: "Every day. *Every* day."

"It almost feels like my first spring training all over again," says the star of baseball's most inspirational show. "And I just thank God every day for it."

March, 2005

Red Sox Contemplate Life After The Curse

AUTHOR'S NOTE: As I set out for the spring training camp of the 2005 Red Sox, I couldn't help but wonder what I'd find. But I knew the universe I'd encounter wasn't the same place I'd left the previous spring. Here's my account of what I found, still unfurled in the present tense, just as I wrote it, so you can fully grasp the unprecedented enormity of what was unfolding beneath the Fort Myers palm trees.

FORT MYERS, FLORIDA—It's a little spooky, living in a world with no curses, no baggage, no ghosts of Bucky Bleeping Dent.

It's a little disorienting, knowing that Life the Way It's Always Been is now permanently defunct, to be replaced by Life After Winning, Whatever That Is.

It's a little scary, staring into a future with a whole new set of mysterious ground rules, built around a concept almost no living human is familiar with:

The Boston Red Sox as your official defending World Series champs.

In actual non-fictionalized life.

Imagine that.

Perhaps you haven't fully contemplated what this means, friends—not just in a baseball sense, but in a truly cosmic sense. What it means, though, is that the universe has changed, in some dramatic and mysterious way.

What we can't grasp—what no one can grasp yet—is exactly how it has changed.

How, after all, *could* we grasp it? We haven't lived in that world. We haven't traveled that highway. We haven't landed on that planet. Until now, that is.

So we wonder, because we can't help it: what lies ahead in this unfamiliar new world?

Too bad that's a question that might be tougher to answer than how the heck this team ever won the ALCS when it was three outs from getting swept with Mariano Rivera on the mound.

"The truth is, we don't know yet," says James Taylor, the great singer-songwriter-philosopher from western Massachusetts, and one of approximately 9.7 trillion New Englanders who have made the journey to this Red Sox spring training camp. "We've just stepped through a new portal into a whole new dynamic, and it's very strange."

Those who look for tangible signs, however, are almost terrified by what they've seen on our planet since the Red Sox won.

"You kind of start to wonder," says center fielder/teenybopper-idol Johnny Damon. "Tsunamis. All those birds flying over Egypt. Major rainfall in southern California. So I don't know, man.

"Hopefully," Damon laughs, "this doesn't mean the world is coming to an end."

Yeah, hopefully. But whatever, it does mean that life in New England, as we used to know it, actually *has* come to an end.

And the first tip-off is the T-shirts.

We remind you what the T-shirts of Red Sox spring trainings past used to look like. They were angry shirts. Tortured shirts. Misery shirts:

"Aaron Bleeping Boone" shirts. "Bucky Bleeping Dent" shirts. "Yankees (Pick a Verb)" shirts.

Funny, you don't see those shirts anymore.

The new shirts tell it all: "Finally" shirts. "Now I Can Die in Peace" shirts. And hundreds and hundreds of 2004 World Champions shirts, worn by people who almost seem to need to wear them, to prove it really happened.

Fred Habib, of Newburyport, stands behind a batting cage, draped in his favorite "Now I Can Die in Peace" shirt, bought for five bucks after the Series, down at the mall.

He still feels the pain of walking home from a friend's house after Game 7 of the 2003 ALCS, after Aaron Boone's homer, seeing his 12-year-old son in tears and thinking, *This may never happen. And now I'm putting my kid through this, too.*

But a year later, there was a very different Game 7 and a very different feeling: He and his buddies, "sitting there and looking at each other," Fred Habib says, "going: 'Our lives have changed.'"

Ah, but how? For every year of his lifetime, for nearly all of our lifetimes, winter in New England meant waiting for the Red Sox to start another this-will-be-the-year kind of season. But this winter, even here in spring training, we sense a different vibe.

"Now," says first baseman David McCarty, "it's almost like they don't want this season to start."

Not only are these people stuck in a moment they can't get out of—they don't want to get out of it.

They'd much rather hold onto a moment they waited for all their lives than move on to the next moment—because how can that moment possibly feel as good as this?

"I've got to admit," says James Taylor, "I feel that way myself a little bit. Can't we just take that one back and run it again in slow motion?"

Well, matter of fact, you can. Just maybe a little too literally. There are two DVDs to watch (one from MLB Productions, the other from NESN). And there are at least 10 books, either already on the shelves or coming soon to a bookstore near you.

So for those who want to bask in what was, the basking opportunities are almost endless. By cueing up the video. Or turning the pages. Or by descending on Fort Myers, in what feels more like a pilgrimage than a spring training camp.

On the first day of full-squad workouts, an astounding 2,500 people showed up. On a Tuesday in February. Mostly just for the privilege of gawking and worshipping their heroes, even if they weren't doing a whole lot.

In theory, the World Series parade ended four months ago. So how come it feels as if it's still going on? Just substitute the palms of Fort Myers for the street lights of Boston.

"Like watching the gallery at Augusta," says pitcher Bronson Arroyo.

"Looked like the line from Space Mountain," says assistant GM Jed Hoyer.

It literally boggles the mind that a mere baseball team could bring joy this intense to this many people. Have there always been this many Red Sox fans in so many places? Or did winning just suck them out of hiding like a gigantic magnetic force?

"It's incredible," McCarty says. "I live right by Oakland [which was still in California last time we looked]. When I lived in Oakland and *played* in Oakland, I used to walk around and not get recognized as much as I do now, playing for the Red Sox."

Was it this way for the Marlins after they won? For the Angels? For the Diamondbacks? Oh, maybe it was for an October hero here and there. But not for everybody—every pinch hitter, every utility infielder, every long reliever. No matter whom you ask, for every Red Sox player, there is a story.

Damon caused such a mob scene at his son's T-ball game recently, "I had to sneak off and jump fences, just to get away," he says.

David Ortiz got swarmed at Disney World, where he'd always thought "people don't even pay attention to see if there are famous people."

McCarty had it happen one day on a ski slope at Lake Tahoe—Red Sox fans materializing out of the snowflakes to say, "Thanks."

You could tell those tales for a month. So if these men didn't sense the power in what they did as they were doing it, they sure sense it now.

Arroyo talks about sitting home one day this winter, watching the HBO special, *Reverse the Curse of the Bambino*.

"You listen to these people talk about their heartbreak in '86 and '75 and '03," Arroyo says. "Then you listen to them talk about what '04 meant. It makes you cry."

Ortiz tells of not quite grasping the full impact of it all until he sat his friends and family down to watch the beautifully crafted MLB Productions DVD.

"I got all my people at home [in the Dominican] lined up, and played that DVD," he says. "And everyone—even the people who don't understand a damn thing—they were like: 'Papi, you did it.' And I'm not even going to tell you about what it was like in my country. Everywhere I went, it was like heaven."

Unlike the real heaven, however, this heaven isn't forever.

Sorry to announce this, but the Red Sox will be forced by proper authorities to play another game. Lots of them. And that's when this saga will get really fascinating.

Once the baseball earth starts spinning for real again April 3 in Yankee Stadium, we'll begin to get some answers to the question we posed many paragraphs ago:

How has the universe changed?

"I have a feeling these people aren't going to worry about a thing anymore," Damon theorizes. "It'll be tough to get those smiles off their faces. People will be, like: 'It's OK. You lost 20 in a row. Things will be fine.'"

"I think there will definitely be a calm about them now," Arroyo guesses. "Last year, we got into a bad streak for two or three months, and everybody was talking about how mediocre we were. I think it will be easier for people to stick with us now. They'll realize, after last year, there's always a chance. Even if we're down 3–0 [in a playoff series], they can remember there's always a chance to win."

"It will be so different from here on out," says Fred Habib, the fan in the "Now I Can Die in Peace" shirt. "A game will just be a game now. It won't have all this baggage attached to it."

We listen to these theories. We rattle them around in our brains. They sound pretty close to plausible.

Then we imagine six games against the Yankees in the first 10 days of the season. Does anybody really believe that if the Red Sox lose five of six, these people will still be smiling, saying: "Things will be fine?"

"The way it looks to me," says Kevin Millar, "is that these people want to win again. We're not the lovable losers here. The Cubbies can go out and have a beer and have a good time. But we've gotta win."

Oh, maybe they won't have to win in quite the same way they had to win when it hadn't happened in 86 years. But you would have to believe in the Tooth Fairy not to believe there isn't some middle ground between the "what-will-go-wrong-next" paranoia of Life Before Winning and the "don't-wake-us-up" delirium of Life After Winning.

"It's not an easy thing to get over something that people haven't seen in

86 years," Ortiz says. "I think it's something people are going to appreciate for the rest of their lives, even if we come out and win five World Series in a row. They're never going to forget about the first one.

"Maybe if we win 10 World Series in a row, people might be [thinking], *OK, we want somebody else to win now.* That's what happened with the Yankees. People got tired of seeing them win—even their own fans."

But the glow from this one—it's as close to permanent as anything in sports ever gets.

"I bet we'd need to win at least five in a row," Ortiz chuckles, "for people to forget about 86 years."

We'll never find out, you know. They're not going to win five in a row. Good as they are, they'll practically need divine intervention to win two in a row.

But we will find out many other things, here in The Year After.

Who knows what can be accomplished with all the energy people won't have to waste anymore doing stuff like digging up the Bambino's piano?

Who knows what it could mean for the betterment of mankind now that it's safe for Bill Buckner to leave the house—and maybe even vacation on the Vineyard?

Now we get to learn all those things, just from studying the citizens of New England as they go about life in a world without curses.

This is where the fun really begins—with 10 miles behind them, but 10,000 more to go.

March, 2006

The Return of Jim Leyland

LAKELAND, FLORIDA—He had been here before. Right here.

In another lifetime, of course.

But Jim Leyland had been here, all right. Running this same drill for his corner infielders, on a back field of the Detroit Tigers' minor league complex, in the middle of the Polk County citrus belt.

A baseball went roaring off a fungo bat down the third-base line. Brandon Inge lunged, working on his best Brooks Robinson imitation. But this ball skipped off his glove.

"That's OK," Jim Leyland shouted. "It's OK, Brad. That's why we're here."

Yes, that's why they were here. But that didn't answer the big question:

Why was Jim Leyland here?

He leaned back at his desk in the Tigers manager's office. But his mind was drifting back to another day, in another office, a long, long time ago.

The date was October 3, 1999. That office was located in the bowels of Coors Field, in downtown Denver.

As he took off his uniform that day, Leyland remembers thinking, *I may never manage again.*

The Rockies had just scored two runs in the bottom of the ninth to beat the Giants on the final day of Leyland's first and only season as manager in Colorado. The last baseball wound up in Leyland's hand. He decided to keep it.

But all that dramatic win did was help his team avoid its 91st loss of the year. All it did was keep Leyland's Rockies within 28 games of first place.

"It was certainly anticlimactic," Leyland would say seven years later. "It wasn't like Earl Weaver or Sparky Anderson stepping down, that's for sure. I don't think anybody really gave a [hoot], to be honest with you."

He remembered the owners stopping by the office to shake his hand. But he was almost embarrassed to shake back "because I'd disappointed the hell out of them. That's one of the biggest regrets of my life, the way I let all those people down."

And when everyone was gone, Jim Leyland began to peel off his uniform, after the final day of his 36th consecutive season in professional baseball. The best words he could find in retrospect to describe his emotions at the time were *empty* and *sad*.

He tossed his uniform into a pile of dirty clothes. He never thought he would wear another one.

"I absolutely did not," he said. "Under no circumstances did I think I'd ever be back."

Over the previous six baseball seasons—as the Tigers were losing 585 games (the most in baseball during that span), as his old team in Florida was winning another World Series (and holding another fire sale), as his onetime leadoff man in Pittsburgh, Barry Bonds, was mashing 263 home runs—all Leyland managed was to be a dad. And a husband. And a special-assignment scout for his good friend, Tony La Russa.

He made it to the Little League games. And he made it home for dinner. Unless the Pirates were at home. In which case Leyland was out at the ballpark, scouting. And sitting next to his predecessor in the Pirates manager's office, Chuck Tanner.

"Chuck said, 'Jim, you'll manage again'—like he knew," Leyland chuckled. "He's pretty sharp, as sharp as ever. He said, 'You just enjoy those kids right now. But you'll be back.' And sure enough, he was right."

The other voice in Leyland's ear belonged to La Russa, a man who has referred to Leyland a thousand times as "the best manager I ever managed against." La Russa made sure Leyland

> **TRIVIALITY**
>
> In 22 seasons as a big-league manager, Jim Leyland took his teams to the postseason eight times. Only four managers since World War II got to October more than he did. Can you name them?

got a taste of spring training, reached out to him in the postseason, shrewdly tried to remind Leyland of all the best parts of the job.

In retrospect, Leyland said, there was no moment when he knew it was time. But nothing was more responsible for relighting his flame than "being around Tony," he said.

"He always encouraged me," Leyland said. "He said, 'You should be a manager.' We'd talk for hours, just talk about the game."

And next thing Leyland knew, he could feel his adrenaline flowing again. So in the fall of 2004, he quietly nudged his friends into floating his name for the opening in Philadelphia. He charged into the interview with so much fury and honesty, people in the Phillies' organization suggest he actually intimidated then-GM Ed Wade.

The Phillies hired Charlie Manuel instead. But there it was—Leyland's name was out there. And one guy taking notes was Tigers GM Dave Dombrowski.

They had worked together with the White Sox and then again in Florida, where they won a World Series in 1997 and suffered together through the painful job of selling off all their championship parts before the confetti had even been swept up.

"That experience would have been tough on anybody, but it was especially tough on Jim," Dombrowski said. "He'd waited so many years to have a championship club—I should say a world championship club, because he won enough [NL East] championships in Pittsburgh. And as soon as he won, it was basically taken away from him...That took a lot out of him. I kind of wish now he'd taken a year off at that point."

Instead, Leyland grabbed an offer from the Rockies, overheated through a disastrous season, and found himself asking, "What am I doing?"

"When you're managing," Leyland said, "you've got to put out fires...But I got to the point where I knew I was shortchanging them. I couldn't attack it. I couldn't put out the fires anymore. And I think that was sending me a message."

The message flashed before his eyes so relentlessly, he told the Rockies he couldn't accept the $4.5 million they owed him over the next two years. Which was honorable on one level, but certainly wasn't portrayed that way around the ski slopes.

Over those next six years, Dombrowski was one baseball friend who always stayed in touch, always keeping his antennas pointed in Leyland's direction. So in 2005, as Alan Trammell lost his grip on a crumbling 91-loss team, Dombrowski began wondering if Leyland's hard drive had been fully reformatted.

He was invited to interview. But Dombrowski had only one question that mattered.

"I just wanted to be convinced he had the fire back," the GM said. "And it took about two minutes. To me, if he wanted to do it, which he did, and he had the fire back, which it became clear he did, there was no question in my mind he was the guy, because he's one of the best."

As ready as Leyland was, though, he wouldn't have come back to manage just anywhere. But here, he was managing for Dombrowski. And he was managing the Tigers, back where it all began.

Back to the team for which he'd played all six seasons of his minor league career, plus one as a player-coach. Back to the team that gave him his first shot to manage, for 11 minor league seasons. And finally, back to the team that gave him the chance to rewrite a final chapter that had gnawed at him throughout this millennium.

Leyland stampeded into spring training and took charge, making sure his players knew there would be order in a clubhouse that split into chaos the year before.

"He has a presence," Dmitri Young said. "You knew, right from the get-go, he was the manager, and what he says goes."

His new closer, Todd Jones, sensed the same dynamic: "He's told us, I don't know how many times, 'Guys, don't push me—'cause you'll lose.'"

Leyland had been able to keep control of clubhouses that held the likes of Bonds, Gary Sheffield, and Kevin Brown. So there was no reason Pudge Rodriguez or Kenny Rogers should terrify him.

But Leyland also had taken steps to do something he didn't do enough of in Colorado—reach out to his players and listen to what they thought.

After his full squad arrived, he held a team meeting to set the rules. But he left some of those rules up to the players. Did they want music in the clubhouse or a dress code on the road? Their call.

"With the big stuff, he tells us the way it's going to be," Jones said. "But on some of the not-so-big stuff, he gives players a little control so we have some input. It's like: 'Here's an olive branch. Let's see what you do with it.' He makes you feel like it's not a totalitarian dictatorship."

They're quite a match, this team and this manager. In his first 14 seasons as a manager, Leyland was never given a team capable of winning and not won. Go back and take a look some time. The Tigers, meanwhile, hadn't had a winning season—with any manager—since 1993, under Sparky Anderson. That was seven managers ago.

But Leyland's first-base coach, Andy Van Slyke, saw the same guy he played for in Pittsburgh, laying the same groundwork that drove the Pirates to three straight NL East titles.

"He hasn't changed his commitment to the fundamentals of the game," Van Slyke said. "He hasn't changed his commitment to the integrity of the game. He hasn't changed his work ethic. He hasn't changed his demand that his players play the game right. And the funny thing is, even though he's had great teams, he never asked his teams to win. He just asked them to do those four things I just mentioned."

Not all of his teams were as capable of doing those things as others, unfortunately. So it would be fascinating to see how this team responded. And it would be just as fascinating, Van Slyke said, to see if Leyland's recharged batteries came equipped with longer-lasting tolerance cells.

Nevertheless, Leyland had brought his own personal heat wave to March. Asked if he was a different guy than he used to be, Leyland waxed almost poetic.

"I'm the same guy who managed my first game in Pittsburgh," he said, eyes twinkling. "I'm not the same guy who managed my last game in Colorado. Now, I'm ready to put out the fires."

Dombrowski watched him bursting from field to field—mouth constantly moving, brain waves constantly flowing—and couldn't help but observe: "You know, he's only 61. People think of him as a lot older because he's been around the game such a long time. But there's no reason he can't do this for an extended period if he wants to."

Well, he wanted to. Yeah, it was only March, and he was still undefeated, and he hadn't taken his first multi-time-zone road trip yet. But Leyland made it a point to announce, without anyone asking: "I'm ready to go. I don't want to just manage for two or three years. I hope I'm managing a lot longer than that."

His players would have something to say about that, naturally. But when Leyland thought about the script he was beginning to compose, he obviously had a lot more to prove than you might think. And he clearly wanted to be judged by more than wins and losses.

"I would definitely say that I'm not some grumpy old man coming back into baseball. I'll tell you that," he said. "I'm not some grumpy, old-school guy. Hell, I don't know what old-school means.

"I'm a baseball person who happens to manage. I've managed a long time, and now I'm back at it again."

And then he said the three words that made you understand that intermission was over, the show was going strong, and why the heck were we all traipsing through his office, asking why he's here. He's here, he said, because he's a manager. That's what he is.

"No…big…deal," said Jim Leyland.

February, 2007

How the Tigers Changed Their Stripes

LAKELAND, FLORIDA—As we strolled around the Tigers' 2007 spring training camp, it hit us.

Here in America, we measure winning in the wrong place:

The standings.

If we were really in tune with what sports is all about, we would know there's a better way.

We would measure it with the sight of 2,000 people, huddled around a back field in Tigertown at 10:30 on a wind-chilled Florida morning, watching pitchers fielding ground balls off a fungo bat.

We would measure it with the crazed scramble to find a decent March hotel room in exotic Lakeland, Florida.

We would measure it with the laughs we hear in a transformed clubhouse, a place that is no longer looked upon as a room where losers hang out.

The 2007 Tigers were walking, talking proof that the 97 games the standings say they won in 2006 don't begin to express what they *really* won.

What their World Series journey in 2006 really did was change their franchise. And change their lives. You just had to ask them.

"It does change lives. It changes communities. It changes cities," said first baseman Sean Casey.

"When you win, it really does bring people together. If you're out walking around the mall and you just see a guy with a Tigers hat, it starts a conversation. It brings fans together. It brings fathers and sons out to a game. It brings friends together to watch games on TV. You see it everywhere."

And you do. You saw it imprinted on faces all over Lakeland, never before regarded as a fashionable spring training destination.

You saw it at the ticket windows, where this team sold more Grapefruit League tickets than it had all spring in 2006—before it had even played an inning.

And you could see it in the upbeat demeanor of the people who drew paychecks from this team—a team that had become a laugh track in spikes after 12 straight losing seasons.

"It used to be, if you got released out of the Tigers, you had a problem getting a job," said closer Todd Jones, whose history with this club dated back to 1997. "Because the street cred around the industry was, if he can't cut it in Detroit, how's his career looking? The same thing [happens] with other teams now. But it's just nice to be on this end of the cycle—for once—and not be the butt of a joke, or an afterthought."

Twelve losing seasons in a row. Twelve. No team in history had ever spent that many years below .500 and then pole-vaulted all the way to the World Series.

So how could we properly measure the transformational tidal wave unleashed by a turnaround like that? We asked the people in the middle of it to document and describe it for us. That's how.

The Mind Games

The GM/CEO/club president arrived back in 2002. It didn't take long before David Dombrowski realized he had a mess on his hands.

He didn't merely have to stop the losing, or the how-bad-are-the-Tigers jokes. He had to undo the damage all that losing had inflicted on the brain waves of the people around him.

"One of the goals—and we used to talk about it all the time—was to change the mind-set of the people in the organization," Dombrowski said. "Not that they were losers. They just accepted the losing too easily."

What happens when your team loses for 12 years in a row? That's what happens. So this World Series team that Dave Dombrowski built, he had to begin by building in the mind. In many minds.

By 2007, he could talk about all the plans, the strategies, the goals. He could talk about the people who were brought in and the changes that had to be made. It all had a purpose—this purpose. It all felt right. But there was no way to prove it was right—until a World Series season provided the only proof the planet would take seriously.

"You can talk about building," Dombrowski said. "You can talk about young players. You can talk about quality young players…But they don't get recognized until you win. You've got to win."

It was only a year earlier that Dombrowski came across a list of the top 25 pitching prospects in baseball. It seemed to him that list was missing a prominent name:

A fellow named Justin Verlander.

The day he read that list, we happened to run into him on the same back field in Tigertown. We'll never forget him venting: "If there are 25 better pitching prospects than Justin Verlander, I'll…"

He decided not to finish that sentence. But we got the idea. A year later, it's clear exactly why Verlander didn't make that list.

"You don't get the recognition," said Dave Dombrowski, "until you win."

The Credibility Factor

It was the place nobody wanted to play, and the place nobody wanted to stay.

When he first arrived, Dombrowski said, "you'd try to sign players, and they'd give you reasons why they didn't want to play for you. 'You're not drawing well. You're not winning. Cold-weather climate. Players don't come from there.' I heard all those reasons—and many more.

"I remember one [free agent] who was doing everything he could to not accept our offer. He just kept stringing us along, hoping something else would come up, even though we pretty much knew we were the only team that had made an offer. Even the agent was saying, 'We're just waiting.' And it went on a long time. I mean, months."

Not anymore.

Once a World Series had cast its glow on the franchise, it was almost shocking to hear the marquee future free agents—Pudge Rodriguez, Carlos Guillen, Kenny Rogers—just about begging this team to sign them, extend them, keep them around.

You saw a Sean Casey, jumping at the Tigers' offer, not even a week into the free-agent signing period. You heard a Pudge Rodriguez saying: "Everyone wants to come here right now." So how magical was the power of winning? That said it all.

"Really," Dombrowski said, "that's the difference between one extreme and the other—why people don't want to play with you, versus why, all of a sudden, they do. You've got the same franchise…except you win."

The Closer

The Closer was a Tiger back in the days of Deivi Cruz and Melvin Nieves and Omar Olivares. Todd Jones first joined the Tigers in February 1997, the spring after a 109-loss nightmare.

He hadn't been a Tiger for all 10 seasons since then. But he went back in time further than anyone around him. He saw a once-great franchise disintegrating in front of his eyes. He'd known nothing in this town but losing and more losing.

Until 2006.

When the Tigers brought him back, after a four-and-a-half-year, seven-team intermission, for this.

"My whole career," he said, "my knock was: 'He can't get big outs. He can't pitch in big pressure. He's just a second-tier closer.' Well, being on a good team gives you the avenue to debate that point."

As recently as March of 2004, he'd gotten released by the *Devil Rays*. So imagine the feeling of this man at age 38, finding himself back in Detroit in October 2006, in the middle of a celebration he never thought he'd live to see: A celebration by a team that had just won the ALCS and now had an appointment with the World Series.

It was so overwhelming that, more than an hour after the last pitch, "I went back out on the field," Jones said. "And I sat on the back of the mound—for five minutes, 10 minutes…just sitting there, freezing, in this empty ballpark… knowing I was going to the World Series. And it was such a fulfilling moment."

Later that night, he and his wife went out to dinner—and got a standing ovation. For the next week, as the Tigers waited for the Series to start, he could hardly walk down the street without experiencing another head-on collision with rampant euphoria.

"People were just happy," he said. "We made them happy. People just wanted to come up and say thanks. They didn't want anything. They didn't want you to sign a picture or anything. They just wanted to say thanks. It was an awesome feeling.

"To be a part of that kind of team, that hits such a chord with people, I mean, *that*," said Todd Jones, "is why you play."

The Bond

When do you see this—ever? When do you see a baseball team, in this age of money and mercenaries, bring back just about every player from the year before?

But that's what the Tigers did after the magic of 2006. They lost one reliever (Jamie Walker) to free agency. They traded for Gary Sheffield and signed Jose Mesa. But other than that, this was exactly the same team that played in the World Series the year before.

Hey, it sure wasn't broke. So why would they fix it—or even redecorate it?

And the men in that clubhouse were totally conscious of who was back, because the eight and a half months they spent together in 2006 represented an experience very few humans outside their sphere can relate to.

What they lived through together—the exhilarating games they won, the memories they made, the magic carpet they rode—was the ride of a lifetime. It was a giant magnetic force, bonding them to each other for the rest of their lives.

"People always ask what I like about playing," said catcher Vance Wilson. "Well, I love the competition. But more than that, I love being a part of something. It's always special. But last year, to be a part of something like that, man, it was extra special."

When a baseball team gets so tight that the men in uniform hate to leave the ballpark, it's a sign they've enrolled in a whole different chemistry class than most teams these days. But that was the 2006 Tigers, a group that had a tough time telling the difference between the comforts of home and the comforts of the home office.

After home games, they found themselves hanging around the clubhouse sauna—just to "make fun of each other, laugh about the game, talk seriously about the game," Wilson reported. "Our sauna was just that place where we'd kid around and call it a team meeting."

And even on the road, "it's amazing to think back on how many times the bus had to wait because we weren't ready yet," Wilson laughed. "We had to delay the bus because guys were eating, talking, drinking beer together, all these things…It was almost like an inconvenience, forcing us out of the clubhouse."

So as that heart-thumping voyage kept going and going, they would never forget the feeling of not wanting it to end.

"When we lost to the Cardinals," Wilson said, "I remember us all sitting there in the clubhouse. You look around, and you see all these guys, and you're thinking, like, *Man, I can't believe I've got to go home now*…It's an emotional time. You kind of want to lay on the ground and start crying—not only because you lost, but because you're fixing to leave your teammates, who have become your best friends."

They were forced out of that clubhouse, too, obviously. But a few months later, they were back, staring into the same faces, savoring the rare opportunity to do it again.

Their manager, Jim Leyland, wasn't into rear-view mirrors. So he told them to stuff the good times into their memory banks and take them off the shelf some other time.

But even as they looked ahead, they knew they'd been transformed by the season they left behind. So even the same old spring training drills felt different than before.

"That bond is still there," said Todd Jones. "So it's a different kind of preparation, and a different kind of expectation, because you don't want to let your teammates down, let your friends down who you connected with. And those guys don't want to let you down.

"You know, I've been around a lot of guys that will do extra because they're free agents, because they want to get paid. But I've never been around guys who want to do it because the other 24 are watching them, and who know what it took to get to the World Series last year. We want to make sure that, if all our pieces are back, we don't want to be the reason that it doesn't happen again…

"I guess it's because it takes so much from everybody that you can walk around that clubhouse and look at every player that you played with and remember something they did during the playoffs. Or something that they did during the season to get us there. And that just puts a good feeling in it."

So he was savoring that good feeling—every second of it—because he knew that other feeling, that *old* Tiger feeling, all too well.

"I guess when you've got the most to lose," said Jones, "that's when it feels the best when you win."

Not Just Another Hurdle for the Pirates

AUTHOR'S NOTE: We know now exactly how Clint Hurdle's unique blend of strength, stature, philosophy, and decibels left its mark on the Pittsburgh Pirates. We know now that three seasons into his tenure, they got a scintillating trip to October out of the deal, and that Hurdle got a Manager of the Year award out of it. But we didn't know that back in the spring of 2011, when Clint Hurdle first burst through their door. We only knew this man was already blowing people away with his presence and his wisdom. Here's exactly how it looked and sounded at the time.

Nearly every night, the emails arrive in the inboxes of dozens of employees of the Pittsburgh Pirates.

Amazingly, they aren't written by any Nigerian princes, telemarketers, or online poker champs. They are written by the new manager in town, a fellow named Clint Hurdle. And they all have the same purpose:

Inspiration.

His players get them. His bosses get them. Employees who have barely laid eyes on him get them. These must-read pearls of wisdom may not guarantee the Pirates a single win this season or any season. But they do guarantee that everyone who reads these words will have something to think about—until the next email arrives.

The messages Clint Hurdle delivers via email are the same sorts of messages that come pouring out of his soul—not to mention his vocal cords—just about every minute of every day:

Why not us? Why not now?

You have to eat the elephant one bite at a time.

To win a ballgame, you only have to be better than the team you play that night.

This is how Clint Hurdle talks. This is how Clint Hurdle thinks. This is how Clint Hurdle lives life—and leads people.

Which explains what he's doing in this job in the first place.

The Pirates have run across many hurdles over the last 18½ years, since Sid Bream crossed home plate, and Barry Bonds fled for the West Coast, and all the winning stopped. But this is one Hurdle they have no trouble embracing, because it would be hard to find a franchise in professional sports in more need of inspiration than this one.

Think of all that's transpired since the last time the Pirates had a winning season. Twenty-seven of the other 29 teams have played at least one postseason series. The Yankees have played 152 postseason games. Ninety space-shuttle missions have circled the planet. The Steelers and Penguins have gone to the finals of their sport a half-dozen times...

And five different managers have tried, and failed, to lead the Pirates to the summit of Mount .500.

Yet 22 months after his firing by the Rockies, Clint Hurdle came bursting through his new team's door with no trepidation over the challenge, with no fear of the moment. And he's obviously not faking it—because in his case, the Pirates didn't just choose him. He chose them.

"I think in life, you come to crossroads," he says, in his ever-booming baritone. "And you have opportunities. And you choose the one that fits you the best, the one where you can have a chance to make a difference."

So he passed on the chance to return as the hitting coach for a World Series team in Texas. He declined a second interview for the Mets' managerial job. Instead, he zeroed in on the Pirates, grilling both his friends around the sport and the people who were supposed to be interviewing him about where this franchise was headed.

"They asked tough questions of me, sitting across the desk," he says. "And

I asked tough questions of [them]."

And enough of the right answers came back that here he is, because "these opportunities don't come along very often," he says. "There's not a greater opportunity in all of sports."

We can't tell you—and neither can he—whether this is the man who will finally end the Pirates' unprecedented streak of 18 straight losing seasons. But we can promise you this:

Clint Hurdle *will* make a difference.

For one thing, he couldn't possibly represent more of a difference from the manager who preceded him—the relentlessly low-key John Russell.

For all his baseball smarts, Russell was a man who took the term "soft-spoken" to a whole new level of quietude. So not only were the people of Pittsburgh never too sure of what he was all about, they were barely even sure what his voice sounded like.

But let's just say lack of volume won't be an issue for the new manager.

"He's a big man, with a big voice," says outfielder/first baseman Steve Pearce. "He's a loud guy. But when he talks, people listen."

And in this case, the Pirates *want* people to listen—hope, in fact, that they can't stop listening. When it came time to hire this manager, says team president Frank Coonelly, "the force of his personality was very important to us."

At this point in their history, the Pirates needed a manager who could do a lot more than write out a lineup and flash a squeeze sign. They needed a face, a voice, a presence. They needed a manager who could sell their team and their vision of the future to a fan base that, in Hurdle's words, has been "so beat down for so many years…they don't even care who the manager is."

The idea, of course, is not to make them care who this manager is, either. The idea is to charge toward a brighter tomorrow, behind Andrew McCutchen, Pedro Alvarez, Jose Tabata, and a core group this team is trying its best to dream on. But until that dream comes true, Clint Hurdle's innate magnetism will just have to do.

"We all look forward to the time when the players become our face," says general manager Neal Huntington. "But until then, if Clint is out front, that's great."

At age 53, Hurdle is still a hulking, dominating, figure—a guy you definitely wouldn't want to get into an arm-wrestling duel with. But somehow, it's still that thundering, ring-announcer's voice that overpowers you more than his solid, 6'3" tight end's physique. And that's saying something.

"We have a joke in the organization," Huntington laughs, "that we don't ever want to follow him when we have to give speeches."

Now, as Hurdle found out personally, by living through five straight losing seasons in Colorado before he finally steered the Rockies into the World Series in 2007, the power of personality can only take any manager so far. So just because he's a forceful man with a forceful message, he doesn't want anybody thinking he can charm his way to October.

"The thing you want to watch out for is trying to be the knight on the white horse," he says, "because that's not reality."

And just to reinforce that point, he's also quick to quote one of the most heroic figures of his lifetime—the legendary Popeye the Sailor Man.

"I need to be who I am," Hurdle says. "I can't be somebody I'm not. So I shared a quote from Popeye the other day: 'I am what I am, and that's all that I am.' In other words, don't be somebody you're not. Bring *your* skill set. And bring it every day."

So Hurdle has been serving up his own innovative skill set since the day he showed up beneath the Florida palm trees.

He's given history lessons on Bill Mazeroski and the Lumber Company, to remind the troops that Pirates history began 129 years ago, not 18 years ago. He's brought in "live" base runners from the minor league camp to add real-life urgency to rundown drills.

He's sent every one of his coaches to that minor league camp for a day to work with kids who once felt forgotten. He logged a day in that camp himself, and allowed 73-year-old minor league coach Woody Huyke to manage the big-league team in his place. And Hurdle has charged his entire coaching staff with this mission: bond with these players. Do whatever it takes to forge a connection that keeps this entire locomotive steaming down the same track.

"I'm not talking about a Kumbaya campfire thing," Hurdle quips. "We just want to make sure, from a coaching standpoint, we don't have any 'oh, no' coaches here. And by that I mean, we've all had a coach in our life where, when you saw this guy coming, the first thing you thought was, 'Oh, no. Here we go again.' We want to open up the line of communications where they see us walking up to them and they go, 'I wonder what he's got for me today.'"

And what he's got is an ability to relate to just about anything any of them can possibly experience—because he's probably experienced it himself, along a 35-year winding road that began with a *Sports Illustrated* cover spot at age 21, curled through 10 big-league seasons, and kept spinning until it found its way to this time and place.

"There isn't much that's happened in the game that I haven't faced," he says. "Good. Bad. Sideways. Up. Down. Personal adversity. Professional adversity. All those things. And personal triumph."

And then there was a slice of his history that especially appealed to the Pirates—namely, defying all the cynics who said nobody would ever be able to win anything in the Coors Field ozone. So this wouldn't be his first Mission: Impossible.

"In Colorado, we were told we couldn't win at that altitude," he says. "And you know what? The players ended up winning the National League championship. In Texas, you [supposedly] couldn't win because it's so freaking hot… And we wound up doing something very significant."

But Colorado and Texas were just the warm-up acts for his present assignment. Now he has to try winning with a team that's compiled the longest streak of consecutive losing seasons in North American professional-sports history. A team that went 6–32 on the road after June in 2010. And a team only a few months removed from getting outscored by a terrifying 279 runs in one season. Yikes!

Now *that's* a challenge. But it's one Clint Hurdle can't wait to arm-wrestle.

"I don't know how long this is going to take," he says. "I can't worry about how long. I have to keep pushing us forward one day at a time. I'll use the expression we talked about earlier: how do you eat an elephant? You eat an elephant one bite at a time. If you look at the size of the elephant, it can be overwhelming. But if you just take a bite every day, and you keep these guys believing in themselves, through the rain and the storms and the challenges and the hard times…we can do this together.

"I've told them numerous times," he roars on, "that I'm here because I believe in the players here and what's in place. And I'm not going to get overwhelmed by other people's opinions. I know what's at stake. I know the challenges. I'm also aware [of] the reward. When we get good here, it's gonna be a whole lot of fun. It's gonna be so special and so significant for so many people."

He gets so evangelical about all this, you almost hate to mention how much has to happen for that fun to begin. But there's barely enough room in cyberspace to sum it all up. This team needs many more pieces, a vastly upgraded pitching staff, and, to be honest, a lot more time.

But for the first time in years, there's hope, at least. And the new manager has delivered more than his share of it.

In fact, he delivers it nearly every night—directly to the inbox of the people who need to cling to that hope most.

Greatest Spring Injuries of All Time

Every once in a while, there comes a time, in the sportswriting business, that the stars, the planets, and every asteroid in the heavens line up to pretty much command you to write a column you've been born to write.

This week in March, back in 2012, was one of those weeks.

You didn't have to be a descendant of Carl Sagan that week to detect we had a full moon shining on spring training. All it took was this:

Rays ace David Price had to leave a game with a neck spasm—because he was toweling off between innings, got the towel caught on the hair on the back of his head, and spun his neck around like he was auditioning for a remake of *The Exorcist*.

"We might need more fabric softener in the towels," manager Joe Maddon told *Tampa Bay Times* dugout-linens aficionado Marc Topkin.

Then there was Yankees setup king David Robertson, who sprained his foot—while carrying boxes down the stairs—and had to deny that his wife was chasing him down the stairs at the time.

Hey, it's always a thrill to welcome mishaps like these into the Spring Injury Hall of Fame. And since I've been compiling these calamities for something like 20 years now, it's time to put them in perspective—by presenting the 10 Greatest Spring Training Injuries of All Time, according to a distinguished committee comprised of, well, me.

10. Carlos Baerga cut his finger in 2003 when he went to hand money to his cousin to pay for gas at a gas station, and got the car door slammed on his hand. Just one more reason to pay at the pump.

9. Rich Harden strained his shoulder in 2004 trying to turn off his alarm clock. Turned out that, for once, this was one Rich Harden injury that was nothing to be, ahem, alarmed about.

8. Mo Vaughn missed a game in 2000 after a piece of leaky ceiling dropped into his eye. "We're meeting that curse head-on," said manager Mike Scioscia. "We're not going to let a little drywall stop us."

7. Cardinals pitcher Cliff Politte missed a start in 1998 when he stepped on a pair of pliers he was using to tighten his spikes. Just one more reminder that it's always good to avoid a little tightness in the spring.

6. Rays pitcher Bryan Rekar burned two fingers in 2000—on his lawn mower. That's an injury that ought to be impossible in spring training, except in the case of the only team in baseball that was training (at the time) in its hometown. "Usually," said manager Larry Rothschild, "you'd be in a hotel, and you wouldn't have to mow the carpet."

5. You'd think it would at least be safe to travel to spring training. But it didn't work out that way for Blue Jays pitcher Huck Flener in 1997. He was flying to Florida when a briefcase flew out of the overhead rack, drilled him in the shoulder, and chipped his collarbone. Guess he should have driven.

4. Padres reliever Jay Witasick missed a week and a half of spring training in 2003 after straining his elbow—while throwing out a trash bag. It still ranks as the worst, um, waste pitch of his career.

3. Talk about having a rough day at the office. On the same day in 2004, Marlins pitcher Bryce Florie pulled a rib-cage muscle while throwing, then had a bad dream in the middle of the night that caused him to jump out of bed and slam into the window on his sliding door. He wound up in the emergency room and had to have 15 stitches to stop a cut in his chin. "I need to drive back home and start all over again,"

he told the *Miami Herald*'s Clark Spencer.

2. Phillies pitcher Amaury Telemaco was just minding his own business in 2000, working out on a back field behind the late, great Jack Russell Stadium, when teammate Rico Brogna smoked a BP home run that flew over the right-field wall—and drilled him on the arm. I bet he's still wondering how *that* happened. "Tons of people cross by that same spot every day," he told me at the time. "They come. They go. They never get hit. I used to be with the Cubs, and Sammy [Sosa] hits all those bombs on Waveland Avenue. Everyone there is OK. So why me?"

1. And the Greatest Spring Training Injury of All Time comes to us from Brewers knuckleballer Steve Sparks, who will never live down this 1994 classic. After the team brought in a group of motivational speakers whose routine included ripping up phone books to demonstrate mind-over-matter techniques, Sparks decided to try the same trick—and dislocated his left shoulder. Not only was this one of the freakiest injuries ever, trainer John Adam told the *Milwaukee Journal-Sentinel*'s Tom Haudricourt, but it was also one of the most annoying—"because I had to look up a number later."

March, 2004

Reggie Sanders' Guide to Spring Training

AUTHOR'S NOTE: I love spring training for many reasons. And one of the biggest is that it allows me to write off-kilter pieces like this one, about a baseball player who only wanted to find a home—but instead kept landing in a different home every spring. As Reggie Sanders embarked on his eighth consecutive spring in a different town, I got the brilliant idea to let him spin his very own travelogue. Let's just say Lonely Planet couldn't have spun it any better.

JUPITER, FLORIDA—He has seen enough palm trees to join the cast of Survivor.

He has reported for work in enough different spring training zip codes to get a job with the Postal Service.

He is Reggie Sanders, outfield nomad. And if the Travel Channel ever calls, looking for the perfect spring training tour guide, he could host a 12-hour special. Because this guy is the Arthur Frommer of spring training. If not the Jules Verne of spring training.

He has dodged alligators in exotic Plant City, Florida. He has zig-zagged through the cacti in Tucson. He has hung out with Mickey, Pluto, and Chipper Jones in Disney World.

You name the Florida or Arizona metropolis, Reggie Sanders has trained there. Go ahead. We dare you.

He's a St. Louis Cardinal now. You might have missed that. Which means he's no longer a Pirate, Giant, Diamondback, Brave, Padre, or Red. You might have missed that, too.

That also means he will now be employed by his seventh team in seven years, all in the same league (National), all without ever changing teams once in midseason.

That's a distinguished place in history topped by only one player who ever played—the well-traveled Shorty (Rent, Don't Buy) Radford, who toiled for eight teams in eight years from 1885 to 1892, while never playing for more than one club a year.

Ah, but nobody—not even Shorty—can top Reggie Sanders' place in spring training history (if only because we're pretty sure no one had stopped shoveling snow long enough to invent spring training back in Radford's day).

Sanders' current spring address, in beautiful downtown Jupiter, Florida, is his eighth different spring training site in eight years. And yeah, we did the math on this.

Not only did he get to chill in Bradenton with the Pirates, Scottsdale with the Giants, Tucson with the D-backs, Lake Buena Vista with the Braves, Peoria with the Padres, and Sarasota with the Reds, but...

He also got a bonus site—since the Reds finally figured out a way to escape Plant City in his final season with Cincinnati. He's still celebrating that escape, by the way.

As with everything in life, Reggie Sanders says there's a good side and a bad side to his eternal orbit of the spring training universe.

The good side, he said cheerfully, is that "you really get a chance to see how different organizations work." How many different ways are there to practice those cutoffs and relays at 9:00 AM? Reggie Sanders now knows them all.

And the bad side? Hey, that's easy. You get lost a lot.

Heck, that first day of camp, every single freaking year, you don't even know how to get into the stadium. But after eight years of this drill, Sanders has the answer to that predicament figured out, too.

"I just stay in the car," he laughed. "I wait till somebody else goes in. Then I go in."

Yes, he has seen the best of spring training. And he has seen the worst of spring training. So since the Travel Channel hasn't called yet, we talked him into telling all. All about spring training, that is.

So here it comes, friends, ready or not—Reggie Sanders' Totally Exclusive Guide to Spring Training Sites around the baseball globe:

Best Ballpark: "Disney. It's like a mini-version of a major league stadium."

Worst Ballpark: "Plant City. Aw, the field was OK. Just, there was nothing to do in Plant City." (Pay attention now. There may be a recurrent theme here.)

Best Restaurants: "Disney. You had that Adventure Island. Lot of choices."

Worst Restaurants: "Plant City. The only thing I enjoyed was getting some fried catfish. I must have eaten catfish at least three times a week."

Best Single Restaurant: "Sushi 10 in Tucson. I love eating sushi in spring training."

Most Meals, One Restaurant (or Chain): "Cracker Barrel. I ate a lotttttt of breakfasts at Cracker Barrel."

Best View From Spring Training Condo: "Tucson. I could look out at the mountains *and* the desert. Beautiful."

Worst View From Spring Training Condo: "Plant City. My only view was I-4." (Well, it was either that or a bunch of strawberry plants.)

Best Traffic/Commute: "Jupiter. I live on the golf course, right up the road."

Worst Traffic/Commute: "Sarasota, because I lived at home, in Tampa, and drove it every day. There were a lot of trucks out there, and I got behind every one of them. And there was always construction."

Best Golf After Workouts: "Scottsdale. Of course. Can't beat that."

Worst Golf After Workouts: "Plant City. You can't even play."

Best Ballpark Hitting Background: "Disney. They had a big wall in center. You could really see the ball well."

Worst Ballpark Hitting Background: "Bradenton. They had no background. There was nothing there. So the ball came right out of the sun. If I had bad spring numbers there, that's the reason."

Shortest Workouts: "Braves. Disney. As long as you got your work in, you could get out of there [by noon]."

Longest Workouts: "Probably the Pirates. Bradenton. Lloyd [McClendon] had some long ones." Asked if the Pirates get a lot of twilight golf rates thanks to those workouts, Sanders chuckled, "You do, as a matter of fact."

Best Description of the Weather in Arizona: "Consistency."

Best Description of the Weather in Florida: "Humidity."

Place He Wished He Could Have Bought a Condo if He'd Known He Would Have Been There More Than a Year: "Jupiter. Right here. I hope this is it." (The Cardinals did, in fact, give him a two-year contract—but no no-trade clause.)

Place He's Grateful He Never Bought a Condo, Even if He'd Known He'd Train There 10 Years: "Plant City, because you can't get your money back."

What He Remembers About Spring in Plant City: "Probably getting the opportunity to play with Schottzie 02." (Yeah, he really said that.)

What He Remembers About Spring in Sarasota: "Windy. Very windy. But a good teppanyaki restaurant."

What He Remembers About Spring in Peoria: "My first spring training in Arizona. Loved it. There's just something about the sand and the mountains together."

What He Remembers About Spring in Disney: "The amusement park, man— and my kids loving it."

What He Remembers About Spring in Tucson: "Going to play golf with Steve Finley a lot. Uh-oh. I guess I should be talking about baseball, huh?"

What He Remembers About Spring in Scottsdale: "My all-time favorite place. I actually live there now."

What He Remembers About Spring in Bradenton: "It reminded me of a retiree place."

His Impression of Spring in Jupiter: "I have a feeling this will be a good place for me. Jupiter is the beginning of a two-year journey. I like the sound of that."

And after all those one-year cameo appearances in all those Plant Citys and Bradentons, this is a man who deserves a two-year journey—even more than another $4.49 breakfast at Cracker Barrel.

The Invited to Spring Training All-Stars

AUTHOR'S NOTE: It wouldn't be true to say I've written a version of this column every spring for th-e last 20 years—but it's close. Is there any concept more bizarre in sports that "inviting" a guy to stop by and maybe help you win a World Series? But it happens every year. So there's always a cool story to tell behind every one of those mysterious "invitations."

ST. PETERSBURG, FLORIDA—When most of us get an invitation, we're honored. Possibly delighted. Maybe even downright teary-eyed.

And that's just at the thought of lining up at an open bar.

But in baseball, the only "invitations" we've run across don't tend to be quite that inspirational. No tears are shed. No vows will be exchanged. No gifts are allowed.

That's because in baseball, the only place a player ever gets "invited" is to spring training. And a rough synonym for "invited," in this case, would go something like:

Just be glad you're not unemployed and shoveling snow.

As we've mentioned before this time of year, we always love that expression, "invited to spring training—as in: "Atlanta Braves Sign IF-OF-C-RHP Mike Glofenstofferhof and Invite Him to Spring Training."

For Mike Glofenstofferhof, you understand, this probably means his only other offer was from Walmart. So this "invitation" was actually just his way of postponing real life for at least another month and a half.

But it's still a fascinating way to describe that phenomenon—with a festive word like "invites." We bet you've wondered about this yourself. Is there a little RSVP card included that a guy has to send back in a pre-stamped blue envelope?

"I'll put it this way," said nonroster Twins quotesmith Andy Fox. "If you're a nonroster guy, your aspirations for winning the MVP are nil. So you go for the RSVP."

But in fact, this whole concept of "inviting" guys to spring training has always appeared to be a massive hoax. No one we know has ever found his invitation in the mail, enclosed in a fancy embossed envelope that probably cost more than his contract.

Fortunately, our favorite baseball problem-solver, 2005 Yankees invitee Doug Glanville, had gotten to the bottom of this enduring sporting mystery.

"People are missing the boat on this," Glanville reported. "It's the era of cyberspace. If they didn't get their invitation, they probably didn't submit their email address. It turns out, you need a password. Then they send you a code. You go through six websites, pass through a couple of firewalls, and you're there.

"It's a little complicated, so a lot of guys don't get it…But I used my engineering background and called some of my professors from Penn, and they gave me some tips on how to decrypt. So that's how it works. People just aren't thinking outside the box. They're waiting by the mailbox. But nobody sends mail anymore."

So there you have it. There is an invitation involved. You just need to consult a few of your favorite Ivy League faculty members to locate it.

Nevertheless, even if you ever do get that invitation, we wouldn't advise counting on any open bars.

"Well, we do get lunch," Glanville said. "We have a lot of spaghetti and meatballs here in camp. That's free. But an open bar? That might be a little dangerous."

Every year in spring training, we find hundreds of extra players roaming the free-spaghetti lines, looking—to the untrained eye—almost exactly like the Derek Jeters and Carlos Beltrans of the baseball universe. Or wearing the same uniforms, anyway.

But the trained eye can pick out many of those invitees in about 1.2 seconds—if only because there's a good chance they're wearing a number higher than their salary.

"My first year I was an invited guy, in Cincinnati, I came to camp and I had No. 56," says by-invitation-only Marlins pinch-hit specialist Lenny Harris. "When I got my first at-bat, I was out in the on-deck circle, and I heard a guy say, 'Hey, Lenny Harris—you're a good player, but you've got to get rid of that Bengals number.'"

So in this particular spring, Harris was feeling a little better—since he was wearing No. 10. Which at least means that, if he wound up with the Dolphins, they might let him play quarterback.

"If I ever came in and they gave me No. 97," Harris says, "I'd just turn back around and go home."

Nobody we know has ever done a scientific study on the uniform numbers of players invited to spring training. But we'll go with Lenny Harris' highly unscientific conclusion: the lower your number, the better chance you have of making the team.

"I didn't know what number I was going to get," says Glanville, who does know that the Yankees' supply of low numbers is kind of limited. "I just figured when I did put it on, I'd better make sure that Tiki Barber wasn't behind me."

But that wide receiver job can wait, because Glanville was handed No. 26. So he knew there was hope he might still be wearing it in April.

There were no guarantees of that, though. Which is part of the gig when you're invited to spring training: No perks. No glory. No tee times. No promises.

And no complaints.

"This is a totally different spring training than any I've ever had," says Dean Palmer, once a Tigers star, in 2005 a Tigers invitee. "You don't start a game, then get the next day off. If you do start a game, the next day you go in late for defense. You make every road trip. And you don't ever get a day off. But you know what? It's kind of fun."

It wasn't so long ago that Palmer was an All-Star—a Silver Slugger third baseman who averaged almost 30 homers per year from 1993 through 2000. But by the spring of 2005, at age 36, the only All-Star team he qualified for was ours—the Invited to Spring Training All-Star team.

In fact, Dean Palmer just might be the ultimate Invited to Spring Training All-Star—because this wasn't merely a comeback he's mixed up in. It was practically a reincarnation.

Remember the last time Palmer got 500 at-bats in a season? Probably not, since it was back in 2000. He hit 29 homers and drove in 102 runs for the Tigers that year. The next spring, his shoulder started throbbing. He needed rotator-cuff surgery by July. And over the next four and a half seasons, he accumulated a total of 12 hits. Which is, essentially, about one weekend in the life of Ichiro.

Palmer headed for the disabled list to stay on May 10, 2003. Even *he* thought that was the last we'd ever see of him.

Uh, apparently not. In the fall of 2004, he felt that itch again while watching the playoffs. And he noticed his shoulder didn't hurt anymore. And then this saga took a really insane twist.

It isn't every Invited to Spring Training All-Star who is lucky enough to have his five-year-old twin sons end up in the same class at school as the son of a real, live major league general manager. But that happened to Dean Palmer.

That GM was the Tigers' Dave Dombrowski. And because of that connection with their kids, "I see him all the time," Dombrowski said.

So one day, Dombrowski wondered whether Palmer might be interested in a job as a coach or a scout. Palmer said he had a better idea.

"The way I went out of the game before, it wasn't the way I would have picked," Palmer said. "I thought it would be a situation where you just say you've had enough and walk away. But I hadn't had enough.

"This way, if I go through spring training and it turns out that's it, at least I was playing. I was on the field playing, and I just didn't have what it takes to play in the big leagues. And I could accept that."

Palmer knew when he arrived in camp that there probably was no roster vacancy for him to step into. But the Tigers never did treat him like a guy with no chance. They gave him a ballplayer's number (17). He even got his old locker back.

And 24 at-bats into his Grapefruit League audition, he was hitting .292, with a homer and three RBIs. So after eyeballing him for a few weeks, his manager, Alan Trammell, was ready to say that when he looks at Dean Palmer, he saw "a major league player."

All that means is a couple more weeks of having to prove himself. But when you're an Invited to Spring Training All-Star, having to prove yourself all spring is an unwritten clause in the contract.

"I always tell people I like it like that," said Harris, who may have set an all-time record by going to camp as a lowly invitee for the sixth straight year. "My dad used to say, 'Nobody gives you anything in life. You have to earn it.' So that's what I want to do—earn it. If anybody ever gives me something, I might relax. I don't want that."

So while the big boys go play golf at noon, the Invited to Spring Training All-Stars go out to take batting practice in a group full of guys wearing No. 78 or 86.

While the big boys jet into spring training first-class, "I get 20 bucks for mileage from Miami," Harris chuckled. But still, it sure beats real life.

"You can't come in and expect to be treated like a superstar," Palmer said. "You've gotta be humble."

But for some of the humbled ones, if the breaks fall right and the bloopers fall safely, they'll find themselves riding on that airplane when it heads north. And they'll get to head for the ballpark, not a PTA meeting.

"Even my son's been amazed by this," Dombrowski said of the fellow PTA father now wearing his uniform. "We were at a game the other day, and Landon was saying, 'That's Casey and Bryce's dad. Is he really playing for the Tigers, Dad?'"

Well, yeah he was—for the moment, anyway. And who knows? If this works out, you might find GMs sending their scouts to a bunch of parent-teacher conferences next winter, looking for next spring's greatest Invited to Spring Training All-Star.

"Hey, we're open to any way we can find players," said Dave Dombrowski. "You never can tell."

Chapter 3
Champions

The 2009 Yankees

NEW YORK—They stood together, arms around each other's shoulders, on a makeshift podium in the middle of a still-packed stadium as euphoria rained from the sky.

Mariano Rivera. Derek Jeter. Andy Pettitte. Jorge Posada.

They had done this before. And not just once. But somehow, this time was different. This time was special. This night was one that made them want to freeze time and hold onto a moment that was nine years in the making.

The clock had already blown past midnight on the night the New York Yankees won their 27th World Series. And the Gang of Four who connected two Yankee generations were going to savor this one for many more ticks of that clock.

So Derek Jeter held the World Series trophy in his hands and looked out at the ecstatic masses.

"Now," he said, cradling that trophy as if he might never let it go, "this thing is right where it belongs."

Behind the four of them, the scoreboard told the tale of the final World Series game, the final baseball game, of 2009: Yankees 7, Phillies 3.

But scoreboards never tell you the whole story. And for these four men, this was a night that couldn't have followed a more perfect script if George Steinbrenner had been able to personally sign the big script-writing free agent in the sky to an $8-zillion contract.

The Great Mariano got the final five outs. Derek Jeter slapped three hits. Andy Pettitte won the clinching game of a postseason series for the *sixth* time. Jorge Posada was the man catching that first pitch by Pettitte and that final pitch by Rivera.

There was something fitting about that—the four of them finding their names in this particular box score—because they are the men who connect all the dots in the Yankees' universe.

You might have trouble convincing a Cubs fan or a Giants fan or an Indians fan that it had been a long time since the Yankees had themselves a night like this. But it was longer than you think.

The last time the New York Yankees did this, the men squirting champagne all over the Gang of Four were long-lost names like David Justice, and Denny Neagle, and even Jose Canseco. It feels like those guys haven't played in the big leagues in 90 years, not nine. But the last time the Yankees floated down the Canyon of Heroes, those men were riding right along with them.

In between titles, Mike Mussina came and went. Jason Giambi came and went. Even Raul Mondesi, Rondell White, and Karim Garcia came and went.

But Derek Jeter and Mariano Rivera and Jorge Posada kept putting on those pinstripes day after day. Pettitte bolted for Houston, then found his way back. And it was all about waiting for this night to arrive again.

So by the time it did, they understood this wasn't their birthright, wasn't as automatic as their teams had once made it look.

"It makes it sweeter, no doubt," said Andy Pettitte, "because you don't know if you're going to go back. I realize I'm 37 years old. I realize I'm getting older. I realize I'm toward the end of my career. And that makes it sweet.

"The first one is always sweet, because you live your whole life, you want to win a championship, and when you're able to do it that first time, that's sweet. But when so many years pass, you don't know if you're ever going to be able to do it again. So it's just very gratifying to be able to do this."

We understand this is no tale of some plucky underdog battling to this place against all odds. This was a $208 million baseball team we're talking about. This was a team that paid its four infielders alone more money ($81.225 million) than 16 of the other 29 franchises paid their whole *team*. This was a team that had spent nearly $1.9 billion hard-earned Steinbrenner-family dollars in between trips to the Canyon of Heroes.

But contrary to popular belief, it's never dollars alone that make that happen. You need talent. You need brains. And you need people—people who understand what winning is all about, what leadership is all about, what being a teammate is all about.

So these Yankees needed the Gang of Four—even more than they ever needed them back in the day when they were winning four of these titles in five years.

"On those teams [that won in the '90s], those guys were young," said GM Brian Cashman. "They weren't veteran guys like they are now. They had different roles. Derek Jeter wasn't a leader back then. Jorge Posada wasn't a leader then. They were the guys looking to the David Cones, the Paul O'Neills, the Scott Brosiuses, the veterans around them. But now this is those guys' team. They've taken over that leadership role. And they've proved they can deliver a championship with a whole new cast."

That cast included the World Series MVP, Hideki Matsui, a man who would drive in a record-tying six runs in the Series clincher. And it included a fellow who had spent his entire Yankees career listening to the amusing debate about whether he was a "true Yankee," Alex Rodriguez. And it included the latest batch of Yankees free agents who will eventually earn more money than the Gross National Product of Trinidad and Tobago—Mark Teixeira, CC Sabathia, and A.J. Burnett.

But those pieces never could have fit if the leaders on this Yankees team didn't do what had to be done to make sure they fit. And the Gang of Four made sure.

"You know what?" said Burnett, still sopping from the Moet & Chandon shower he had to show for his first season in New York. "These guys are very classy individuals—Jeter, Mariano, Pettitte, and Posada, especially for me, in my first year here, being a pitcher. They're guys who really showed you how to be a New York Yankee.

"And they do that by being themselves. By showing class. And being the most humble human beings I've ever been around. They're all Hall of Famers, but you wouldn't know it, man. They come in here, and they're just one of us. They're humble people who play this game one day at a time, one game at a time. And that rubbed off on everyone else."

But this was a night to recognize that the Gang of Four was still—even now—way more than just a quartet of nostalgic figures from the '90s who hung around the clubhouse, telling stories about the good old days.

Jeter may have reached age 35, but he was coming off a season in which he hit .334. Spewed 212 hits. Finished third in the league in on-base percentage (.406). Then his seventh World Series rolled around, and all he did was bat .407, hit safely in all six games, and just miss tying the record for most hits in a six-game World Series.

"This is what you play for," Jeter said, on the night he passed Lou Gehrig on the all-time World Series hits list. "When you're six, seven years old, you're out on the field, thinking about being in the World Series, winning the World Series. And it's always something special to be able to do it."

This one meant he had now won more World Series as a Yankee (five) than Babe Ruth (who "only" won four). And he was so consumed by the quest for a ring that he didn't watch a single World Series game he wasn't playing in over the previous eight years. And why was that? Because "it makes me sick" not to be there, he said.

This night came 13 years and 33 days after the first winning postseason game Derek Jeter ever played in. So what were the odds that the same pitcher started this game who started that one—Andy Pettitte?

Pettitte's manager, Joe Girardi, took a big gamble on a 37-year-old left-hander, starting him on three days' rest in a game of this magnitude. But Pettitte made his manager's I.Q. look MENSA-ready, by firing five two-hit, one-run innings before tiring in the sixth.

Nevertheless, Andy Pettitte did enough to become the oldest starting pitcher to win a World Series game on short rest since 1958 (Warren Spahn). And the oldest to win a Series clincher on any amount of rest since 1931 (Burleigh Grimes). And the first pitcher in the wild-card era to start and win the clinching game of all three postseason series in the same year.

"I just feel very fortunate, very blessed, to be healthy right now and to be able to pitch in the postseason here and help this team win," he said.

You might say the man who caught him on this night, Jorge Posada, had done that a few times before. Like 202 times to be exact—22 of them in the postseason. Of Pettitte's 229 career regular season wins, Posada had been the starting catcher in 95 of them. Of Pettitte's 18 postseason wins, Posada had caught 11 of those. They're the only pitcher-catcher tag team in history with that many postseason wins together. Astounding.

Meanwhile, the first postseason start Pettitte ever made came way back in Game 2 of the 1995 Division Series. The young reliever who got the last 10 outs of that game? It was a kid named Mariano Rivera. Who else?

So how could it be that 14 years later, there was Mariano again, getting the final five outs of another Pettitte start on another postseason stage? This was the fourth time Rivera had thrown the final pitch of a World Series clincher—twice as many as any other pitcher in history. And even at age 40, his aura still shone as bright as it ever has.

Let the historians note that it was 11:14 PM, Eastern Steinbrenner Time, when the bullpen door swung opened and out he came.

Camera flashes sparkled around him as The Great Mariano began the long jog to his home office—to do what he does better than anyone has ever done it.

To finish what Andy Pettitte had started…

To end the reign of the defending champions…

And to complete the nine-year journey of the only franchise he has ever thrown a pitch for.

This, for the New York Yankees, is what victory looks like—what it's looked like for a dozen years.

Asked if this game felt as if it was over in his mind when Rivera popped out of that bullpen, Jeter laughed and said: "It's over in *everybody's* mind."

"I mean, he's human," Jeter said of his buddy, Mo. "He's going to give up some runs here and there. But a four-run lead? C'mon man. We could have gone on and played another nine innings [and he wouldn't have blown that lead]."

And Derek Jeter ought to know. He had watched this man pitch in 88 post-season games. And never once, in any of those outings, did Mariano Rivera give up as many runs (three) as the closer on the other side, Brad Lidge, allowed in a span of four *hitters* in Game 4 of this World Series.

These four men—Jeter, Rivera,

TRIVIALITY

Derek Jeter and Jorge Posada played in 29 World Series games together. Of course, it was helpful that they played for the Yankees. Can you name the only two players in the Division Play era who have appeared in at least 29 World Series games but never played for the Yankees?

Pettitte, and Posada—have played in six World Series together. Before this group (and Bernie Williams) came along, no other foursome on any team had played in that many World Series together since Mickey Mantle, Whitey Ford, Elston Howard, and Bobby Richardson shared seven, between 1957 and 1964. The all-time record is eight, by Mantle, Ford, Howard, and Yogi Berra.

So for the men who make up the Gang of Four, it wasn't winning alone that they celebrated on this night. It was winning together.

"It's special," Jeter said. "We've played together for what—17 years, 18 years? We were together in the minor leagues coming up. And you don't see that too often, especially with free agency. You don't see guys staying together. We're like brothers. And to get an opportunity to spend all these years together and win another championship, it really feels good."

They've won more titles together than Ruth and Gehrig, than Gehrig and Joe DiMaggio, than DiMaggio and Allie Reynolds. Think about that. Sure, you can say this group had timing on its side. But was that luck? Or was it more? When four players this great share what these four have shared, it's not just about good fortune. Not anymore.

So Derek Jeter, Jorge Posada, Andy Pettitte, and Mariano Rivera haven't merely hung out together on a baseball field all these years. They've defined their generation. And on the night they won again—side by side—after eight empty Octobers, they understood the power of the moment.

TRIVIA ANSWER
Pete Rose (34, for the Reds and Phillies) and Lonnie Smith (32, for the Phillies, Cardinals, Royals, and Braves).

"It's amazing," said Rivera. "I mean, I tried to never forget [what it felt like]. But when you're in there, you know how much you miss it. You find out, definitely, how much you miss it to be in this position."

He may have been the closer for a $208 million baseball team. But "to be the last team standing and to be on the mound and win the whole thing," said Mariano Rivera, "that's priceless."

October, 2004

The 2004 Red Sox

St. Louis—A hundred years from now, how will we make people understand what just happened here?

How will we ever make them understand what happened The Year the Red Sox Finally Won the World Series?

There was no way they could ever do this the good old normal way. Never. They're the Red Sox.

They had ghosts to blow away, and lots of them. They had curses to blow away, and not just any curse.

They had fathers and grandmothers and many a lost generation to redeem, to heal, to shower in tears of joy.

So their work wasn't easy. They always understood that. But who ever figured on *this*? Who ever figured it would take the most amazing week and a half in the history of sports?

Nobody goes from humiliation to annihilation in 10 insane days. But the 2004 Red Sox did.

Nobody goes from sweep-ee to sweep-er in 10 life-altering days. But the 2004 Red Sox did.

And then there they were, on the final Wednesday night in October, in a big round stadium in Missouri, doing what we once thought we would never live to see. And allowing us to type a sentence we once thought we would never live to type:

The Boston Red Sox won the World Series. We saw it with our own eyes.

"They can take that curse thing now and put it where the sun don't shine," said Keith Foulke, the man who threw the final pitch of the 3–0 victory that completed a four-game obliteration of the St. Louis Cardinals. "That curse is over. Now we'll never have to hear about that thing again."

Well, not in the present tense, anyway. But as long ago as 1918 seemed on this night, the evening of October 17 might have seemed even longer ago.

Tell us this really happened. Tell us that, on October 17, 2004, this team was really three outs away from getting swept by the Yankees, and the only way to stay alive was to score a run off the Greatest October Closer in the History of Mankind, Mariano Rivera.

And then tell us *this* really happened. Tell us that, just 10 days later, with no pinstripes within a thousand miles, Pedro Martinez would be racing around the outfield of Busch Stadium lifting the World Series trophy above his head. And hundreds of Red Sox fans wouldl remain transfixed in their seats in this strange stadium in this strange land, chanting in unison at a 1.8-trillion decibel level: "Red Sox Nation! Red Sox Nation!"

OK, it really happened. We have witnesses. But how? In 10 days? This wasn't a comeback. This was a reincarnation.

Rack your brain. Tell us any team ever, in any sport, ever had a week and a half like this team had just had. From down 0–3 in one series—to sweeping the World Series?

"Never," said Doug Mientkiewicz. "It would be hard to do it again. I know that. But I think one thing this group never stopped doing was believing it could win. Even down 0–3, guys were standing in this clubhouse saying, 'Don't let us win one, because we just might get on a roll.'"

A roll? Heck, it was more like a tsunami. But as it turned out, it wouldn't be 100 percent true to say that *everyone* believed back then. We have witnesses for that, too.

"I understand," GM Theo Epstein confessed, "that certain people in this organization were literally writing their concession speeches around the seventh inning of Game 4. Not me, of course. But people were putting together speaking points—about how deeply disappointed we all were, things we'd be working on to get ready for next year. I mean, it didn't look real good."

Yeah, you might say that. But even as that ninth inning began that night, as the great Mariano flipped his warm-ups toward home plate, the men in the other dugout were already plotting just how the world was about to change.

"We knew if we could just get one guy on, we could get Dave [Roberts] in the game," Mientkiewicz said. "And Dave has the ability to steal second, even when everyone in the world knows he's going. And then that's just how it worked out. It just seemed like every time our backs were against the wall, we had the right guy in the right place to do exactly what he was capable of doing."

Could you possibly sum up this improbable week and a half better than that last sentence? Right guy? Right place? Right everything? From that moment on—for 10 days, for eight mind-boggling baseball games—everything went right.

For the Boston Red Sox.

In October.

What a country.

For a week and a half, it seemed as if all that Stuff That Always Happened to the Red Sox was suddenly happening *for* the Red Sox.

Who knows how? Who knows why? Who knows who pulled what switch to make everything change in the universe?

But it changed, all right. Did it ever.

So *of course*, Kevin Millar drew a walk against Rivera. And *of course*, Roberts pinch-ran for him and stole second. And *of course*, Bill Mueller slapped a single past the sprawling Mariano to tie the game. And *of course*, David Ortiz bombed a walkoff homer in the middle of the night to win it.

And so the tidal wave began. The comeback against Rivera again the next day (well, actually *that* day). The Ortiz blooper that won Game 5 in the 14th. The astounding masterpiece pitched by The Man with the Bloody Sock (Curt Schilling) in Game 6.

The Game 7 call that somehow went their way—*in Yankee Stadium*—when A-Rod played The Karate Kid. The Johnny Damon–Derek Lowe Show that fueled that historic Game 7 wipeout.

And then on to the Series, where the big wheels just kept on turning. Damon doubling to lead off the first inning of Game 1. Ortiz homering to make it 4–0. Four errors. Manny's Divot. Red Sox 11, Cardinals 9. And little did we know—this Series was over.

"I was worried, after New York, that we wouldn't have enough juice to get back out there and grind it out and do it again," Mientkiewicz said. "But this group never stopped believing. We just kept saying, 'It's our time.'"

And that's exactly what it was—their time. The Cardinals won more games than any team in baseball in 2004. The Red Sox made them look like the Canton Crocodiles.

It's hard enough to sweep a team that won 105 games. But the Red Sox didn't just sweep these Cardinals. They dismantled them.

The Cardinals became the first team in the history of the World Series to trail at some point in *every* inning of *every* game. The most feared lineup in the National League hit .190 for the World Series, .143 after Game 1. Of the last 84 Cardinals hitters to come to the plate, 74 of them made an out. Over the final three games, they had *one* multi-hit inning.

Schilling won again in Game 2. Pedro turned back into Pedro in Game 3. And then there they were in Game 4, one win away.

From the moment Damon smoked the fourth pitch of the evening into the Cardinals' bullpen, for the first Red Sox World Series leadoff homer in 101 years, you knew. It was their time. Really.

Two innings later, Trot Nixon got a 3-0 green light, with two outs and the bases loaded—and squashed it halfway up the right-field fence for two more runs. It was their time. Wasn't it?

"Not at all," Nixon said. "Not with the kind of lineup those guys have. We knew we were still going to need a great pitching performance…When you've got the enemy on the side of the cliff, you need to step on his hand and let him fall. You don't give him the opportunity to get his hand back up on the mountain."

But the innings went by, and the hand still hung on that mountain. A half-dozen Red Sox hitters came to the plate with a chance to put this thing away, so all those paramedics all over New England could go home. But nobody could get that hit.

They *had* to leave 12 runners on base—seven in scoring position. They *had* to. They're the Red Sox.

"I'm telling you, man. That was gut-wrenching," Nixon said. "I couldn't take it. I probably won't sleep for three days after that. But that's just the way we go about it around here."

On this night, though, Lowe wouldn't let that lead shrink. He pounded those Cardinals with sinkers for seven brilliant three-hit innings. Then he passed the ball to Bronson Arroyo, who passed it on to Alan Embree, who handed it to Foulke. Who got to do what Calvin Schiraldi and Bob Stanley and Dick Drago never got to do:

Throw *that* pitch. The pitch that ended an 86-year nervous breakdown.

"I don't even remember it, to tell you the truth," Foulke would say later, drenched in champagne from his head to his socks. "What kind of pitch was it? It was an out. That's all I know."

It was an out. That's all that mattered.

Just minutes before, Foulke had stood there, 60 feet away from the man who would make that out (Edgar Renteria), thinking about how shocked he was to feel as calm as he felt.

"It was probably a lot tougher, sitting in the stands, or watching on TV, or watching from the dugout," he said. "It was a lot easier to have the ball in my hand than it was to watch."

If he only knew. The tying run was on deck. All across the universe, the hearts of all those Red Sox fans—young or old, husband or wife, son or daughter, uncle or aunt, grandma or grandpa—were pumping faster than hearts should be allowed to pump.

And then Edgar Renteria was one-hopping That Out right back to the mound. Right to Keith Foulke. Who stabbed it out of the air. And began trotting toward first base. Where he flipped it to Mientkiewicz. And at that moment—10:40 PM in the Central Time Zone—the world became a whole different place.

The Boston Red Sox had won the World Series.

"It didn't take long to sink in," Foulke said. "At first, it was a strange thing. You never know what's going to happen until the last out is made. But after it's made, I found myself saying, 'Whoa. We did it.'"

Whoa. They did it. We saw it. You saw it. It must be true.

But when our memories begin to fade, how will we explain this? How will we make people understand what happened here? How will we make *ourselves* understand what happened?

How can anyone ever explain the most amazing week and a half in the history of sports? Was it really only 10 days earlier they were three outs away from another one of Those Winters? It suddenly seemed like 10 years ago.

"I'll tell you what," Epstein said. "I think I was only 14 during that Angels series, it seems so long ago. I can't even remember that anymore."

Aw, but who cares? He'll remember this night. Who won't?

It was The Night the Red Sox Won the World Series. The night they set the ghosts free.

"We knew it wasn't going to be easy," Mientkiewicz said. "So we had to do something different. We had to do something that never happened before."

They had to. They're the Red Sox. And on this remarkable night of goose-bumps and champagne, they were something they hadn't been for 86 para-lyzing years.

Finally, unbelievably, they were the champs.

The 2005 White Sox

HOUSTON—Just one month earlier, no one ever would have bet it would end like this.

Just one month earlier, as they were watching a 14-game lead shrink all the way down to a 1½-game lead, the debate about the 2005 Chicago White Sox never seemed to involve whether they belonged in the same sentence as the '27 Yankees, or even the '99 Yankees.

No, the debate back then was whether they were heading for the same sentence as the '64 Phillies—a *life* sentence, that is. In confinement with the great collapsers of all time.

"Yeah, a month ago, they were calling us chokers," said White Sox poet laureate A.J. Pierzynski on this magical night in October. "But now they can call us something else that starts with a C-H—champions."

The Chicago White Sox…Champions. How 'bout *that* for a stranger-than-heck phenomenon?

Until this night, it was a phenomenon that only about 14 living humans were familiar with—for the same reason that you no longer run across many members of the Eddie Cicotte Fan Club.

In other words, 88 years ago was a long, long, lonnnnggg time ago. Even longer than that six-hour World Series game these White Sox had played just the night before.

The last time the Chicago White Sox won a World Series, there were no radio stations to listen to it on. And no such thing as a national anthem to sing before every game. And no such animal as a commissioner of baseball to hand them their trophy.

The last time the Chicago White Sox won a World Series, it was 1917. And the best part of winning it *that* year was that they never had to hear a soul complain about crummy TV ratings.

One of these years, or one of these decades, or one of these centuries, you knew some White Sox team was bound to win another one. But who among us thought it would be this team, in *this* year? (Sorry, members of the Guillen and Konerko families are ineligible to answer that question.)

But on this night, it didn't matter what anybody thought of these White Sox in February. All that mattered was the 27th out that landed in the glove of Mr. White Sox, Paul Konerko.

The out that finished off a 1–0 win over the Houston Astros.

The out that finished off an improbable sweep of an improbable World Series.

The out that ended 88 years of Wait Till Next Year seasons for a franchise that had spent every one of those seasons living in the shadow of another team in its own city.

"I've been here for seven years," said Konerko. "And on this team, I've been here the longest, along with Frank [Thomas]. But compared with all the fans and all the people who put up with the frustrations of this team for all those years, that's nothing. Those are the people who have suffered for a long, long time.

"But when you win, people don't forget you. So now, we'll always be remembered as part of the team that finally jumped over that wall."

When this team jumped that wall, however, it was one giant leap for White Sox kind, because here's the thunderous way in which they did it:

- They swept the World Series—for the first time in franchise history.

- They won their final eight games in a row—tying the 2004 Red Sox for the longest winning streak any team has had in a single postseason.

- They went 11–1 in their 12 postseason games—tying the '99 Yankees for the best postseason record of the 11-season wild-card era.

- They played six road games in this 2005 postseason—against teams (Boston, Anaheim, and Houston) that finished a combined 69 games over .500 at home—and won *all six.*

- And they became just the third team in history to sweep a World Series after a season in which they were in first place *every* day of the season. Those other two teams were the 1990 Reds and the fabled '27 Yankees.

"The '27 YANKEES?" gulped Pierzynski after hearing that news. "I don't think we're exactly the '27 Yankees. We've got no Babe Ruth. We don't even have a Roger Maris. We do have the Three Stooges, though—me, [Joe] Crede, and [Aaron] Rowand: Ro, Mo, and Yo."

But if that's what it took to shake off 88 years of ghosts and demons, no one on the South Side of Chicago would have cared if their double-play combination was Laurel and Hardy, or their starting rotation was the cast of *American Pie.*

"We're different than a lot of teams that win the World Series," said Konerko. "We don't have a lot of All-Star type guys. We've got a bunch of low-maintenance, low-key guys here. I don't think that when we're done, we'll have any guys who will make you say, 'That guy was the best player in the league at his position.'

"But we're proof that you don't have to put together an All-Star team to win it, like some teams that went down along the way. I don't have to mention their names. You know who they are. We're not a team that was a lock to win. We could start the playoffs again tomorrow and get knocked off in three games, because we aren't some unbelievably great team. We're just a team that played our best baseball when we had to."

This was a team whose claim to fame all year was its ability to win those 2–1 games that supposedly went out of style about 1968. This was a team that, amazingly, won 15 games in which it scored one run or two—the most by any World Series champ since the '88 Dodgers.

And this was a team that, including the postseason, went an insane 68–35 in games decided by one run or two—the best record in baseball.

So how fitting was the final chapter to this team's story? How fitting was it that the White Sox wound up sweeping a World Series in which they never led by more than two runs at *any* point in *any* game?

How fitting was it that they outscored the Astros by only six runs over the entire World Series and still managed to sweep it—tied with the 1950

Yankees for the smallest margin by any sweepers in history. And how fitting was it that the grand finale was one last 1–0 game?

"Our first game of the year was 1–0," Pierzynski said. "Our first game of the second half was 1–0. And our last game of the year was 1–0. You couldn't ask for a better script."

It was a script that included the first World Series game to roll into the eighth inning with a 0–0 score since Jack Morris versus John Smoltz, Game 7, 1991.

It was a script that revolved around the brilliance of one more White Sox starting pitcher—in this case, Freddy Garcia (seven innings pitched, four hits, zero runs).

And it was a script that turned on the efforts of yet another member of this team's bench crew—the increasingly legendary "Group 4" scrubeenies who spent their October in relentless obscurity.

In this case, the special Group 4 guest star du jour was infielder Willie Harris, who was sent out to pinch-hit for Garcia to start the eighth—against a man nobody would have wanted to hit against after three weeks without an at-bat: Houston closer Brad Lidge.

But Harris poked a single into left—for his first hit in 23 days. His teammates moved him along to third with a bunt and a ground ball. And then the World Series MVP, Jermaine Dye, knocked him in with a single up the middle.

So all of a sudden, the team with the 88-year drought had a one-run lead—and only six more outs to get.

"Unbelievable," said Group 4 ringleader Geoff Blum, the guy who had hit the game-winning homer just the night (or morning) before. "It took eight stars to get us here—and Group 4 to get us over the top."

Relievers Cliff Politte and Neal Cotts got the first three outs, squirming out of a two-on, one-out jam in the eighth. So then, in the ninth, it was Bobby Jenks' turn.

Jenks is another guy who seemed to sum up this team's year. Claimed on waivers over the winter. Pitching in Birmingham in April. Then standing on the mound with a World Series to finish in October. Perfect.

He'd thrown 41 exhausting pitches in Game 3, less than 24 hours earlier. But there was "no way in hell I wasn't coming in" to pitch *this* game, he said.

Of course, he had to make it as terrifying as possible, though. *Of course*, as his teammates crowded around the top step of the dugout, he had to give up a bloop leadoff single to Jason Lane—followed by a Brad Ausmus bunt that moved the tying run to second base.

"What an inning," Blum would say later. "It was scary. It was quixotic. What's that mean, anyway—quixotic?"

Hey, you've got us. But it sounded good. Whatever, it was Jenks-otic. And that was the last thing anybody in Chicago needed, after all the Bartman-esque things that have gone on there for the last 88 years.

"You know, if we'd won this game 10–0, that would have been great," said Konerko. "But it wouldn't have been right. That's not us. So I was waiting for them to tie it up in the ninth, so we could say, 'OK, let's go. Extra innings.'"

Turned out that wouldn't be necessary, though—thanks to Jenks and his trusty shortstop, Juan Uribe.

With that tying run on second, Jenks dueled pinch hitter Chris Burke for six stirring pitches. Burke lofted the last of those six toward the seats beyond third base. It sure looked as if it would float out of play. But there was one guy on the field who didn't think so—Uribe.

He scrambled toward the stands, lunged precipitously, and careened into the crowd, like some character in a Road Runner cartoon. But a moment later, he emerged with the baseball. And the White Sox were one out away.

If Derek Jeter had made that play in a game like this, it would turn into a major motion picture, coming to a theater near you. That won't be happening for Juan Uribe. But his teammates knew what this play meant.

"That play pretty much sums up our team," Konerko said. "Juan is probably the one guy on this team who's capable of making that play. But *every* guy on this team would do that—crash into those stands if that's what it took."

Crash or no crash, though, Jenks still needed to get one final out.

His teammates were just about bursting out of the dugout by then. The stadium P.A. system blared out, "We Will Rock You," as Orlando Palmeiro dug in.

Jenks surged ahead of Palmeiro 1–2, then stood on the rubber and heaved one final big gulp of oxygen. Then he fired his final fastball of the night.

Palmeiro chopped it into the sky. Jenks leaped for it, then realized the most disastrous thing he could have done was deflect it. So he pulled his hand back and watched it hop over his head.

It looked, for an instant, like an infield hit waiting to happen. But here came Uribe one more time, charging, scooping, firing the baseball toward Konerko at approximately 866 miles per hour.

Thwack. The ball hit the glove. *Frrrummphh.* Palmeiro's foot hit the bag. First-base ump Gary Cederstrom pumped the out sign toward the Great Lakes. And 88 years of agony melted into the past tense.

"I knew I caught it in time," Konerko said. "But I still sneaked a look over at the umpire—because I didn't want to get caught celebrating prematurely."

"I'm not sure what happened after that," said Jenks, "other than a whole lot of loudness—and a bunch of guys hitting me on the head."

Then he looked up and saw his catcher, Pierzynski, sprinting toward him—and (yikes) leaping into his arms.

"I knew he was coming," Jenks said. "I just had a feeling. I saw it in his face: 'Here I come!'"

"Hey, I knew he wouldn't drop me," Pierzynski said. "He might be the only guy in the league who's fatter than me."

"It didn't matter how big he is," Jenks said. "I could have picked up a car right then."

Then they all dissolved into a gigantic group hug—a hug that stretched from the pitcher's mound all the way to a famous lakefront in Illinois.

A team from Chicago had won itself a championship. And it didn't require the services of Michael Jordan, Mike Ditka, or Jim McMahon to do it.

Drew Barrymore wasn't around to run around the field, chased by any Hollywood producers. Stephen King wasn't around, to dial his friendly neighborhood publisher. The Cubs weren't around, to remind the champs who was really No. 1.

No, this wasn't about any of those teams these White Sox were always being compared to. This was *their* moment, *their* time, *their* trophy. And the second-longest championship drought in the history of professional sports was no more.

The Chicago White Sox...Champions. How 'bout *that* phenomenon?

"Who," grinned A.J. Pierzynski, "would have thunk it?"

The 2010 Giants

ARLINGTON, TEXAS—Barry Bonds...Willie McCovey...Orlando Cepeda.

They never got to do what this unlikely cast of Giants—Cody Ross and Andres Torres and Edgar Renteria—finally were able to do on a star-spangled baseball field in Texas.

Will Clark...Matt Williams...Robby Thompson.

They never got to feel this feeling. Never got to meet this moment. Never got to see this dream come true.

Juan Marichal...Gaylord Perry...John "The Count" Montefusco.

They never got to say the word that Tim Lincecum and Matt Cain and Madison Bumgarner got to utter, on a night they will never forget:

Champions.

Every once in a while in sports, something happens on one of these fields of dreams that transcends the normal course of athletic events. Every once in a while, you find yourself watching something that no one has watched before, saying words that no one has ever said before.

And this night in Arlington, Texas, was one of those special times—the first time any living human could ever say this:

The San Francisco Giants won the World Series.

They'd moved out of New York and found a home by the Golden Gate 52 long years earlier. Dwight Eisenhower was president. A postage stamp cost three cents. If there was a TV screen in your parents' or grandparents' living room, it was black and white and grainy, and it sure wasn't flat.

And the San Francisco Giants would spend the next half-century employing many, many of the greatest baseball players of their time—or any time.

But for 52 seasons, all those men had one thing in common:

Their baseball seasons always ended with someone else doing the celebrating, someone else spraying the champagne, someone else riding the parade floats.

Until now.

Until 9:30 PM, Texas Daylight Time, on this night…when Brian Wilson stared in through his jet-black beard at Nelson Cruz, settled into the stretch, and unleashed the final cut fastball of this magical mystery tour of a season.

And when that baseball sailed past one last mighty flash of Nelson Cruz's bat, the San Francisco Giants had done it. They'd wiped away the ghosts—of Willie McCovey's 1962 line drive, of Scott Spiezio's heart-breaking 2002 homer, of the 1989 rumblings of the San Andreas Fault.

The giant scoreboard read: Giants 3, Rangers 1. And the sign, held by a grateful Giants fan standing above the visiting dugout, said it all:

TORTURE HAS ENDED.

It ended thanks to Tim Lincecum, who outdueled the great Cliff Lee in the biggest game of his 26-year-old lifetime.

It ended thanks to Edgar Renteria, who sent a heart-stopping, game-changing, MVP-award-sealing three-run homer flying through the night in the seventh inning of this game—just a few hours after telling his buddy, Andres Torres: "Today, I have the feeling I'm going to hit a homer."

And it ended when Brian Wilson threw the pitch that no Giants closer before him had ever been lucky enough to throw.

Not Rod Beck…Not Robb Nen…Not Gary Lavelle or Greg Minton.

The pitch that ended the World Series.

"I dreamed it to happen, and then it happened," Wilson said, his heart still pounding as he stood on this strange baseball field a thousand miles from AT&T Park, with hundreds of Giants fans still frozen in their seats around him, basking in this moment. "So I can't really explain it."

He'd spent his life watching other men throw That Pitch: Mariano Rivera… Brad Lidge…Keith Foulke. And then the heavens all aligned, and the earth spun him—Brian Wilson—into this out-of-body experience, throwing The Pitch That Ends the World Series. And even after he'd thrown it, seen it, lived it, he admitted it was difficult to comprehend this had really just happened.

Asked if this was what he always thought this moment would feel like, he shook his head.

"I didn't know what I expected it would feel like," Brian Wilson said, "because I always woke up before the final out."

But not this time. Not in this dream. This time, he and one of history's most unlikely champions were wide awake—and trying to digest the magnitude of what they'd all done.

"The years I've been here," said center fielder Aaron Rowand, "it's all been about bringing a world championship to San Francisco. And now we did."

But when a team like this wins, it isn't just for the men inside those uniforms. You understand that, right?

When a team like this wins, it's for all those generations of Giants fans who bundled up to survive the piercing breezes of Candlestick Park, who wore the scars of all the summertimes that broke their hearts, who lived through all those Wait Till Next Year seasons that didn't end this way.

And when a team like this wins, it's for another special group, too. It's for all those players, great and not-so-great, who put on this uniform, praying a season like this one would drop in their laps some day.

Rich Aurilia…J.T. Snow…Jeffrey "Penitentiary Face" Leonard.

"This puts to bed the ghosts of 2002," said Snow, from the champagne-drenched clubhouse of the first championship team in San Francisco history. "We were so close. Seven outs away. As a player, that never goes out of your system. But this is the next best thing for us."

And J.T. Snow wasn't the only ghost of Giants past to witness this coronation, either. Shawon Dunston was there. Will Clark was there. They'd been invited weeks earlier by the Giants' brass to travel with this team, bond with this team, share wisdom and memories and October insights, with this team. And in the end, they came away with the feeling that the 2010 Giants had done as much for them as they'd done for the 2010 Giants.

And the great Juan Marichal was there, too. Officially, he was in this ballpark as a broadcaster. But inside his chest beat the heart of a Giant. So there was no bitterness in his voice, or in his soul, that he and his great Giants teams of the '60s never got to do this.

"I don't mind," said Juan Marichal, who won 238 games for his Giants over 14 remarkable seasons. "I don't care. We couldn't do it in those days. But I knew these kids could do it. That's baseball, you know? That's baseball."

Jeff Kent…Felipe Alou…Jack Clark.

That's baseball, all right. Is any other explanation possible? For half a century, the Giants put together teams talented enough to employ players who won nine MVP awards, three Cy Young awards, four Rookie of the Year awards—and won no World Series.

And then *this* team—a team that lovingly described itself as "the castoffs" and "the misfits"—turned out to be The One? The one that ended the third-longest current title drought in baseball, and the eighth-longest in the history of baseball? How does *that* happen?

Hey, that's baseball. That's how that happens.

And those castoffs and misfits couldn't have been prouder to be marinating in champagne after making it happen. Asked which of those labels fit him best, their cleanup hitter du jour, Cody Ross, could only laugh.

"Which of them am I? Both of them, I think," he said. "Actually, I don't know which I am. Either one, man. I'm just glad I'm one of them right now."

A little over two months earlier, he'd joined this team practically by accident. By the last game of the World Series, he'd become their leading postseason home run hitter. And he found himself doing something in this game he never did *once* all season—bat cleanup. According to the Elias Sports Bureau, no National Leaguer had done that—hit cleanup in a World Series game after never hitting fourth all year—since Pepper Martin in 1931.

But naturally, the names on Bruce Bochy's lineup card would line up in exactly the right order. Again. Hadn't they done that through this entire postseason?

So as the top of the seventh inning dawned, it was Cody Ross due to lead off against Cliff Lee in what was still a taut 0–0 game. Lee had allowed three hits. Lincecum had given up two. No one had reached second base all night. And as two tremendous pitchers sliced through dominating inning after dominating inning, visions of Jack Morris–John Smoltz were beginning to occupy the minds of everyone in this ballpark.

"I was thinking that, too," said Giants pitching coach Dave Righetti. "You found yourself saying, 'Here we go,' especially in an American League park, because you're not going to [pinch] hit for either guy. So yeah, I started to think about it. You start to wonder how far they both can go."

And so, for that matter, were the hitters who had to face them.

Asked what his mind-set was as he dug in to battle Lee in the seventh, Ross replied: "At that point, I was just thinking, *Do anything. Please hit me. Anything to get on base.*"

Lee declined that invitation to drill him, but Ross managed to slap a single up the middle. And the Giants had something going.

Next it was Juan Uribe's turn. Not so long ago in this postseason, he and Ross had been the Giants' Nos. 7-8 hitters. Now, in the game in which they won the World Series, they found themselves as the Nos. 4-5 hitters. Does that sum up this team, or what?

Five years earlier, Uribe had been the shortstop on a White Sox team that ended 88 years of title-less misery. By the end of this night, he would become the first man ever who could say he was a regular on two teams that blew away more than a half-century worth of curses. But first, he had to fight off an 0-2 pitch, serve it into center, and give the Giants two base runners in the same inning for the first time all night.

So it was first and second, nobody out. And in a 0–0 game, that would ordinarily mean: bunt. Except in this case, the hitter was Aubrey Huff, a fellow with this claim to fame:

He'd accumulated 5,505 at-bats in his big-league career without ever laying down a sacrifice bunt. Only one active hitter has been to the plate more without a SAC—Vlad Guerrero.

But before Huff even looked down to third base for the sign, he already knew what he had to do—end this sac-free streak right here. It was either that or take his hacks against Cliff Lee. And he didn't like his odds if he did *that*.

"I'll be honest," Huff said. "When I went up there, I didn't feel like I had a chance. So even though I got the bunt sign, I was going to do it anyway."

So he laid one down, got both runners over, and sprinted back to the bench ecstatically. But the ecstasy didn't last long, because the next hitter, Pat Burrell struck out—for the 10th time in 12 at-bats in this World Series. There were two outs.

Never fear, though. Mr. Nov-Edgar was here.

As Renteria smoothed the dirt and settled into the box, he inspired an incredible sense of confidence in his teammates. It was 13 years since his epic, game-winning, extra-inning Game 7 hit in the 1997 World Series. But this was still Edgar Renteria's time of year.

He worked the count to 2–0, then stepped out for a quick gulp of breath as Lee waited on the rubber for him to pivot back to work. Renteria tapped the outside of the plate, then the inside of the plate and rocked into his trademark closed stance, as the noise swelled around him.

Lee wound, fired, and threw his worst pitch of an otherwise-spectacular night—a cutter that hung up there around Renteria's waist. And the man at the plate was all over it.

As the baseball disappeared—barely—over the fence in left-center, Cody Ross leaped into the night, Rowand pumped his fist in the on-deck circle, and a dugout full of Giants looked for someone to hug. In the dugout, Andres Torres found it hard to believe he'd just seen what he'd seen.

"When we were in the clubhouse today, he told me he was going to hit a homer," Torres said. "Then we went to the cage, and he said it again. He told me, 'Today, I've got the feeling I'm going to hit a homer.' And he never says that. But he told me twice, 'Kid, I'm going to hit a homer.'"

Remember now, Edgar Renteria was a man who'd hit precisely two regular season homers after April 9. But a voice in his head told him he was going to hit his second home run of this World Series. So he believed.

"Edgar, he's been a mentor for me," Torres said. "I saw him do it in '97, and now here. That ball just kept going and going, and I got so excited. That was unbelievable, because he told me. So I said to him, 'How'd you do it? You told me, and you did it.' And he looked at me and he said, 'Kid, I told you.'"

So how many three-RBI games did Renteria have all season? Not a one. Of course. But he'd just driven in three with one swing, in Game 5 of the World Series. Who writes these scripts?

Lincecum would give back one run of his lead by allowing a solo homer to Cruz in the bottom of the seventh. But on the night when he became just the fifth pitcher to pile up double-figure strikeouts in the clinching game of a World Series, that would be that.

This game, this duel with Lee, this special moment in championship time, was all the inspiration Tim Lincecum needed. Was there any question that all of that brought out the best of him on this historic evening?

"I think it did," said Righetti. "Obviously it did. He definitely had a look about him. But he had it last week. After he came out of that first game in San Francisco, he told me in the dugout, 'I *will* be better next time.' And he sure was."

Lincecum got them through the eighth. And then those bullpen gates opened in the bottom of the ninth, and here came Brian Wilson.

He and his beard had saved 53 games in 2010, between the season and the postseason. But he knew exactly what this one meant.

"I know the crowd loves the ninth-inning guys—Rod Beck, Robb Nen," Wilson said. "That's the history of the ninth inning for this franchise. So for me to take the mound and do something they were never able to do—it means a lot."

Down went Josh Hamilton. One out. Down went Vlad Guerrero. Two outs. Then Wilson ran the count on Cruz to 1–2, then 2–2, then 3–2. He understood how much was riding on this next pitch. He just wasn't sure how he could make himself throw it.

"It's kind of hard to comprehend," he said. "You're in another world out there. I don't care who you are. You're not in your normal spot when you're out there in the final game of the World Series, 3–2 pitch. So you tell yourself, 'Just throw a strike. Get your leg up. Find your release point. Throw it in there. And let God do the rest.'"

Up there in the heavens, they must have wanted this to happen. It had been 52 years since the great move west. Nineteen different franchises had won a World Series since the last time the Giants won one. But this was the right man throwing the right pitch for the right team at the right time.

So Nelson Cruz swung. Nelson Cruz missed. And the San Francisco Giants had won the World Series. Finally.

In the previous 10 years, they'd seen the Red Sox win. They'd seen the White Sox win. They'd seen the Phillies win. But now, at last, it was the Giants' turn.

For 52 years, it had been The Story hanging over their otherwise-great franchise. And now it would never be The Story again. Hopefully.

"Yeah, hopefully," said Brian Wilson, "we'll win another one before another 50 years is up."

The 2011 Cardinals

St. Louis—Even after it was over, they still couldn't grasp it.

Even as the fireworks shot through the sky, even as the World Series trophy sat on a podium at second base, they still weren't sure exactly what they'd done or how they'd done it.

Mere humans can only comprehend so much, you know. So how were the 2011 St. Louis Cardinals supposed to comprehend this?

Only 24 hours earlier, they were down to the last strike of their magical season in two different innings—and lived. And now here they were, hugging everyone within hugging range, pulling on their championship T-shirts, spraying that sweet Mount Pleasant Brut Imperial.

Here they were, the most improbable World Series champions who ever lived, a 6–2 Game 7 win over Texas etched in the scorebooks, the championship caps already perched on their heads. And it still didn't make sense—even to the men who had made this impossible dream come true.

"It has to be destiny. There's no other way to explain it," said center fielder Skip Schumaker, on the night his team won the World Series. "I can't believe it happened. I feel like it went so quick. It hasn't really had a chance to sink in, what we're really doing here. I just hope in the next couple of days, we'll have a chance to think about what just happened. It's amazing."

Amazing is as good a word as any for it, too, because there has never been a World Series champion like the 2011 Cardinals. It's that simple.

They should have been dead, buried, forgotten weeks ago. They should have spent October in a golf cart or a fishing boat, miles from the seats of Busch Stadium. They had no business still playing baseball. But the cool thing was, no one was more aware of that than them.

"We're supposed to be home, watching the World Series," said a jubilant man by the name of Albert Pujols, on an evening he'll never forget. "And now we're world champions."

And what could possibly have summed up their improbable saga better than a phrase that now will bond them all forever:

One strike away.

In the history of baseball, only one other team had ever done what these Cardinals had just done. Only one other team—the '86 Mets—ever tumbled into that one-strike-away abyss in a World Series and survived to pop the champagne bottles.

So think about that. In the first 106 World Series ever played, just those '86 Mets ever got down to their last strike and then won it all. Then *this* team found itself in that mess twice in two *innings* in Game 6.

But for this group, what more fitting script could these men ever have written for themselves—in a season where they were 10½ games out with 31 to play, 8½ back with 21 to play, and three games out with five to play? No team in modern history could possibly have understood the expression, "near-death experience," better than this one.

"[Game 6] was our shining moment," said Lance Berkman, a guy who was responsible for one of those two life-saving "one-strike-away" hits. "That game was a perfect reflection of what this team embodies—just that never-say-die mind-set. Keep fighting until they finally put you away. But nobody could put us away. And that's why we're standing here."

As he stood on the outfield grass and uttered these words, thousands of Cardinals fans were still frozen in their seats an hour after the final out, unable to pull themselves away from this field where impossible dreams came true, unwilling to let go of this powerful, joyful moment. And how could you blame them?

But for all Lance Berkman and his friends knew, these people might have been there since Game 6 ended the night before, still attempting to absorb the greatest World Series game of their lifetimes.

"A lot of people I talked to couldn't sleep after that game," Berkman said. "It was just such an emotional thing. And a lot of people in this [uniform] couldn't sleep very well, either."

And he was one of them. He plopped into bed afterward and lay there for an hour, the adrenaline still flowing, he said. Then he bolted out of bed a few hours later, at 8:00 AM, swept up again in "all the emotion of where we were."

We took an informal survey of the clubhouse after this game. We found many players who said they couldn't go to sleep until 4:30 AM, 5:00 AM. And there was one guy who couldn't make his eyes close until after the sun had come up.

"I got like 45 minutes of sleep last night," said the man who had just become the latest World Series MVP, David Freese. "I didn't get to sleep until around 8:00 AM. It was hard, man. I just couldn't understand what was really going on."

Every one of them, it seemed, carried the magic potion of a special night with them when they burst through the ballpark doors that night—"and I don't think it ever really went away," said their hitting coach, Mark McGwire.

"I still had it this morning," McGwire said. "I walked around the city earlier today, and there was still that aura in the city. And I don't think it left. There was just that buzz. There was just that feeling, that energy. People were so *up*."

Then they all lugged that aura right back into the ballpark with them—and watched their team go out and win the World Series. Show a little faith, and there's magic in the night. And this was one magic act these people will be cheering forever.

As this team for the ages took the field on this night, the men who trotted out there were still swept up in that feeling, that this was where they were supposed to be.

"If this team was supposed to win this thing," said second baseman Nick Punto, "we were *going* to win it in a Game 7. Right? I mean, there was no other way. The story was written."

And if you believe in destiny, as so many of these men had come to believe, then what were you supposed to make of the raindrops that came splattering out of the sky two days earlier?

How could you not wonder about the meaning of a rainout that would push back this World Series for a day—a day that made it possible for the Cardinals to start their ace, Chris Carpenter, in a Game 7 that would define their season? If there had been no rain, there would have been no Carpenter. Freaky.

"The baseball gods," said Schumaker, "were working in our favor."

Unfortunately, there were a few minutes where they weren't sure about what those baseball gods had in mind. Starting on three days' rest for only the second time in his career, Carpenter scuffled with his command in the first inning, allowed the first four hitters to reach base, and fell behind 2–0 faster than you could say, "Here we go again."

But then Freese—who else?—doubled in two runs in the bottom of the first to tie this game up. And Carpenter began to rediscover his rhythm and control of all three pitches. After that, he would spend the rest of his night reminding America of why he's arguably the best big-game starter of his generation.

This would be his ninth postseason victory—more than any active pitcher. He went 4–0 in this miraculous October. And his win on this night would make him only the second Cardinals starter in the expansion era to win more than one winner-take-all World Series game in his career. The other? That would be Bob Gibson (in 1964 and '67).

"When he starts a game like this, we feel like we're going to win," said his buddy, Adam Wainwright. "His competitiveness, his ferocity out there, is probably unmatched."

Until this night, no pitcher in history—not Pedro Martinez, not John Smoltz, not Curt Schilling, not a single October legend of the division-play era—had ever won two win-or-go-home games in a single postseason. But not anymore.

Just three weeks after outdueling Roy Halladay in a Game 5 showdown in the Division Series, Carpenter would perform a historic encore by squashing the Rangers, even without his killer stuff.

After those first four hitters, the Texas lineup would go just 3-for-18 against him until he exited in the seventh inning. And by then, he and his team had this game in nearly complete control—for a change.

Finally, at 10:15 PM in the Central time zone, the closer, Jason Motte, emerged out of the bullpen gates and began the long trot to the mound where he would finish this off. Camera flashes sparkled. Rally towels spun.

The ballpark felt like an earthquake. This was it.

Down went Nelson Cruz on a fly ball to center. One out. Down went Mike Napoli on a bouncer to third base. Two out. Then David Murphy would loft a fly ball toward the track in left, and Allen Craig began running across the outfield grass, waiting for this baseball to come down.

"Honestly, when he hit it, I turned the wrong way," Craig said. "And then I had to look over my shoulder to pick it up again, and it was bouncing. And I was, like, 'Just catch it, please,' so we could win it. I mean, I knew I was going to catch it. But it was one of those moments where it's just slow-mo, and all I could think was, *Just catch it.*"

But finally, this baseball would in fact return to earth. And finally, Allen Craig would squeeze it so tight that an hour later, he still hadn't let go. And finally, the St. Louis Cardinals had done what once seemed un-doable to everyone but them.

They had won this World Series. Just don't ask them how.

No team had ever won a World Series after finding itself 10½ games out of a playoff spot on August 25 or later. No team had ever won a World Series after finding itself 8½ games out in September. No team had ever won a World Series after being one strike away from extinction in back-to-back innings of the same World Series game. But this team was special.

These Cardinals needed the Phillies to sweep the Braves in the last week of September just to make this tournament at all. But it happened. These Cardinals had to beat Roy Oswalt and Roy Halladay in Games 4 and 5 to topple the Phillies in the Division Series. But it happened.

These Cardinals had to find the strength to roar back to life after crushing losses to the Mets and Cubs and Astros down the stretch. But they found that strength. And the longer the rest of the sport let them keep breathing, the more dangerous this team became.

"It just kept going, kept going, kept going," said Schumaker. "So, I mean, I knew there was a reason for this season. I just couldn't figure out what it was. Just certain things kept happening. And there's a reason for everything."

And then, on a crisp Friday night in October, in a city that worships them, they came to understand just what that reason was. Little did they know it was exactly what their manager, the one and only Tony La Russa, had been telling them they were up to for weeks.

"It's history," said Allen Craig. "That's what it is. It's history. That's what Tony would say to us. It's history. Our whole ride to the playoffs. Just what we did to get here. It's improbable. It's unbelievable. All I can say is, we did it."

In four months, when this team would finally get the band back together in Jupiter, they knew that they might not look the same or feel the same. That there might be no La Russa in the manager's office. That there might be no Pujols in the No. 3 hole. That there might be a very different feeling than the one that swept over them at Busch Stadium on this night.

But that didn't change what had just happened to them. They may never truly understand how it happened or why it happened. But this was a team that had just completed one of the most amazing rides into the history books in the annals of this or any sport. All they had to do was win this one last Game 7 to make it happen.

"We had to win tonight," said Mark McGwire, "because it doesn't become history unless you finish it off."

Chapter 4
October Classics

October 27, 2011

The Greatest World Series Game Ever

St. Louis—It ended with a baseball soaring through the October sky.

Soaring toward a patch of resplendent green grass, located just beyond the center-field fence.

Soaring toward its place in the storybooks and the history books.

Soaring to its rightful spot alongside the most famous World Series walkoffs ever hit—alongside Mazeroski, alongside Fisk, alongside Carter, alongside Gibson.

This was how Game 6 of the 2011 World Series would end on the final Thursday night of October…

With a man named David Freese hitting a home run that will never stop flying.

With fireworks exploding in the night.

With teammates sprinting toward home plate to meet the man who had saved their season.

With the 47,325 lucky humans who made up the largest crowd in the history of Busch Stadium fighting back the tears, not to mention the over-powering urge to phone their cardiologists.

With the giant scoreboard in right field flipping the score one last time, to Cardinals 10, Rangers 9, in 11 innings of unforgettable madness.

But this was merely the final freeze frame in what we could easily argue was the greatest World Series game ever played. Describing this one last picturesque swing of the bat, painting a picture of this euphoric scene, was the easy part. These were the everlasting images in this vivid October picture book that, in David Freese's own words, "become memories."

What, though, will these St. Louis Cardinals tell their children and their grandchildren about the long and winding four-hour-and-33-minute road that led them to this incredible finale? What will they tell the next generations about the greatest World Series game ever played?

Well, here's where they ought to start:

- They should say they were a part of the first World Series game in history in which a team got down to its final strike, its final breath, *twice*—once in the ninth inning, once in the 10th inning—and somehow won.

- They should say they were a part of the first World Series game ever played in which any team trailed *five* different times—and still came back to win.

- They should say they were a part of the first World Series game ever in which a team found itself losing in the ninth inning *and* extra innings—yet still found a way to win.

- They should say they played in the first World Series game in history in which *two* different players—Josh Hamilton for the Rangers, then Freese for the Cardinals—hit go-ahead home runs in extra innings.

- They should say they were the first team in the 1,330-game history of postseason baseball to score in the eighth, ninth, 10th, and 11th innings of *any* game.

- But mostly, they should say this: that they played in a baseball game that reminded all of them why they play, why we watch, and why sports can be such a powerful force in all of our lives—because the term "baseball game" doesn't begin to do justice to this remarkable life experience.

"The greatest game I've ever played in," said the right fielder, Lance Berkman.

"In the 31 years I've been alive and the 11 years I've been in the big leagues, this was pretty special, man," said The Franchise, Albert Pujols. "This is what baseball is all about."

"I don't know how to describe this game," said the center fielder, Skip Schumaker. "I almost want to tell people, 'You have to see the video.' It's one of those games you have to watch. It's one of those instant classics on ESPN, just because of the magnitude of the game…I'm only 30 years old. But I know it's the best World Series game I've ever seen."

Well, it may not matter how long you've been alive. It may not matter how many October baseball games you've watched in your lifetime. You would have a very, very, very difficult time making a case that any of them were better than this one—because an extra-inning walkoff home run was almost a secondary plot line, to the sight of a team coming back from the dead. Twice.

"It's just an exhilarating feeling," said Berkman, whose game-tying 10th-inning hit was part two of the late-inning CPR, "when you're like Lazarus and you come back from the dead."

That's not to say this game was some kind of work of art or anything. It would be tough to ignore the five errors, the unearned runs that scored in three different innings, the base running mistakes, and the miscommunications that left potholes all over the highway for the first half of this extravaganza.

Long before Freese turned into Mr. October, for instance, he clanked a routine pop-up, and failed to catch another catchable foul ball while impaling himself on a railing beyond third base.

"I felt like I was part of a circus out there," he would say later, "bouncing balls off the top of my hat a little bit."

But all that goofiness was kind of entertaining in its own right. And fortunately, at least it was confined to only the first act of this show.

"Really and truly, this was an ugly game for about six or seven innings," said the relentlessly honest Berkman. "But then it got beautiful, right at the end."

No kidding. And by our calculations, it was about the seventh inning when the Louvre acquisitions committee should have lurched to attention. One second, this was a 4–4 game. The next, Adrian Beltre and Nelson Cruz were launching back-to-back homers to springboard the Rangers back into the lead. And here's all you need to know about how rare that was:

According to the Elias Sports Bureau, had the Rangers won, it would have been the first time a team hit back-to-back home runs to take the lead that late in a clinching game since two nobodies named Babe Ruth and Lou Gehrig hit a game-tying bomb and a go-ahead shot back-to-back in the final game of the 1928 World Series. Pretty cool.

And by the time that seventh inning ended, the Rangers led 7–4 with six outs to go and three of their most trusted pitchers—Derek Holland, Mike Adams, and Neftali Feliz—lined up to nail down those six outs. Now here's how secure a spot *that* was:

According to the invaluable website, whowins.com, 41 previous home teams had trailed by three runs after seven innings in any game of a best-of-seven postseason series—and only one of them had ever come back to win. That was the 2008 Red Sox, against Tampa Bay, in Game 5 of the ALCS. So obviously, no team had ever survived a mess like this and won in a World Series game.

But these 2011 Cardinals are no ordinary team. We don't need to retell the story of their season. But if there ever was a team that wouldn't be inclined to look at a deficit like that and decide it was hopeless, it would be an outfit that trailed by 10½ games in the last week of August, by 8½ with 21 games to go, and by three games with five to play.

"We've been playing must-win games since August and September, when we were 10½ back and 8½ back," said reliever Jason Motte. "So we've been there before. These guys just don't give up."

Nevertheless, when the bottom of the ninth rolled around, they were still trailing by two runs, 7–5. Then Feliz marched in and blew away Ryan Theriot with a 98-miles-per-hour scorchball. And The End was two outs away.

But then Pujols pounded a double up the gap, and Berkman walked. And the tying run was actually on base. But when Feliz punched out Allen Craig with a vicious 2-2 breaking ball, you could feel the energy begin to drain out of a charged-up ballpark.

Then Feliz jumped ahead of Freese, 1-2. So here was Texas, one strike away.

Rangers players climbed to the top step of the dugout. Feliz walked to the back of the mound and stared out to center field, then left field, picturing the pitch that was going to finish off the first championship season in Rangers history.

Freese leaned on his back foot, watching, waiting, and thinking, he would say later, *What a great way to have my first career AB off Feliz.* But he also reminded himself to keep his swing as short as possible. And when he found another 98-mph fastball headed his way, he "didn't miss that one."

He practically flicked this baseball 350 feet toward deep right field. But Nelson Cruz appeared to have a line on it. As he drifted back, almost casually, toward the warning track, his teammates were practically into their victory celebration. Then, to their horror, the ball sailed to the right of Cruz's glove and clattered off the wall in right. Triple. Tie game. Cue the first wave of pandemonium.

It was just the third RBI hit in World Series history by any player whose team was one out from heading home for the winter. (The other two came from Otis Nixon in 1992 and Josh Devore in 1911.) But Freese was an excellent candidate to add his name to that, or any, list of October clutchiness. By the time this game ended, he found himself hitting 8-for-18 in the 2011 postseason with runners in scoring position, with three doubles, two homers, that heart-thumping triple, and 15 RBIs.

"He's just got 'it,'" said Berkman. "I don't know exactly what 'it' is. But he's got it. He's one of those players who can perform when it matters most. He may not always come through, but the moment is never bigger than he is."

The stadium must have rattled continuously for the next five minutes after this stunning turn of events. But the elation didn't last long, because three hitters into the top of the 10th inning, Josh Hamilton pounded a towering two-run homer off Motte that seemed, once and for all, to settle this deal.

What the heck. How many times could one team come back anyway? When a team has already made four leads disappear, performed an act of reincarnation when it was one strike away from elimination, and *still* finds itself two down in the 10th inning, that's not what you'd call a real good formula for how to win the World Series.

So out in right field, Berkman admitted he thought, just for a moment, about what an amazing story it would be for Josh Hamilton, a man with a positively cinematic life story, to be the hero of this World Series. But his very next thought, he said, was, *Let's fight back and see what happens.*

And whaddaya know, this game would come down to him.

There were two outs in the 10th. It was a 9–8 game. The tying run was on third, thanks to a not-exactly-textbook bunt by—don't even ask how it came to this—a pitcher (Kyle Lohse) who was pinch-hitting for another pitcher (Edwin Jackson) who was announced as the pinch hitter for a third pitcher (Motte). And Pujols had just been intentionally walked by the Rangers for the fifth time in three games.

But Berkman said he felt "really calm, really at peace as I was walking up to the plate" to face Scott Feldman, a guy he'd seen enough to go 4-for-10 against, with a .500 on-base percentage.

"I actually felt pretty good about it," Berkman said, "because I figured I was in a no-lose situation."

And why was it a no-lose situation? Because nobody could possibly have expected *this*, right? Not after all this team had been through over the last eight weeks. Not after already surviving one near-death experience just moments before.

So once again, the count went to 1-2, and then 2-2. Feldman stood on the rubber and tried to blow warmth into his fingertips. Berkman wagged his bat, as those rally towels spun and the P.A. system pounded.

Feldman rocked, fired, and tried to jam Berkman with a cutter that had just enough movement to break Berkman's bat. But somehow, he was able to stroke it into center, in front of Hamilton. And once again, this was a tie game—at (gulp) 9–9.

Asked later if this was a moment he'd dreamed of as a kid, Berkman quipped: "When you're a little kid and you're out there, you don't have a bunch of reporters and fans that are ready to call you a choking dog if you don't come through. So when you're a kid, you don't realize what a big moment that is. I'm just going to caution all little kids out there: Be careful what you wish for."

That's excellent advice, kiddies. But the truth is, what you're wishing for is this:

You're wishing for the chance to be David Freese, standing there at home plate in the 11th inning—bat wagging, crowd erupting—as the seventh Texas reliever of the night, Mark Lowe, stared him in the eyeballs.

And then here came the 3-2 changeup—the 383rd pitch of this astounding ballgame—that was going to rewrite the script of his entire life.

David Freese's bat flashed through the electrified Missouri night. And then…

There went the baseball, soaring through the October sky.

And back went Josh Hamilton…back…back…until there was no place left to run.

And the incomprehensible had happened. In real life.

The St. Louis Cardinals were alive—and heading for the first World Series Game 7 since 2002. Alive. Somehow.

They knew they'd just been a part of something unique and everlasting. But for those four and a half grueling hours they were out there living it, they hadn't had a second—not one—to savor it. How could they?

Asked if he'd taken a step back at any point to appreciate what they'd all been a part of, Berkman laughed and said: "Heck, when you're down to your last strike, no one ever thinks, *Boy, this is great!*"

But in retrospect? Boy, this was great. And the best part for these men was that it had a chance to be something greater.

To find the last team that was in the Cardinals' position—a team that had just won Game 6 at home—and then *lost* Game 7 at home, you had to travel all the way back to 1975, to the Red Sox, who lost Game 7 at Fenway against the Big Red Machine.

Since then, seven teams had gone home, down three games to two, and won Game 6. And all seven of them won Game 7 as well.

So history said that, for this team, this just set them up to do something greater. The only trouble was, they still had to go out and actually do it.

"The reality," Berkman said, "is that if we don't win tomorrow, this game becomes just a footnote to a nice season.

"But if we win tomorrow," said Lance Berkman, "this is the stuff of legends."

October 17, 2005

Pujols' Homer

HOUSTON—As the baseball soared through the electrified night, you almost wanted the world to stop spinning—just for a moment—so you could digest what was unfolding before your eyes.

It was only one swing of Albert Pujols' bat. It was only one baseball, heading for history. It was only one moment in the life of two franchises.

But it was a swing, a baseball, a moment that seemed to change the world.

In an instant, in one click of a camera lens, in one quick gulp of air, in one flash of Albert Pujols' bat, victory dissolved into defeat. Euphoria transformed into disbelief. Ear-drum-rattling noise turned to how'd-that-happen silence.

And the Houston Astros' trip to the first World Series in the life of their franchise had just taken an unexpected detour—back to a nearly defunct stadium in St. Louis that had been abruptly rescued from the implosion button for one more night of baseball. Or more.

What just happened? Did we really see what we just saw?

We could have sworn we saw the great Albert Pujols hit a season-saving three-run home run off the unhittable, untouchable, unbeatable Brad Lidge. With two outs in the ninth inning. But were we sure this was real?

These are questions you always ask yourselves at moments like this, when the impossible has just turned possible. So it shouldn't surprise us that even Pujols' teammates, men whose lives had just taken a ride right along with that home run ball, were feeling the same thing.

"When he hit that ball, I didn't react," said the man on deck, Reggie Sanders. "I didn't react, because I didn't know what to do. I couldn't believe he just did that. So I froze. I just froze."

Eventually, though, he unfroze. Eventually, we all unfroze. Eventually, we convinced ourselves it was time to contemplate several questions: How long will we remember this moment? How long will we talk about this magical wave of Pujols' bat? How long will we talk about a game in which the St. Louis Cardinals, one strike away from the fishing hole, would save their season with a staggering 5–4 victory over the Houston Astros—and a pitcher they kept calling "the best closer in the game"?

"I know we'll be talking about it for a long time," said the Cardinals' Larry Walker, his retirement plans suddenly delayed by Pujols-esque forces beyond his control. "But I think it will get talked about a lot more if we win two more games."

Two more games. That's how many the Cardinals still needed to win in this National League Championship Series.

But it seemed eminently possible all of a sudden. Didn't it? When you've witnessed an event this improbable, anything seems possible. Anything.

The list of men who have done what Albert Pujols did on this night is a list that flips the switch on a video reel inside your brain. You know these men. You know these moments. You know these two-out, ninth-inning homers that turned October defeat into unforgettable triumph:

Kirk Gibson off Dennis Eckersley, Game 1, 1988 World Series.

Jack Clark off Tom Niedenfuer, Game 6, 1985 NLCS.

And Dave Henderson off Donnie Moore, Game 5, 1986 ALCS.

The closest parallel to this one is Henderson—because, just like Albert Pujols, his team was trailing that series 3–1. And just like Albert Pujols, his team had been one strike away from The End.

And just like Albert Pujols, the team Henderson was losing to (in that case, the Angels) was about to head to the first World Series in its history—and celebrate it in front of its very own fans.

The only difference is that, after Henderson's homer gave the '86 Red Sox a one-run lead, the Angels came back to tie the game in the bottom of the ninth, only to lose in 11.

But details, schmetails. It's close enough to know that Albert Pujols' home run will be traveling through the history books for as long as October matters.

We could still recall all the teams in those history books that were one strike away from going home—and then didn't: We remember those 1986 Red Sox (thanks to Dave Henderson). We remember the 1986 Mets (thanks to Mookie Wilson and Bill Buckner). We remember the 1992 Braves (thanks to the legendary Francisco Cabrera).

And we would remember this—no matter how this series turned out.

"Now I can appreciate Joe Carter and Kirby Puckett and all those guys," said Sanders. "Because this was the exact same thing."

OK, so it wasn't the *exact* same thing. But we get the idea. Because these take-your-breath-away October home runs don't happen every day. And when they do, they stick inside all of our memory banks for as long as the banks stay open.

So what will we remember about this night?

We'll remember Lidge sprinting out of the Houston bullpen at 10:24 pm Central Daylight Time, as an entire stadium rattled.

We'll remember Lidge striking out the first two hitters in the ninth—John Rodriguez, then John Mabry—on two carnivorous sliders. We'll remember that the sound that erupted after those two strikeouts was so monstrous, you needed a Richter scale to measure it.

And we'll remember, as much as anything, the peskiest leadoff man alive, David Eckstein, walking up there and taking two 96-mph smokeballs for the strikes that left his team one strike away.

But as grown men and women shrieked and leaped and hugged all around him, Eckstein took a deep breath and stepped back in to hit, feeling amazingly serene.

"The one thing I didn't want to do was get into any type of jumpiness," Eckstein said. "Any type of anything in my body besides just focus on the baseball. And it's pretty calming to step into at the plate in that situation. I have no idea, no reason why."

His teammates, watching him, were shockingly calm themselves. David Eckstein just had that effect on people.

"When David gets two strikes, you still know he'll put the ball in play," said Walker. "David doesn't have bad at-bats. Ever."

And he didn't have one here. Lidge tried to put him away with one final slider. Eckstein slapped it toward the left side. The third baseman, Morgan

Ensberg, lunged. But the baseball, somehow, veered just beneath his dive. And the Cardinals were alive.

Next was Jim Edmonds, the same Jim Edmonds whose ejection the day before had been the talk of baseball for the next 24 hours. Lidge got him to take one ugly hack at a 1-0 slider. But Edmonds then laid off three straight fastballs, each one harder than the one before it.

And when plate ump Larry Poncino called the last one ball four, that man on deck, the menacing Mr. Pujols, was suddenly marching toward the box, representing the winning run.

If there was a word that best described Minute Maid Park at that point, that word would be nervous. Those roars of ecstasy had softened into mumbles of worry. Those leaps of joy had turned into squirms of fear.

One moment, the Cardinals had been peering into the other dugout, taking mental notes as the Astros players themselves began to celebrate. After all, they'd lost *one* game all year when they took a lead into the ninth.

In fact, they'd lost one game like that since June 15, 2004. And they'd gone 136–1 in that situation since—much of it thanks to the brilliance of Brad Lidge. So who could blame them for celebrating? Well, the Cardinals could, for one.

"We were looking over to their bench, and guys were high-fiving," Walker said. "A couple of guys were even dancing. But until that fat lady sings, you can't do that."

You especially can't do that when there's a chance Albert Pujols could get to hit. And now—voilà—here he was.

"Any time we go into the ninth with the bottom of the lineup coming up," said Jason Isringhausen, "all we're trying to do is get a hit, get a walk, get a couple of guys on—because we know we've *got* to get Albert up there."

It hadn't been one of Pujols' better nights. He was 0-for-4. He'd left five runners on base. He'd even struck out against Andy Pettitte in the third inning with men on first and third and nobody out. It was only the fifth time all season Pujols

> **TRIVIALITY**
>
> Albert Pujols is one of 44 players in history who have hit a walkoff home run in a postseason game. But just two of those 44 players have hit a walkoff postseason homer twice in their careers. Can you name both of them?

had struck out with a runner on third and less than two outs.

But none of that mattered now. This was the game. This was the season. This was history.

"Unbelievable," said Cardinals starter Chris Carpenter. "I'm sitting there thinking that we've got the best closer in the game on the mound—but we also have the best hitter in the game at the plate…It was an unbelievable feeling."

Pujols tapped the plate with his bat, dug in, and took a messy, off-balance swing at a first-pitch slider for strike one. The noise began to build again. Towels waved everywhere you looked. Thousands of ThunderStix crashed together. Pujols stepped back in to hit.

"I was just thinking, *Don't swing at the same slider that I swung at the first pitch*," he said. "He's probably the best closer in the game besides Mariano [Rivera] right now. He has probably the best slider in the game. I just want to get a good pitch to hit and just put my best swing."

He waved his bat loosely once, then twice. Then he cocked and loaded, rocking gently in the box, as Lidge wound and fired. Pujols even told himself, he would say later: "Don't try to be a hero. Don't try to hit a three-run home run." How ironic was that?

But this was one Lidge slider that didn't plummet as if it were dropped out of an airplane. This was one Lidge slider that hung like the Mona Lisa. And the second it crashed against Albert Pujols' bat, it felt as if the entire stadium was spinning through some kind of surreal Cuisinart.

The baseball climbed and climbed and climbed some more, like one of those missile launches across town. It cleared the scoreboard, cleared the inviting Crawford Box seats where so many heroic Astros homers had been landing for weeks.

It cleared the boxed-in Cardinals bullpen, which sits underneath the stands. So the relievers sitting there watching had no idea where it was heading: Austin? San Antonio? Mars?

"It just disappeared," said left hander Ray King. "But when it disappeared, we knew that was good."

It cleared the left-field façade, complete with an auxiliary video board and all those Astros pennant flags. It even cleared the train tracks that sit atop the left-field wall.

Finally, with nothing left to clear except planet earth, it splattered off the glass next to the light towers, about a thousand feet away.

And as it clanked off that glass, the most staggering sound of all was the sound of silence where, just seconds before, there had been such a head-pounding din.

"I've never heard 43,000 people shut up, just like that, in my life," Walker said. "One second, you could barely hear in here. And the next second, all that noise was gone. And the only noise you could hear was on our bench."

"When that ball flew over our heads," said King, "I turned to Mike Mason, our bullpen coach, and said, 'That's why they pay that guy 100 million bucks.'"

And that is, in fact, why. But even 100 million bucks doesn't guarantee you that any man can deliver a moment like that one. So as Pujols slowly ambled up the first-base line and watched his ulti-mate homer fly, even he had to make himself understand the magnitude of what he'd done.

> **TRIVIA ANSWER**
> David Ortiz (Game 3 of the 2004 ALDS, Game 4 of the 2004 ALCS) and Bernie Williams (Game 1 of the 1996 ALDS, Game 1 of the 1999 ALCS).

"I just couldn't believe," he would say later, "that I did it."

But he did it, all right. And now he can never undo it. Cue up the video tape. Write another line in the October history books. It's in there. Forever.

October/November, 2001

The Mr. November World Series

Game 4

NEW YORK—Are we sure it's still The House That Ruth Built?

There are nights when it seemed like The House That Francis Ford Coppola Built. Or The House That David Copperfield Built.

And needless to say, this epic Wednesday night at Yankee Stadium was another one of those nights. It was Yankees 4, Diamondbacks 3, in 10 indelible innings. It was as breathtaking a sporting event as you can ever witness.

But what else was new? This was life at Yankee Stadium, autumn after autumn, postseason after postseason, even when October was turning into November before your eyes.

The cinematic moments never seemed to end. The magic tricks seemed to get more unbelievable every year.

Things that couldn't happen still found a way to happen. Games the Yankees couldn't win somehow turned into games they did win.

"As much as it's happened," said Mike Stanton, after Tino Martinez and Derek Jeter had performed long-ball CPR on this Yankees season, "you still don't expect it to happen. You'd think, after it happens time after time, you'd start to expect it. But you don't. It's just amazing to watch."

We knew, thinking logically, that sooner or later, this dynasty would end. We knew, logically, that sooner or later, this team would reach for one more miracle and find the miracle bin out of stock. That's reality. That's life.

But how do we explain why it didn't happen in this game? How do we explain where this latest miracle came from?

On this night, the Yankees were one out away from being buried in this World Series, three games to one. Four games into the Series, they were hitting .143, with almost twice as many strikeouts (36) as hits (19). With runners in scoring position, they were batting .067 (1-for-15)—over *four* games.

They were one out away from being blown away by the astonishing Curt Schilling and the Frisbee-master closer, Byung-Hyun Kim, to the tune of a 13-strikeout four-hitter. Kim had just struck out his fourth Yankee in 1⅔ innings.

One out away from a 3–1 loss. Once-hopeful eyewitnesses trudged toward the exits. A dozen Diamondbacks leaned on the dugout rail, ready to celebrate. They were one out away from needing to win just once in three games, with Schilling and Randy Johnson all lined up to start two of them.

One out away. Here came Martinez. He had never faced Kim in his life. He was 0 for the World Series (0-for-9). He came to the plate enveloped by a silence in this stadium that said it all.

One out away. Paul O'Neill stood on first base, having dumped a broken-bat single into left. But where was he going? Where all these Yankees base runners kept going, all night, all Series—back to the dugout after another inning of frustration.

And then it happened. Kim lurched into his windup, arms flying every-where. He whirled one final first-pitch fastball toward the outside corner. But this one wasn't one of those unhittable sailers that devour every hitter alive. It stayed flat and true and out over the heart of the plate.

Martinez coiled and swung, and another miracle began soaring toward history. Center fielder Steve Finley tried to climb the fence until there was no more fence to climb.

The baseball dropped into the land of hopes and dreams that always seemed to come true for this team. This game was tied. These Yankees were rising from the dead again.

Stanton, who was this one swing away from being the losing pitcher, and fellow reliever Mark Wohlers watched on TV in the clubhouse. They watched this home run disappear beyond Finley's desperate leap. They looked at each other in disbelief.

"You shake your head," Stanton said. "We did it again."

"These are the days you dream about when you're five or six years old, swinging a bat in your backyard," O'Neill said. "These are the nights you play out in your mind."

Except this night wasn't over. They would head for the 10th. The clock would pass midnight. The scoreboard would flash a greeting never before seen in a major-league ballpark: WELCOME TO NOVEMBER BASEBALL.

And Jeter would march to the plate. Never had he looked any worse in any postseason than he had looked these last two weeks. He was three for his last 32. His only hit in 15 World Series at-bats was an infield single.

He'd felt so confused just by the sight of Kim in their first go-round, in the eighth inning, that he'd tried bunting for a hit, with no luck.

"He's weird, man," Jeter said of Kim. "The way he throws, it takes a while to get used to."

So Jeter gave himself a while, grinding out an exhausting nine-pitch at-bat, barely fouling off three two-strike pitches, almost falling down to avoid hacking at Kim's duck hooks just off the plate.

And then Kim wound again and delivered his 62nd pitch of the night—the most pitches he'd thrown since September 26, 2000—85 appearances ago. He seemed to let go of this pitch from six inches above the ground. It was designed to rise like an ascending jet and elevate north of Jeter's bat.

But after four games of watching the Diamondbacks jam him to take away his inside-out stroke, Jeter got one he could extend on—and thumped it toward the right-field foul pole.

Had a Diamondback hit it, had a Mariner hit it, had anybody from Boston hit it, you know it would have hit the top of the wall. But this was the World Series. This was the Yankees. This was Derek Jeter.

So of course, it cleared the fence by the approximate length of Jeter's after-midnight stubble. And of course, it stayed fair. And of course, the Yankees had won a game they couldn't win. Because it was the specialty of their house.

And it was Derek Jeter's specialty. Always. It wasn't enough this time just to win. This time he had to become the first-ever Mr. November.

"I guess he is," Stanton said. "There's not a lot of competition right now for that award."

Jeter floated around the bases, fist pumping, his smile as wide as Queens, his teammates sprinting toward home plate. He ran until he reached them, then leaped into their arms, leaped into the magic of the night.

"There's a lot of emotion involved when you play in a World Series," O'Neill said. "If you can't have fun out there when you win a game like that, there's something wrong. We weren't trying to show anybody up. But a game like that takes you back to Little League."

We'd seen it before. They'd done it before. We'd seen Jim Leyritz homer and Chad Curtis homer against the Atlanta Braves. We'd seen Bernie Williams' game-tyer against the Mariners and Alfonso Soriano's trot of a lifetime.

If it wasn't one Yankee, it was another. It was who you expected. It was who you didn't expect. It was the hottest Yankee. It was the coldest Yankee. What did it matter? In the end, it all came out the same: Yankees win.

"The one thing you realize after a while," Jeter said, "is that in these games, the stats don't matter. Who cares what the scoreboard says your stats are when you come to the plate? The beauty of the postseason is that, regardless of what you've done, every time you come up, you have the opportunity to do something special."

So they did. You could almost get the impression they didn't know how not to anymore. This was the ninth straight World Series game they'd won at Yankee Stadium. They'd won 11 straight one-run games in the postseason. They'd won nine straight one-run games in the World Series.

When they'd taken a lead into the ninth inning over these last six post-seasons, these Yankees had gone 41–1. When they'd even taken a lead into the seventh, they were 37–1.

But in that same period, this was the third time they'd won when they trailed in the ninth inning. They'd also won nine times when they trailed as late as the eighth and four more times when they trailed as late as the seventh. So that's 16 games in which they were *losing* in the seventh or later—and *won*.

And this one might have been the best of them all.

"Some day, when we look back on this, there will be a few games that really, really stand out," O'Neill said. "I'm sure this one will be fresh in every-one's mind."

"A lot of guys were saying," Stanton chuckled, "that this one will be on ESPN Classic—*tomorrow*."

Yeah, if it took that long. To find the last World Series game in which a team won after trailing by two runs in the bottom of the ninth, you had to travel all the way back to 1929, when the old Philadelphia A's did it in Game 5 against the Cubs. It was also done once by the 1911 Giants. But that's it.

Until this. When you watched them do this stuff, you began to think this couldn't be happening in real life. Real life doesn't work this way—not for anybody else.

"It almost feels like Billy Crystal wrote this one," Stanton said. "Regardless of how many times you see this happen, you still shake your head and say, 'That's unbelievable.'"

After six years of these miracles, there was no other word for it. So we asked Stanton if he thought that some day, when he told his grandchildren about these things he's seen, *they'd* believe it.

"Hmmm," he pondered. "I'll probably have to break out the video."

Game 5

NEW YORK—And for their next trick...the Yankees activate Don Zimmer for Game 6 of the World Series...and he hits a 500-foot game-tying homer off Randy Johnson with two outs in the ninth.

Ridiculous, you say? Impossible, you say? For the New York Yankees, there was no such thing as ridiculous, no such thing as impossible anymore.

You couldn't doubt them. You couldn't stop them. You couldn't beat them.

And you apparently required a court order to get a 27th out against them.

None of us needs to call M.I.T. to ask what the odds are of a team coming from two runs behind with two outs in the bottom of the ninth inning two nights in a row to win a World Series game. We already know the odds.

The odds are *zero*.

That can't be done. It had never been done. And even though we'd seen the New York Yankees do what can't be done, we still don't believe this was mathematically possible, logically possible, or humanly possible.

Except that we really did see Scott Brosius bash a two-run miracle into the left-field bleachers with two outs in the ninth inning of the first November

World Series game ever played.

And we really did see Chuck Knoblauch slide home with the winning run in the 12th inning, as a seemingly perfect throw to the plate made sure to hop over the nearest catcher's mitt.

And we really did see the numbers on the scoreboard change to read: Yankees 3, Diamondbacks 2, at 12:39 AM.

And we know we really had seen almost an identical baseball game the night before.

So if the first game was off-the-charts impossible, what was the second game? A science-fiction novel?

"Last night was a night dreams are made of," said the most poetic of all Yankees, reliever Mike Stanton. "But tonight? Wow. You don't even dream that."

Eventually, the Arizona Diamondbacks would remember that they were privileged to take part in two of the most historic, most exhilarating, most improbable back-to-back World Series games ever played.

But all they knew after this night was that they were losing this World Series, three games to two, when they should have been busy figuring out which cactus plants to parade around.

"I've never seen anything like this," said Arizona pitcher Brian Anderson. "I've never heard of anything like this. Two times with two outs in the ninth? We could be celebrating a world championship right now. Instead, we're behind the 8 ball.

"If we come back and win the Series now, it would be like we beat them six times in seven games. That's a tough thing to do—put them one out from losing six times in a seven-game Series."

No kidding. But it was that last out that was killing them. It was that last out that was adding astonishing lore to that Yankees legend. It was that last out that turned a fun little World Series into the greatest sporting event of the 21st century.

"We were saying last night that they should just put this game right on ESPN Classic tomorrow," Stanton laughed. "After tonight, ESPN might as well just put the whole series on as soon as it's over. Just have World Series Day and play the whole World Series over and over."

It is rare when you find athletes in the middle of an event this close, this exhausting, this riveting, who realize they are taking the ride of a lifetime. But these men sure realized it.

"It's remarkable. It's unbelievable," said Knoblauch, who, of course, got his first hit of the World Series in the 12th inning to put himself in position to score the winning run. "To have two different nights both have almost the exact scenario? To get a home run to tie the game when you have one out to play with? It's very strange, very weird."

"We're all just kind of blown away by what's happening out there," said Paul O'Neill, after the final game he would ever play in Yankee Stadium. "It's a storybook Series. You keep hearing, 'New York needs it.' Heck, *everyone* needs it. The World Series is for the fans, and this is as good as it gets."

"Just when you think you've seen it all," Knoblauch said, "it happens again. You can't say it was out of nowhere because it just happened last night. But the odds of that happening are slim and none."

No. The odds of that happening would be slim and none if that were the Babe in left, DiMaggio in center, and Gehrig on first. But when you start looking at the extenuating circumstances involved in *this* team doing something like this two nights in a row, you ought to upgrade those odds to none and none.

After all:

- In 101 seasons on the baseball earth—several of which have turned out fairly happily—the Yankees had never hit game-tying home runs with two outs in the ninth inning in back-to-back games. We're talking about more than 15,000 games, too, friends.

- No team had ever won two games it trailed in the bottom of the ninth inning in the same World Series, let alone won two like that in two nights.

- No team in 72 years had trailed a World Series game by *two* runs in the bottom of the ninth inning and won—and then the Yankees did it two nights in a row.

- Byung-Hyun Kim—the Arizona closer who gave up these homers to Martinez and Brosius, plus Derek Jeter's 10th-inning game-winner the night before—had given up two home runs all year to right-handed hitters. Both to Jeff Cirillo—at Coors Field.

- If these games were 26 outs long instead of 27, the Yankees would still have had *no* two-run innings in this entire World Series. So how could they possibly have come from two runs behind with one out to play two nights in a row, on these mind-blowing two-run homers by Martinez and Brosius?

- And as Brosius came to the plate with two outs in the ninth, this team full of champions and drama majors was 1 for the World Series (1-for-24) with runners in scoring position. Whereupon it then went two for its next two—the game-tying hit by Brosius, the game-winner by Soriano.

- Brosius, as was the case with Martinez the night before, was a free agent who knew he was probably playing his final game as a Yankee in this stadium, so the schlock meter was at its all-time pinnacle.

- Meanwhile, Brosius was 7-for-49 (.143) in the postseason, 21 for his last 101 (.208) over the previous seven weeks. He'd hit one home run since July 26. And he then homered off a pitcher who'd held right-handed hitters to a .152 batting average.

And because he did, as the clock blew past 12:30 AM, the storied stadium in the Bronx remained nearly full. At an hour when they should have been snoring, more than 50,000 people stood, mesmerized by this fantasy they were watching.

And then there was Soriano in the 12th, lining a single to right field off emergency reliever Albie Lopez. Knoblauch, at second base, was off at the thwack of the bat.

Right fielder Reggie Sanders charged and seemed to make a perfect throw to the plate, a throw that was going to arrive home just before Knoblauch did.

Except that, for no apparent reason other than the fact this was the Yankees, the baseball took what Arizona's Mark Grace would call "a kangaroo bounce." And so, when catcher Rod Barajas went to swipe it out of the sky and apply the tag, he found himself applying that tag without the baseball.

Plate ump Jim Joyce signaled safe. Knoblauch sprung out of the dirt and leaped into the night, both fists pumping with a sense of ecstasy these Yankees never seemed to get tired of.

"Last time I jumped that high? I don't know," Knoblauch said. "Probably trying to dunk a basketball about 20 years ago. But hey, it doesn't get any better than that. This is the World Series. Just to be a part of it, to score the winning run, it's a great feeling. These games are so exhausting, physically and mentally. And this whole series, it's been so difficult to score runs…

"At least," he couldn't help but add, "until two outs in the ninth."

We know there were millions of Americans who were tired of watching these Yankees win and win and win again. But the hardest thing in sports and in life is to be great for any period longer than an instant. So how could you not admire, at least in some way, a team that never grew tired of building its legend one hit, one win, one miracle at a time?

After six years of miracle-making, this made 17 postseason games since 1996 that the Yankees had won after trailing at some point in the seventh, eighth, or ninth innings. Meanwhile, the bullpens that had to face them in those six postseasons had run up a record of 3–15, with 13 blown saves in 21 tries—while the Yankees' bullpen was 18–3, with one blown save in six years (33 chances).

And so, after this final night of Yankee Stadium magic in 2001, the Yankees somehow found themselves *winning* a World Series in which they'd been outscored 19–10, and their team batting average was .177.

And with every impossible dream they fulfilled, their stadium would shake a little harder, their city would smile a little wider—at a time when it needed all the joy its baseball team could provide. And down on the field, the men who played the games could feel that passion.

"I can't tell you what it's like to be out on that field, doing these things, listening to this crowd, seeing all the lights from the flash bulbs," O'Neill said. "You look around, and you see the joy in these people—it's a great feeling to be out there."

After all this, by the way, they still hadn't won this World Series. All these games had earned them was the right to fly to Phoenix and try to find a way to beat Randy Johnson or Curt Schilling in Games 6 and 7 in Arizona.

But regardless, they'd just spent two of the most thrilling, breathtaking nights any team had ever spent at any ballpark, two nights even Hollywood couldn't make up.

After the first of those games, Stanton had said: "It felt like Billy Crystal wrote this one." So who, he was asked the next night, wrote the encore?

"I don't know," Stanton answered. "It would have to be somebody who writes fairy tales—because this is a fairy tale. It really is."

Game 7

PHOENIX—This is the story of a baseball game that made hearts pound.

That made a 42-year-old baseball player pray.

That turned a 6'10" starting pitcher into the world's tallest closer.

That somehow ended with the team that always wins trudging off the field while somebody else celebrated.

This is the story of a World Series that reminded the planet why there is no better sport on earth.

That made the impossible seem possible.

That left the poets and historians searching for ways to digest where it fit into the fabric of the great sporting events we have witnessed in a lifetime.

This was a game, this was a World Series, that explained why they play and why we watch.

"This was a World Series that had it all," said Mark Grace, after his team with the purple pinstripes, the Arizona Diamondbacks, had knocked off the Yankees in the ninth inning of the seventh game of the World Series 3–2. "So I don't think it surprised anybody that the seventh game of this World Series ended crazy. It didn't end normal because it couldn't end normal. I don't think anybody expected it to."

Well, anybody who did sure wasn't paying attention. For the week that led up to this breathtaking finale, the normal had turned abnormal, and the impossible had turned routine. So why wouldn't we expect this one to end with one more astonishing plot twist in the bottom of the ninth inning?

With the ultimate closer, Mariano Rivera, finally meeting a postseason lead he couldn't hold?

With a broken-bat blooper flying over a drawn-in infield?

With the dynasty of a great champion toppling in a brief, stunning instant, with the vision of history's third-ever four-peat dangling just over the horizon?

"Hey, somebody told me we just beat the New York Yankees and Mariano

Rivera in the bottom of the ninth inning," Grace said, looking as if he'd just taken a raft ride down a river of champagne. "I still don't believe it. But here I am, wearing this shirt that says, WORLD SERIES CHAMPIONS. So it must be true."

Oh, it's true, all right. You can look it up. Forever.

There will be a line in every World Series record book and every encyclopedia that says the New York Yankees finally did lose a World Series. But that line won't tell the whole story, because it is a story even George Lucas would have trouble dreaming up.

Three of the last four games in this World Series ended with the final swing of the bat. Four of the last five games were decided by one run. And the grand finale was a game that was instantly locked inside the DVD player in our heads, destined to play on as long as we sit around and debate the epic games we have ever seen.

It was a game in three parts. Part one was Roger Clemens versus Curt Schilling. Two 20-game winners with their gas tanks running low, huffing and puffing, throwing 97-mph smoke and splitters that hurtled out of the sky, refusing to leave, refusing to lose.

"I kept thinking it was the Thrilla in Manila," said Arizona GM Joe Garagiola Jr. "It was Frazier and Ali in the ring. Somebody was going to have to win on points, because you knew they couldn't knock each other out."

They arrived in the sixth inning, tied at 0–0. It was only the third Game 7 ever in which the two starting pitchers got through five innings without allowing a crooked number on the scoreboard. You've heard of the others: Morris-Smoltz in 1991, Gibson-Lolich in 1968.

"No surprise there," Schilling would say later. "I knew he was going to bring his 'A' game. I just had to make sure I brought mine."

Finally, in the sixth, it was Clemens who cracked first, allowing an RBI single to Danny Bautista that shook every cactus bush in the desert.

Schilling, meanwhile, was scary-great, pitching on three days' rest for the second time in a week. After six innings, he'd allowed one hit and faced the minimum 18 base runners—becoming just the fourth pitcher since Don Larsen to do that through six innings of any World Series game, let alone the last one.

But these were the Yankees. You pound them in the kisser. You lock them in a room with no escape hatch. You blindfold them, tie them up, and send them off to sea on a raft. And a second later, they were right back on top of you, with that gleam in their eyes, singing Sinatra.

So they pieced together a game-tying rally off Schilling in the seventh, punctuated by a Tino Martinez single. And you knew they were going to find a way to win a World Series in which they easily could have lost all seven games. Didn't you?

"They played exactly how I expected a four-time world champion to play," Schilling said. "That's an unbelievable baseball team over there."

As soon as Bob Brenly let Schilling hit for himself in the bottom of the seventh, you could smell the next Yankees ambush coming. And it arrived five pitches into the top of the eighth, when Alfonso Soriano nominated himself for the part of Bill Mazeroski in the now-scrapped George Steinbrenner blockbuster production, *Revenge of the 1960 Yankees.*

Schilling worked the count to 0-2 as Soriano led off the inning. Schilling came back with a killer splitter. Soriano fouled it off. Then came a 94-mph flameball. Soriano got a piece of that one, too.

Schilling thought to himself he had this guy right where he wanted him. He shook off a fastball. He reared back and snapped off one more diving splitter that was heading for the dirt when Soriano golfed it out of orbit and lofted it 10 rows deep into the seats in left-center.

In the Yankees' dugout, Joe Torre pumped a fist and remembered to exhale, for the first time in two hours. On the mound, the pain on Schilling's face could be seen from here to New Mexico.

"I felt great," Schilling would say afterward, with the comfort of knowing how it all turned out. "I felt fantastic. That ball he hit out, I shook off to get to. I was happy with the whole sequence. But when that ball went out, I knew it meant we had to go through their bullpen. And their bullpen is so great, let's just say there are not many scenarios that would wind up with me feeling as happy as I do right now."

Soriano hadn't even made it around the bases when out there in the Yankees' bullpen, the greatest closer of our time, Señor Rivera, was already heading for the mound, loosening up to finish a deal he had finished 23 times in a row.

For four straight postseasons, it was a sight that meant the baseball game was over, and the parade could begin whenever they were finished shredding all the ticker tape. But not on this night.

Grace and Brenly converged on the mound to pat Schilling on the head and thank him for sacrificing every tendon in his shoulder for the only cause worth playing for. Brenly and Schilling had had their tense moments in this World Series. But this time, the manager looked his co-ace in the eye and told him, "You're my hero."

As Schilling walked off the mound, the three Arizona outfielders—Bautista, Steve Finley and Gonzalez—converged in center field to talk over how they were possibly going to escape from this giant well they had just fallen into.

"We saw him warming up out there," Finley said of Rivera. "But when we all met out there in the outfield, the first thing I said was, 'We're gonna get this guy. We're gonna get him. We're gonna find a way.'"

Yeah, well, it sounded good. But you could excuse the rest of the world for thinking that way didn't exist. This man had saved 23 postseason games in a row, 19 of them in outings of more than one inning. He had the lowest postseason ERA (0.70) of any pitcher who ever lived.

So if there was a way to beat him that didn't involve a kidnapping plot, no one had uncovered it in four years.

But then this game began spinning in still more crazy ways. Schilling was leaving. Randy Johnson was warming up in the bullpen. Next thing you knew, the Unit was leaving that bullpen to get the last out of the eighth. Next thing you knew after that, he was coming out for the ninth to get three more outs.

And if you'd sworn you'd just seen him *starting* Game 6 the day before, it wasn't the alcohol. He actually did that. Nobody had pitched seven innings of Game 6 of a World Series and then come back in relief the next day since Vic Raschi in 1952. But this was a World Series gone insane. So the Big Unit got his team to the bottom of the ninth.

Rivera had struck out the side in the eighth, marred only by a soft single by Finley. So there was no reason to think his ninth inning would be any different.

"We were very confident when he went out there in the ninth, obviously," said his bullpen cohort, Mike Stanton. "We've seen Mo do it so many times, you know he's got ice in his veins. When he goes out there, he gives these guys the sense they're not going to lose."

But with his second pitch of the ninth, Grace fisted a cutter into left-center field, even as his bat was being given last rites.

"I'm just glad I hit that ball," Grace said, "because I think it would have hit me in the chest if I didn't."

Damian Miller then laid down the bunt that changed the World Series. Rivera fielded it and heard catcher Jorge Posada yell, "second base." But Rivera threw it before he had control of the baseball, and the throw sailed behind pinch runner David Dellucci, into center field. Everyone was safe.

"It was the right place to throw the ball," Rivera said later. "The guy wasn't even halfway to second base. But I didn't have a good grip on the ball, and it just took off."

Rivera then got one out, forcing Dellucci on another bunt attempt, by Jay Bell. So the Yankees were two outs away. Who knew it would be their final out of the season?

Tony Womack somehow fought off a 2-2 cutter and served it into right. Pinch runner Midre Cummings rumbled home. The great Rivera's postseason save streak was over. The baseball game was not.

"We were out in the bullpen," said Brian Anderson, "and the place was shaking, and I was standing next to Mike Morgan. He was going to go into the game next if it stayed tied. I swear, he was like half-crying. He said, 'Lord, I know I don't pray as much as I should. But please get us a run right here, because I don't know if I can pitch.'"

There are some things, though, even prayer hasn't been able to influence. And Rivera is one of them. The odds of getting two runs in the ninth inning off Mariano Rivera are right up there with the odds of going to the moon in a used Hyundai. Can't happen. Never happens.

But it happened. Rivera plunked Craig Counsell with a pitch to load the bases. And up marched Luis Gonzalez, trying to figure out how he could unload them.

Just one inning earlier, Rivera had struck Gonzalez out on a man-eating cutter. And on the way back to the bench, Gonzalez looked over his shoulder at the man who had just thrown this pitch. Was he human, or what?

"The guy's amazing, man," Gonzalez said of that look. "Every time you go up there, you know to keep looking [for the cutter] in. And the more you look in, the more you start to swing early, the more the ball moves on you.

"So when I went up there in the ninth, it was the first time all year I choked up. I said to myself, 'Just put the ball in play and make something happen.' And what do you know, man. It happened."

One more heat-seeking cutter went bearing in on his fists. Gonzalez fought it off and punched it into the air, floating, floating, floating through the night. This wasn't happening. Was it?

Derek Jeter and Soriano turned to stagger after it. But the infield was in. They weren't going to get there. This wasn't happening. Was it?

It was. It did. The baseball fell. Bell could have crawled home with the winning run. A mob scene broke out at home plate. Then another broke out at first base, where Gonzalez was shrieking with joy.

And over their shoulders, the greatest champions of their era walked slowly off the field, one by one, afterthoughts in the shadows of someone else's party. It was only that sight, of Jeter and Bernie Williams shuffling painfully off toward a loser's clubhouse, side by side, that convinced you this was real, that the champs hadn't won, that Rivera hadn't triumphed, that someone else was going to ride in this parade.

"It was a tough moment, definitely," Rivera said, facing this loss and the questions with tremendous dignity. "We have a great bunch of guys here, and I feel sorry that I didn't finish this off. But I'm not perfect."

He's as close as anyone has ever come, though. Which explains the feeling in both clubhouses as the reality of what had just happened to him sank in.

The only word Stanton could find to describe his emotions was *disbelief*— because "you always think Mo's going to get out of it, because he always does. He very rarely gives up any hard-hit balls. And on the rare nights when he doesn't do the job, it's usually jam shots and broken bats that cause it. And it was again tonight."

"They were all broken bats, man," said catcher Jorge Posada. "All of them. Grace, broken bat. Womack, broken bat. Gonzalez, broken bat. What are you gonna do?"

"Nah, I didn't break my bat," Gonzalez said, in full denial. "At least I don't think so. But you know what? If I did, I don't care."

"When Gonzalez got that base hit," Grace said, "the feeling that went through my body is a feeling I never felt in my life. And it's still going through my body. It hasn't sunk in yet that we beat Mariano Rivera, because that doesn't happen. It just doesn't happen."

"It happened, and I knew it was going to happen," Finley claimed, at least slightly seriously. "I saw it rain inside a dome tonight, man. So you knew something freaky was going to happen."

It doesn't get much freakier than Mariano Rivera blowing a save in the ninth inning of the seventh game of the World Series. Except we'd just seen two Yankees hit two game-tying home runs in Yankee Stadium with two outs in the bottom of the ninth. So who's to say, in this World Series, what was freaky and what was sane?

There's no formula you can draw up, no numbers to crunch through the calculator, to measure what makes one sporting event more indelible, more memorable, more classic than the giant heap of events around it. But when you see it, you know it. And this was it.

"I just hope that was as fun to watch as it was to play in," Schilling said, "because that's got to be one of the greatest World Series ever played."

"I haven't slept in a week," Grace said. "This was unbelievable. I don't know how the Yankees do it, man. They do this every year. And this is hard on the old ticker."

"I didn't just come *close* to having a heart attack," said Garagiola. "I think I had one. If they'd have taken my pulse tonight, it would have looked like the Richter Scale in the '89 World Series."

In the end, though, this game and this Series registered on a lot of Richter scales—the scale of baseball, the scale of the heart, the scale in the portion of the brain that seals events like this in a special little corner.

In one crazy week, Mystique and Aura went from Schilling's "dancers in a nightclub," to a magic carpet that carried storybook home runs into the deep recesses of Yankee Stadium, to the missing-persons list on one final nutty weekend in Arizona.

"I know what happened to Mystique and Aura," said Brian Anderson. "They got the night off early tonight—and headed on down to the BOB."

October 14, 2003

The Bartman Game

CHICAGO—We all know in sports that things happen that can't possibly happen. We all know that any time the Cubs are playing baseball in October, the impossible becomes all too possible.

But how do we explain *this*? How do we explain what happened in Wrigley Field on a night when the Cubs were five outs away from the World Series—and wound up in a twilight zone of despair and disbelief?

Five outs away. A 3–0 lead. Mark Prior pitching a ferocious, give-me-the-ball-and-get-outta-the-way three-hit shutout. Cubs fans standing, roaring, basking in the moment wherever you looked—even on the rooftops across Waveland Avenue.

This was not the look of a baseball game about to veer in a whole new historic direction. This was not the sound of a group of people that would soon find itself filing off into the night in shock and confusion.

This was not a recipe even the Florida Marlins would have drawn up for the most remarkable win in the history of their franchise.

But this is the power of sports that makes watching these games so relentlessly addictive. This is the awesome tug of the amazing sport of baseball. And sadly, these are the Cubs. Just when you think they've run out of tragic scripts for their never-ending archives, they even top themselves.

Marlins 8, Cubs 3. Courtesy of an eight-run eighth inning by a team that hadn't gotten a hit with a man in scoring position in three *days*. Couldn't happen. Impossible. Absurd. Inexplicable.

But it happened. Didn't it? Just to make sure, can we watch it again? Maybe if we watch it again, six or 10 or a thousand times, we'll believe we saw it. And maybe if the Florida Marlins watch it again, they'll finally believe they did what they did.

"Brian Banks and I came in here," said left fielder Jeff Conine, in one of the most raucous clubhouses in postseason history, "and looked at each other, and we said, 'What just happened out there?'"

"Honestly," said first baseman Derrek Lee, "I'm in shock. I know we've done this a lot this season. But at some point, you have to say it's gotta run out. I mean, how many times can you do that?"

"We were like, 'When you figure out what happened, fill me in,'" Banks laughed. "Guys came in here and looked at each other, and there was just a sense of shock that what just happened had happened. It was an amazing thing. Whether you were a fan or a player, it was just a shocking situation."

Well, if *they* were in shock after winning, you can only imagine the scene down the concourse in the locker room of the team that lost.

There was silence in that Cubs clubhouse for a long, long time. A half-dozen players sat in the middle of the room, eating. The rest were nowhere to be found, thinking thoughts we'll never know.

For most, this was not a moment in their lives they felt like recreating or dissecting. It was a moment to forget. A moment to shove into a dark corner of their brain where they store the memories they wish would disappear.

"If I go home thinking about this one," said Sammy Sosa, "I'm not going to get any sleep."

The first inclination was to talk about where this game fits in Cubs history, in the ghoulish portion of that Cubs museum—the wing where the baseball was still hopping through Leon Durham's legs 19 years later, where Mule Haas' fly ball was still hiding behind the sun 74 years later, where a goat still roamed the halls 58 years later.

But that would be way too small a way to think. We need to set this game in its place in baseball history, because the only games even remotely like it are among the most talked about baseball games ever played.

According to the Elias Sports Bureau, only four other teams had ever come back to win postseason games in which they'd been at least three runs behind and no more than six outs from calling it a year:

- One was the 1960 Pirates, in Game 7 of the World Series, in what we now know as The Bill Mazeroski Game.

- The next was the 1975 Red Sox, in Game 6 of the World Series, in what we now know as The Carlton Fisk Game (co-starring Bernie Carbo, who hit a game-tying three-run pinch-hit homer off Reds closer Rawly Eastwick in the eighth).

- Then came the 1980 Phillies, in the fifth game of a best-of-five NLCS, in what we now know as The Nolan Ryan Game (because it was Ryan who couldn't hold a three-run lead in the eighth).

- And finally, there were the 1986 Red Sox, in Game 5 of the 1986 ALCS, in what we now know as either The Dave Henderson Game or The Donnie Moore Game (because it was Henderson who hit the home run off Moore with two outs in the ninth that kept the Angels from heading to their first World Series).

But that was it.

Those aren't just baseball games. Those are epic baseball games. They're games you are liable to stumble across on ESPN Classic at 2:00 in the afternoon or 3:00 in the morning, any month of any year.

And then there was this one.

We'll never forget the sound in Wrigley Field in the bottom of the seventh inning, after Mark Grudzielanek singled in the run that put the Cubs three runs ahead. It was a sound you could feel in your rib cage, because it carried a rumble, a clap of thunder, an electric current rippling through every body in the park.

It was the sound of people who were finally certain this was what it felt like to watch the Cubs—*the Cubs*—go to the World Series. It was the sound of people who knew this game was over, because Mark Prior was not going to let them lose.

Even the Marlins heard that sound. They were a team that specialized in the miracle victory, the improbable comeback. But even they were just about resigned to their fate.

They had three hits off Prior. All three were singles. One of them was an infield hit that wound up conking Cubs first baseman Randall Simon on the head. "He hadn't given up *anything*," Lee said, with the utmost admiration.

Prior was 12–1 in his last 13 starts. He was the most dominating pitcher left in the playoffs. This was his time, his night, his way of announcing to the world he had that aura only the best pitchers on earth ever have.

"The way he was dominating the game," Conine admitted, "I thought, *Well, hell, we gave it a great run.*"

Then there was one out in the eighth. Prior had Juan Pierre 2-2. Pierre fought off one 94-mph smokeball. Prior reached back and launched the next one, his 104th pitch of the night, at 96. Pierre flicked it inside the left-field line for a double.

But it felt like just an intermission in The Mark Prior Show. Prior burst ahead of Luis Castillo, 1-2. Then 2-2. And 3-2. Castillo fouled off one 94-mph fastball. Then another. And then it happened.

This was a moment no Cubs fan will ever forget. They will always see this foul ball twisting toward the brick wall that juts out toward the left-field foul line. They will always see Moises Alou angling over, setting himself, leaping, reaching. And they will always see the fan in the blue Cubs hat and the headphones over his ears, cupping his hands, deflecting this baseball away from Alou, keeping this at-bat alive.

Alou spun away in anger, spitting out words we can't repeat. Fans around this anti–Jeffrey Maier, a poor dude we would later learn was named Steve Bartman, began berating him, abusing him, showering him with guilt and beer—but not quite in that order.

Three hundred feet away, in the visitors' dugout, Marlins players looked at each other, wondering if they'd just seen what they'd seen, hoping it meant what they thought it meant.

"Mike Redmond turned to me," Lee said, "and said, 'OK, let's make that kid famous.'"

And after that, everything seemed to change. Prior's next pitch was ball four—but worse. It skipped past Paul Bako, and there were runners on first and third. Then Prior had an 0-2 count on Pudge Rodriguez and tried to strike him out with a curve ball. But he hung it on the inner half of the plate, and Rodriguez roped it into left.

Still, Prior had a two-run lead. And Miguel Cabrera chopped his next pitch toward short, where Alex Gonzalez—the guy who had the highest fielding percentage of any shortstop in the league—was surely going to turn it into an inning-ending, game-saving double play.

But these were the Cubs, masters of the unthinkable. Gonzalez hadn't committed an error in more than *two months*, since August 13. But he chose this time, this unfathomable moment, to have a double-play ball clank off his glove.

"For whatever reason, I didn't catch the ball," Gonzalez said later. "The spin on the ball ate me up."

And after that, the spin on this game ate the Cubs up, eating their World Series dreams alive. Lee doubled. Tie game. Prior exited, after 119 pitches. Kyle Farnsworth entered to try to keep it close. Nope. Intentional walk. Sacrifice fly. Marlins, 4–3. Then another intentional walk. And then the final dagger...

Mike Mordecai, a bench guy who had made the first out of the inning, a man who had only entered this game because of a double-switch the inning before, scorched a three-run double off the ivy in left-center. Three RBIs—equaling Mordecai's RBI total for the previous two months. Of course. And this game was history.

The sounds were different now. Except for the angry mob descending on poor Steve Bartman, there were more tears in this park than words.

"I don't think I've ever heard that many people get that quiet that fast," Mordecai said.

Only once all year had the Marlins scored eight runs in an inning. And only three times in history had a team scored at least eight times in an inning in a postseason game in which losing would have meant elimination. But all of those were early-inning eruptions, by the 1968 Tigers (10-run third), the 1992 Pirates (eight-run second), and 2001 Diamondbacks (eight-run third).

So no team as close to the end of the road as the Marlins had ever had an inning like this. And no team as close to the World Series as the Cubs had ever given up an inning like this.

No wonder then that, in the Cubs' locker room, the ghosts were everywhere—the ghosts of 1984, and 1969, and 1945. The ghosts were riding the wave of every question. Someone asked Alou whether, if he were a Cubs fan, he would find it hard not to think about curses.

"I'm not a Cubs fan," Alou said. "I'm a Cubs player. And I don't believe that crap."

But other men were more philosophical. There were, after all, two teams playing.

"That was crazy," said Doug Glanville. "But so what? Tomorrow's Game 7. A lot of things had to fall our way for us to get this far. But everybody's got to have a story. Every story we have, they have a story. They think they're ordained. We think we're ordained."

But only one of them could come out of this series clinging to their ordination. So it would all come down to one final ballgame—Kerry Wood versus Mark Redman.

Over the last two seasons, Wood and Prior had started back-to-back games 17 different times. Only once had the Cubs lost both of those games. So they couldn't possibly lose two in a row at a time like this. Could they? Uhhhhh, don't ask.

Stuff happens in sports. When *that* stuff happens to the Cubs, it's a tragic tale, all right. But there's always another team, with another story. And on this night, the two of them got mixed up in one of the most mind-boggling games ever to appear in front of our eyeballs.

So very late on a night of a baseball game that will always keep on playing, a group of Marlins—Andy Fox, Brian Banks, Jeff Conine—found themselves looking at each other one more time and shaking their heads. They needed to see this one again, just to believe it. Fortunately, they would get that chance.

"You can bet that game will be on ESPN Classic," Banks said.

"Yeah," Fox laughed. "I think it's on at midnight."

Never Underestimate the Rally Monkey

ANAHEIM—These are the games that don't end with the 27th out. These are the games that keep springing back to life, years after they're over. These are the games that remind us that there's no such word in sports as *impossible*.

It shouldn't have been possible for the Anaheim Angels to be waking up on the morning after a mind-boggling Game 6 with one more World Series game to play. But they were.

It shouldn't have been possible to go into the seventh inning of the sixth game of the World Series five runs behind, your season nine outs from over, and somehow win. But the Angels did.

It shouldn't have been possible to send 22 hitters to the plate over the first 6⅓ innings and get two hits—one an infield single, the other a broken-bat thunker where the bat travels almost as far as the ball—and then have your next 10 hitters get *eight* hits. But the Angels did that, too.

If you witnessed all of that, you know the Angels really did conjure up a miracle to beat the Giants 6–5 in Game 6 of the now-unforgetable 2002 World Series.

And somewhere in there—between the Barry Bonds homer that seemed to carry a World Series trophy on its flight and the Troy Glaus double that changed everything—this 2002 World Series went from being merely fun to something bigger, something better, something classic.

All on the strength of the most breathtaking comeback from the edge of winter in the history of this sport.

No team had ever been five runs behind in a World Series game that could have ended its season and somehow won. We repeat: *no* team. Let alone a team down to its final eight outs.

Even the '86 Mets weren't in *that* bad shape. Even Carlton Fisk didn't have to hit a five-run homer to save the Red Sox in 1975. Even the 1960 Pirates and the 1985 Royals and the 2001 Diamondbacks never found themselves in the kind of mess the Angels found themselves in when the seventh inning of this game arrived.

But no team had ever gone from 41 games out of first place one year to the World Series the next, either. So whatever that thing was that these Angels had inside them, wherever it came from, whatever power truly traveled from the vertical leap of the Rally Monkey to the field where this team weaved its magic, it had given the 2002 Angels a place in the eternal lore of October.

"This," said Angels hitting coach Mickey Hatcher, "was the best game I've ever been a part of."

We need to pause here to remind you that in 1988, Mickey Hatcher was a Dodger. Which means he was in the park the night Kirk Gibson hit a World Series homer that is still traveling.

"People talk about the Gibson game," Hatcher said, "but that was Game 1. There were still four games left to play. This was win-or-go-home. I don't care what happens [in Game 7]. This is the game they'll always be reminded about for the rest of their lives. And it's typical of what this team is all about."

This was a team that had spun 43 come-from-behind wins in the regular season and six more in the postseason. So we know this was a bunch of people who had never seen a mountain they thought was too tall.

But any resemblance between May 29 in Kansas City and October 26 in the World Series is purely hallucinatory. This was the comeback, this was the game that would define this team forever.

"In some way, every single one of these games in this World Series was just amazing," said David Eckstein. "But this game was unbelievable. This was definitely something to tell your kids and grandkids about, about how you made this comeback. This was the one I'll remember above all the games this whole season.

"Making this type of comeback in a World Series atmosphere, when you're facing elimination, is really special. There's no other way to describe it. Every other game we've played this year, we knew there was a tomorrow. Today we didn't know that. So to respond this way was unbelievable."

And it was especially unbelievable because, for most of this game, everything that transpired seemed to be the baseball gods' way of telling the Angels, "Thanks for the memories."

How could they have not known they were going to lose when Shawon Dunston—*Shawon Dunston*—lofted a two-run home run into the first row in left field against them? Shawon Dunston, a man who had hit his last home run more than six months earlier (on April 14).

How could they not have known they were going to lose when Bonds pummeled a frightening home run off their secret weapon, Francisco Rodriguez, in the sixth inning? It was Bonds' fourth home run of this World Series, his eighth home run of this postseason. And it had the look, the feel, of a career-defining home run, roaring down an exit ramp in the right-field stands to give the Giants a 4–0 lead.

And if that didn't do it, how could these Angels not have known they were going to lose when a monstrous center-field shot by Glaus in the fifth settled into Kenny Lofton's glove in the only section of Edison Field where it *wouldn't* have been a home run?

And how could they possibly have thought they still had a chance when Jeff Kent pumped his fist in triumph after the RBI single that made it 5–0 in the seventh—to make it 15 unanswered runs by the Giants over the last two games?

"It goes through your mind," Tim Salmon would admit afterward. "That's just human nature. When they got that fifth run there, the way Russ Ortiz was pitching, you can't help but think, *This game isn't shaping up the way you'd like it to*. But the next thing you knew…"

Yeah, the next thing you knew, Glaus and Brad Fullmer had singled off Ortiz with one out in the seventh. The next thing you knew, out marched Dusty Baker to wave for his trusty bullpen, as Edison Field began to tremble with the first glimmer of hope, and Baker was stuffing the baseball back into Ortiz's hand so he would be able to stuff it into his trophy case. Oops.

The next thing you knew, Felix Rodriguez—a man who had given up just three runs and six hits in the previous six weeks—was locked in a momentous duel with Scott Spiezio that was destined to stand as the turning point of this World Series.

On it went, through eight oxygen-sucking pitches. Spiezio fouled off a 1-2 fastball. And then a 2-2 fastball, clocked at 97 mph. And then it was 3-2, as the ballpark rattled and the Rally Monkey danced and the ThunderStix pounded.

How long did this at-bat last? Three minutes? Five minutes? Ten minutes? Thirty minutes? Even Spiezio—a man who later called it "the biggest at-bat I've had in my life"—had no idea.

"Probably the umpires were mad at me because I was taking so long up there," he laughed. "But at moments like that, I try not to think about time—or anything that would distract me."

Rodriguez—the first man in 22 years to pitch in every one of the first six games of a World Series—whooshed up one more fastball. But this one, he got down and in. Spiezio golfed it toward the right-field corner.

"It seemed like it hung up there for half an hour," Spiezio said. "I was running down to first, praying, 'Please, let it go out.' I saw [Reggie] Sanders out there, running toward the fence. I didn't know if it was going to make it or not."

On the mound, Rodriguez was doing a little praying of his own.

"I saw Reggie going back," Rodriguez said. "And I thought, *Maybe he has a chance.*"

But finally, Sanders banged into the fence. The baseball dropped barely beyond his grasp, in just about the shallowest part of the park. A 5–0 game was suddenly a 5–3 game. And at that instant, what once seemed impossible didn't feel so impossible anymore.

Spiezio floated around the bases trying to comprehend what he'd done. Somewhere on the journey, he became aware of this sound all around him— this thunderclap of elation he had just evoked in his teammates and the 44,000 folks in red who had refused to jump off of this wild ride.

"It was so loud," Spiezio said, "it was like a cannon shot or something."

And to Rodriguez—still standing next to the mound, shaking his head—it felt like the cannonball had traveled right through his gut. He knew this was not a home run in many ballparks—certainly not the one the Giants play in. But a lot of good that did him.

"When you see it in the paper tomorrow," Rodriguez said, "it's not going to say, 'It wouldn't be a home run in San Francisco.' It's still a home run."

It wasn't a home run that won this game. But it sure was a home run that changed this game.

"I knew then," Spiezio said, "we had a chance."

But the Giants' bullpen had been so good, it wasn't a great chance. Scott Eyre was still out there. He hadn't allowed an earned run the whole postseason. Tim Worrell was still out there. He'd ripped off seven straight scoreless October appearances. Robb Nen was still out there. He'd saved seven games this postseason and blown none.

"The only thought we had out in the bullpen," Worrell said, "was, *Time to shut the door.* We've done it this way—Felix to me to Robby—for two-thirds of the season now."

But this night was not going to be like all those other nights. Three pitches into the bottom of the eighth, Worrell left a changeup in the middle of the plate. Darrin Erstad crunched it out to right. And amazingly, it was 5–4.

"He doesn't do that very often," Erstad said of Worrell. "But he did it tonight. Got to take advantage of it."

But *still* the Giants led, 5–4. Worrell took a big gulp of air and told himself, "OK, it's a one-run game. We've done *that* enough times."

By then, though, a one-run lead looked smaller than a mosquito, even in the eighth inning of the sixth game of the World Series. So when Tim Salmon singled, and then Garrett Anderson singled, and then Barry Bonds took a peek at pinch runner Chone Figgins and overran the ball, and then Anderson chugged into second, your eardrums ached.

Baker came to the mound again and pointed to Nen. The tying run was on third. The winning run was on second. There were six outs still to get. Over the previous six seasons, Nen owned exactly *one* six-out save (this July 6, in Arizona). The odds he'd convert this one were tinier than Darren Baker.

"That's a tough job there," said the closer on the other side, Troy Percival. "Basically, he's got to strike out the first two guys or he's going to give up the tying run. That's a situation most people are not going to get out of."

And Nen couldn't, either. He hung a 2-1 slider to Glaus, who went up there thinking, *Hit a ground ball*, and wound up smoking one up the freeway in left-center for a two-run double.

Percival did the rest, finishing a 1-2-3 ninth with a 96-mph inferno that punched out Rich Aurilia for the final out. And it was time for all of us to do our best to digest what we'd just seen.

For the Giants, this game hurt like no other loss could ever hurt. But they couldn't allow themselves to feel that hurt—if that was humanly possible.

The Angels, on the other hand, were looking at a tidal wave it was tough not to ride.

"We all knew we were in a great game out there," said Spiezio, whose homer made him 11-for-17 (.733) with runners in scoring position in this postseason, good for a record-tying 19 RBIs. "We all realized some big things were going on, some huge at-bats…That's an awesome feeling, man. That's the most excited I've ever been from any comeback win. That's the most special game, the most special comeback I've ever been a part of. It was definitely a different feeling from any other game I've ever played."

But when they woke up the next morning, all it would mean was that they had to come back and do it again—in a Game 7 adventure in the land of the Rally Monkey.

Chapter 5

What I Got Right—and Wrong

October, 2003

The World Series Beckons the Cubs

AUTHOR'S NOTE: I don't believe in curses. Do you? I don't believe in jinxes. Do you? Seriously? So on the eve of Game 6 of the 2003 National League Championship Series, with the Cubs up 3–2 and Mark Prior and Kerry Wood lined up to pitch Games 6 and 7, I wrote this piece. I wrote about what it was going to mean for the Cubs to blow away all the ghosts and all the curses, and finally reach another World Series. OK, so that never happened. But it's not my fault! I never threw a pitch. I never sold a ticket to Steve Bartman. I was just writing a column about something that never actually happened. And here it is, word for word.

CHICAGO—The ghosts never sleep at times like this. That's how life works when you're the Cubs. These are the times they get to hear once again about all the years they try so hard to forget: 1984, 1969, 1945, 1918, etc., etc., etc.

Nineteen years ago, another Cubs team was one victory away from winning the National League Championship Series, just like this Cubs team. Nineteen years ago, that Cubs team had three games left and only needed to win one, just like this team. Nineteen years ago, that Cubs team then lost (oops) three in a row.

So now this Cubs team is still hearing about it, even though the pitcher who will start for them Tuesday night (in Game 6), Mark Prior, hadn't even begun kindergarten at the time.

The hitting coach for this Cubs team, Gary Matthews, was the left fielder for that Cubs team. He was asked if he would tell these players about the lessons learned from that legendary collapse in 1984.

"No," Matthews growled. "Why? Why should I? It's well documented. As a staff, as a team, we're not dwelling in the past. We're looking forward to the future."

Look forward. That has been their approach, from the first day of spring training—for the manager (Dusty Baker), the general manager (Jim Hendry), and all these players who have no idea what a "homer in the gloaming" was. Trouble is, when you're a Cub, the future—and the present—are always being tossed into the Cuisinart with the past.

"We have such disdain for that lovable-loser line," said Hendry. "That's not in any of our repertoires around here. That line has hung on for so long. It's time to dispel that…We need to do it—for everybody. For ourselves. For these guys. For those guys that played here in the past. And for the fans."

The longer they journey through this October, the more you begin to understand what makes the Cubs franchise so unique. Despite all those years without a title, despite all those years without even throwing a pitch in a World Series, the bond never snaps:

The bond between players and fans…the bond between current players and former players…the bond between current fans and the people who made them fans…the bond between all of them and the special, ivy-covered ballpark that casts this spell.

Billy Williams—longtime Cub, Hall of Famer, now a Cubs special assistant—has spent October traveling with these Cubs, at the invitation of Hendry and team president Andy MacPhail. He has been living with that bond since the 1950s. He still feels its powerful grip now, stronger than ever.

"Once they grab hold—because of Wrigley Field, Harry Caray, Jack Brickhouse, Ernie Banks, Ron Santo, Billy Williams, Ryne Sandberg, and the people playing right now—they catch onto it," Williams said. "And they're not going to give it up.

"They'll never give up. We could lose every year, but they'll never give up. They support this ballclub. That's the Chicago Cubs fan. And that's why I'm so happy for them."

In other cities, fans jump on the bandwagon when times get good, then hurtle themselves off when the losing starts again. But Cubs fans are different. They jump on—but they never jump off.

"A lot of people who are enjoying this now," Williams said, "are enjoying it for themselves, but also for their father, and their grandfather, and their grandmothers, and their mothers. They're all Cubs fans. It's an unusual thing."

It's hard to even explain. It isn't winning that makes Cubs fans—well, uh, obviously. It isn't just the ballpark. It isn't just Ernie Banks or Ron Santo or Sammy Sosa. For hundreds of thousands of Cubs fans, this is something that has been passed down to them from one generation to the next to the next, almost like the family china.

So when—oh, OK, make that *if* (they're the Cubs)—the Cubs win one more game against the Marlins, that noise you hear won't be your ordinary cheers. It's way more than that.

It's the joys and frustrations, the dreams and nightmares, the close calls and lost seasons, the travails of more than half a century of Cubs soap operatics—all spilling out at once, erupting like the Mount Vesuvius of celebrations.

"This will mean much more to the city than the Bears winning or the Bulls winning," Williams said. "Heck, yeah. Because these people have waited so long."

Oh, they have waited in other places, too. We understand that. As 8 billion New Englanders could tell you, the Cubs don't hold the patent on Not Winning the World Series. But somehow, there's a difference between Cubs fans and Red Sox fans. We've spent enough time around both of them to see it, to feel it.

Red Sox fans are somehow resigned to their fate. They know the next Bill Buckner fiasco, the next Bob Stanley wild pitch, the next gigantic black cloud is right over the horizon. But for some reason, Cubs fans allow themselves to dream.

That's been a big mistake for the last 58 years, of course. But still they do it. They've been imagining what this trip to the World Series might feel like for so long, there's no doubt they'll be real good at enjoying it.

"I'll tell you when it really hit me," Hendry said. "It was the game where we clinched the division. None of us came to work that day assuming it was going to happen [because the Cubs needed to sweep a doubleheader at Wrigley while the Astros lost at home to Milwaukee]…But all of a sudden, it looks like Prior is going to win our opener. And then the score goes up showing that Houston lost. And the atmosphere, from that moment on, was unbelievable.

"I don't know who would have beaten us in the second game. We won easy. But then, an hour and a half, maybe two hours later—at 10:00 or 11:00 at night, after a doubleheader—I bet a third of the people were still in the stands. They couldn't leave."

So, in many ways, that Cubs loss Sunday in Game 5 in Florida could turn out to be a poetic stroke of unintentional genius. If the Cubs are going to the World Series, there's only one place they ought to clinch it. And that place sure isn't next to Exit 2X off the Florida Turnpike.

"It's probably fate," said Kenny Lofton, a Cubs fan as a kid, a Cubs outfielder now. "We get to go back to Wrigley and celebrate at Wrigley."

The coolest thing about that celebration, though—if it happens—is that it won't just be the Loftons and Sosas and Priors and Bakers doing the celebrating. It will be Billy Williams and Ron Santo and Don Kessinger and Ferguson Jenkins. It will be Rick Sutcliffe and Ryne Sandberg and Leon Durham and Bob Dernier. It will be Phil Cavarretta and Frankie Baumholtz and George Altman and Peanuts Lowrey. And of course, Ernie Banks.

"They'll be doing it for themselves, but we'll rejoice in it," Williams said. "We did everything we could to get there, but we didn't get there. These guys are doing it, and we're happy for them. But we're also happy for the fans. And we're happy for ourselves."

They're all links in the chain that brought these Cubs to this time and place. Mark Prior may throw the pitch that sends the Cubs to their first World Series in 58 years. But it will be Banks and Williams and Santo, and three generations of Cubs fans, who will be waiting right there to catch it.

October, 2011

One Win Away

AUTHOR'S NOTE: It's always been fascinating to me how some droughts, some curses—ehhh, the Cubs and Red Sox come to mind—become the stuff of legend and poetry. Yet the droughts and curses of other teams—like the Rangers, for instance—become just more humdrum evidence of The Stuff That Happens in sports. But in 2011, with the Rangers one win away from winning the World Series, it didn't seem so humdrum to me. So I wrote this piece about what it would mean if the Texas Rangers won the World Series. As you might have noticed, though, they're still waiting to find out. Again, this piece is brought to you exactly the way it was written in 2011.

St. Louis—So here they are. After 51 title-free seasons, those Texas Rangers are one win away.

But one win away from what? That's the question.

Look, we know they're one win away from winning the World Series. That's the easy part. That's the part we could see with our own eyes in the next 24 hours, now that the raindrops have stopped splattering and the Rangers and Cardinals can finally play Game 6 Thursday night.

But if the Rangers win this World Series, it will unleash ripple effects that extend well beyond baseball. You get that, right?

This is a franchise that has been around for 51 seasons now. And until lately, it's safe to say it hasn't ever been confused with the Yankees.

We're talking about a franchise that took 36 seasons just to win a postseason game, if you count its 11 seasons disguised as the Washington Senators.

We're talking about a franchise that took 50 seasons—and four trips to October—just to win a postseason series.

We're talking about a franchise that has lost more games (4,272) since its first year of existence, in 1961, than any other team in baseball—and would be 704 games behind the Yankees in the standings if this last half-century had been one giant season.

So what is now within the Rangers' reach is something far more momentous than most of the continent seems to have grasped. After all, did you know that:

- Not a single franchise in baseball has been in existence as long as this one without winning at least one championship?

- Only one other franchise in any major North American professional sport—those Minnesota Vikings—has been in existence as long as this franchise without winning at least one championship? (The Vikings, coincidentally enough, have also been around for 51 years—but are not one win away.)

- There are only two other franchises in baseball that have staggered through a longer title drought than this one? That would be—guess who?—the Cubs (14 or 15 centuries and counting) and the Indians (64 seasons and counting).

So this is big, big stuff. Yet, as the Rangers have closed in on the end of this bumpy road, you might have noticed something.

In Texas, this run has been a good ol' time, a tremendous excuse for a party and a thoroughly joyful experience for hundreds of thousands of people. But…

Unlike, say, when the Red Sox won (for the first time in 86 years) or the White Sox won (for the first time in 88 years) or the Giants won (for the first time since moving to San Francisco), no Doris Kearns Goodwin types have arisen to try to speak poetically for the masses and put this triumph into monumental historical context.

We've seen no succession of front-page stories in the newspapers about kids and parents and grandparents and great-grandparents, all weeping in unison over the end of generations of heartfelt suffering.

We've seen no outbreak of "Now I Can Die in Peace" T-shirt shops.

And we haven't unearthed a single Texan who has stepped forward to take credit for personally ending this long, title-devoid nightmare by digging up Ruben Sierra's piano from the bottom of the Rio Grande.

Not that there's anything wrong with that.

It's just different. That's all. And that's fine.

This is not the Red Sox. And people in Texas, best we can tell, don't even want to be the Red Sox. Especially at the moment.

Remember that, for the most part—except possibly among 12-year-olds—there is no such thing as a "lifelong Rangers fan." Well, just to be clear here, we should probably say there's no such thing as a lot of them, anyway.

"Yeah, there are," said pitcher C.J. Wilson. "They hit me up on Facebook sometimes."

"A couple of people have told me that," said the Rangers' "all-time" hits leader, Michael Young. "But mostly, they tell me how much they've enjoyed this club, and the last couple of years. And I totally understand that."

Nobody, in fact, would understand it better than Young. Even though he wasn't drafted, signed, or developed by the Rangers, he's played for the Rangers longer (since 2000) than anyone else in his clubhouse. So you don't have to spell it out for him that North Texas isn't New England, or that the Rangers' place in Texas culture is a whole different phenomenon than the Red Sox's place in New England culture.

"We flew under the radar for a long time," Young said. "I mean, I don't want to say our team was lost in obscurity, but it's kind of true. Other teams that have existed this long have at least competed for championships, especially the teams that built those winning traditions over years. But it's exciting for us to be a part of the team that's going to kick that off in Texas."

Whether they win or lose this World Series, though, they might already have kicked that off. Nolan Ryan and their ultra-sharp general manager, Jon Daniels, have constructed one of the best organizations in baseball. And they're only just beginning to harvest that field.

In only 12 months, these Rangers have transformed their franchise from an outfit that had won exactly one postseason game in 50 seasons to a team that has played in two World Series in a row. And how amazing is that? The only other franchise in history that went to back-to-back World Series while riding a half-century title drought was the old Brooklyn Dodgers, back in the 1950s. Doris Kearns Goodwin can tell you all about it.

But Texas in the 21st century isn't real reminiscent of Brooklyn in the 1950s, in case you hadn't noticed. Yeah, Dodgers fans had to compete with Yankees fans and Giants fans. But there was no such thing as Them Cowboys in Brooklyn, sucking every sports fan within 500 miles into their practically irresistible gravitational field.

"Think the Mavs are bigger than the Cowboys?" Young asked, with all due respect to the most recent championship team to pass through his neighborhood. "I'd say no. And I give the Mavs a ton of credit. They've been on a great run for years. Then they went out and beat a great Miami team in order to win a championship. But the Cowboys are the top team for reason—because they've got a ton of rings."

So if this love affair with the Rangers—raucous as it's gotten—still doesn't equal Cowboys Fever, "it doesn't bother us one bit," Young said. "I'm a Cowboys fan myself. But I'm pretty sure that if you asked our crowds back at the Metroplex, they're all pretty fired up about our team right now. And that's good enough for us."

It takes more than two special seasons to erase the stuff that used to constitute the most vivid memories of Rangers history (Non-Nolan-Ryan-No-Hitter Division): Jose Canseco deflecting a home run over the fence with his head; Bobby Witt getting yanked in mid-no-hitter (thanks to eight walks and four wild pitches); and the 1977 Rangers ripping through four managers in a week.

And we're not even going to get into the uplifting sight of having the franchise auctioned off in bankruptcy court—at 1:00 in the morning.

But finally winning the World Series? Now that might exorcise all those ghosts.

"It's a lot of fun to be a part of a team that has taken this organization to someplace it's never been," Young said. "Hopefully, we're the group that starts fans passing their love of the Rangers down to their kids, and so on and so on. That's when building traditions gets to be a lot of fun, when it starts getting passed down to generations."

So there's something almost perfect about the scenario the Rangers find themselves in this week—chasing their first World Series title against the Cardinals, a team that has played in, and won, more World Series games than any team in baseball not known as "the Yankees."

"The Cardinals are a classic example," Young said. "Their fans pass it down from generation to generation. And I think we'd like to establish something like that in Texas."

Well, here they are now, just one win away. If in fact, they win that one game, it may not be the tearful, poignant, existence-affirming experience that winning has been in other towns we know. But if these Rangers find a way to win just one more time, life in Texas may never be the same, all-Cowboys-all-the-time universe again.

And in Texas, that's a big, big deal.

October, 2010

San Francisco Will Never Be the Same

AUTHOR'S NOTE: Well, at least I got this one right. This was a piece I wrote on the eve of the 2010 World Series, as the Giants found themselves with a chance to become That Team that won the first World Series in the history of baseball in San Francisco. And since that actually happened, doesn't that prove I'm not a jinx after all? (Again, this piece is presented just as I wrote it back then.)

SAN FRANCISCO—It was well after midnight in the locker room of the brand-new National League champions. And it was here we found the closer for those champs, Mr. Brian Wilson—a fellow much wiser than his inimitable madman-closer persona might indicate—ruminating on the meaning of this amazing moment in time.

Somehow, on this unforgettable Saturday night turned Sunday morning, he was even able to wipe the champagne out of his eyeballs to see far, far beyond these clubhouse walls in South Philadelphia.

"What a sweet feeling," Wilson said, as the 2010 Giants basked in their championship moment. "I can't imagine the streets of San Francisco."

Then, for a brief second, his eyes spun, and his head nodded, and his mouth formed into a knowing smile, almost as if he'd just blinked and viewed the euphoric scene unfolding 2,500 miles from this spot.

Come to think of it, he laughed: "I *can* imagine the streets of San Francisco."

On those streets of San Francisco, they've waited more than half a century for this.

Their wait extends back to a time before color TV, before The Beatles, before humans traveled through space—or cyberspace. Their wait extends back to 1958, the year major league baseball discovered the Pacific time zone, the year the San Francisco Giants were born.

That's when The Wait began. And through all these decades since, while the ever-patient citizens of San Francisco waited, 19 other teams won at least one World Series. The Royals won. The Diamondbacks won. The Marlins won twice. The team that haunts the Giants from the other side of The Bay, the A's, won four times.

But the Giants? Not once.

Willie Mays played 15 seasons in San Francisco. Barry Bonds played 15 there himself. Willie McCovey played 19. Juan Marichal played 14. This team has employed players great enough to collect nine MVP awards, three Cy Youngs, four Rookie of the Year trophies.

But through it all, no Giants team ever found a way to do for this town what this Giants team has a chance to do:

End the third-longest title drought of any franchise in baseball (behind only the Cubs and Indians).

And all these guys have to do to end it is win the World Series that starts Wednesday, against those equally title-starved Texas Rangers. That's all.

So what would it mean to these people if this were the team, if this were the year? Unless you're dining on pot stickers in Chinatown as you read this, we bet you have no idea.

"It would be the same effect we saw with the White Sox in 2005 and the Red Sox in 2004," said always-eloquent Giants broadcast-philosopher Mike Krukow. "It would be the same type of release. It would be closure. It would be validation for all these years these people gave their hearts to this club and their souls to this club."

Now wait, you're no doubt thinking, assuming you can't see the shores of the Pacific or the Santa Cruz Mountains from your living room. How can this man possibly say that? How can this be Boston, cursified for 85 years between titles? How can this be Chicago, title-free (though hardly scandal-free) for 86 years?

How, you're thinking, can one of these newfangled western towns possibly stake a claim to any level of meaningful suffering?

Because this town is different. That's how.

"People on the East Coast think of the West Coast as this new place, but San Francisco is a really old American city," said Brian Murphy, the dulcet morning drive-time sports voice on KNBR radio. "This city has a thriving history that goes all the way back to 1860…So whereas LA, and Seattle, and Portland, and Phoenix are all sort of post–World War II towns, this town's history runs way deeper than most of America realizes."

So the attachment to this team—and the pain associated with it—really does trace back generations, much the way it does in New England and Chicago. Not as many generations, obviously. And not with all these fans, clearly. Definitely not the techies who showed up with their iPads like 20 minutes ago. But there are many, many people in San Francisco whose bond with the Giants goes back a lot further than, say, Game 1 of the NLDS. Trust us.

"So, it's a connection," Murphy said. "It links to their pride—their civic pride, and almost their family pride, too. And I know this really sounds kind of sappy and sort of out there, but the same way the '04 Red Sox brought all of New England to its knees, that's happening here, too.

"Now, we're not them. I'm not saying the Giants are the '04 Red Sox, nor is the fan base like that. But it's in the same area of relativity, of how a fan base relates to its team. So when you combine that generations-deep San Francisco pride with this particular team—so unexpected and '69-Mets-ish—it's more like Philadelphia, more like New York, more like Boston. It really is. And people who don't live here don't understand that. So that's what makes this whole thing so incredibly emotional for all of us."

There's a feeling in AT&T Park these days—a passion, a buzz, a decibel level—that's hard to describe. And it's not just because the World Series is coming to town.

Every once in a while in sports, the right team shows up in the right metropolis at exactly the right time. And it's happened here, with this eclectic collection of no-name scrapmeisters. For whatever reason, this group has locked heartbeats with this fan base in a way that Barry Bonds, Jeff Kent, and their surrounding cast never did.

"I've never seen anything like this," said F.P. Santangelo, who once played with Bonds and Kent, and now does pregame and postgame broadcast gigs. "And you're talking to a kid who grew up a Giants fan as an eight-year-old. Went to Candlestick Park as a kid and sat in the bleachers. Played for the team. Has coached in the minor leagues for the team. Is a broadcaster for the team. I've never seen anything like what's going on.

"We've been doing pregame shows outside the ballpark, and it's bedlam. I didn't know that Giants fans had this in them. This place has been so loud, so energetic, so passionate, I just feel like this is years of frustration, all coming out."

The World Series Giants of eight years ago were a very different group—all Barry all the time. Back then, Barry Bonds was more than just a centerpiece of the 2002 Giants. He was like a human eclipse, blocking all sunlight from shining on anyone or anything around him.

So no wonder these folks find this team so much more lovable. Barry at his greatest may have been mesmerizing viewing—but "lovable" wouldn't be in the top 8,000 words you'd use to describe him.

This team, on the other hand, is like one of those schlocky Hollywood stories about a pickup team, full of guys nobody else wanted, that somehow gets on one of those crazy rolls and beats the state champs. They've been impossible for this town not to embrace.

"You know how in Little League," said Giants president Larry Baer, "everybody always says, it's about the team, it's about the team? With this group, it really is about the team. But this is professional sports. It doesn't usually work out that way. In professional sports, you've got Kobe. You've got LeBron. You've got Brett Favre or whomever. It just doesn't turn out that way. Well, this, if you just look at our position players, is turning out that way. They really are the essence of 'team.'"

And that's a concept any fan would be happy to wrap his arms around. So all of a sudden, the lovefest wells up out of the seats of AT&T Park every night, the way it never has before.

"These last two months have been so intoxicating that if you get here and you're tired, by the time you leave for home you're jacked up again," Krukow said. "There's an energy. I live across the street. So I'll come over here sometimes and walk the dog at 11:30, 12:00 at night, when there's no one here. And I'll go back up on the mound, and I can still feel the crowd. I can still feel the energy. And I'm not making that up. You want to come tonight? You're more than welcome to come with me."

Just so you know, we didn't take him up on that. But thousands and thousands of San Franciscans *are* coming along with him, one way or another, every night these days.

Murphy tells stories about the Giants fans who call his show from far-flung places like Italy and Ireland, because they need to share the joyous experience of falling in love with this team. Santangelo hears the sounds of everyone around him talking baseball round the clock, and it reminds him of his days playing winter ball in Latin America, where life was one big obsession with baseball.

"You might as well be in Maracaibo or San Pedro de Macoris," he said, "because that's how much this city loves baseball right now."

But this story isn't only about the "right now" part of this experience. As any Red Sox fan could tell you, to truly savor the taste of winning, you need to wear the scars of all those years that ended with Ace bandages instead of fairy tales. So if that's a requirement at times like this, don't underestimate the suffering of Giants fans.

Don't forget Willie McCovey's line drive landing in Bobby Richardson's glove for the final, deflating out of Game 7 of the 1962 World Series. Don't forget the Giants' disastrous one-game-away NLCS collapse of 1987, or the painful sight of a 100-win team getting shocked by the Marlins in 2003.

Don't forget The Earthquake that rattled Candlestick Park minutes before Game 3 of the 1989 World Series. And just as Red Sox fans will always have Bucky Bleeping Dent and Aaron Bleeping Boone, the Giants may never get over Scott Bleeping Spiezio and the nightmare of 2002.

"You know what? You go through something like that and it takes time to get over," said Ron Wotus, the Giants' bench coach then and now. "I mean, you have to move on in this business. But when you want something so bad, and you work so long for it and so hard, and you're so close, it takes time. You go home and there's an empty feeling…It stays with you. It stays with you as you go forward. There are just moments in time in this game that don't ever really fade away."

But what those moments do, ultimately, is bring a perspective and an appreciation for *these* moments—the beautiful baseball moments almost nobody saw coming. And in a time when the economy stinks and politics divide and the local football team forgot how to win, what better time for this unlikely baseball team to come along and bond so many people in a way nothing else in life can?

Now these folks know the team they're playing isn't exactly the Yankees, too, of course. They know no one has ever seen "World Series" and "Arlington, Texas," in the same sentence, either. So it probably isn't fair for San Franciscans to get into a big debate over which team and which fan base "deserves" to win more.

But naturally, they're plowing into that debate, anyway—with their vocal cords in flames.

"I don't mean to denigrate the Texas Rangers," said Brian Murphy. "And I love Ron Washington. And I hope Bengie Molina gets the standing ovation he deserves…but I'm going to be brutally honest here. Let's just say it: Texans do not truly value baseball. Texans value football. And it's as simple as that.

"I understand there will be some happy people there. But Texas is a football state all the way—3,000 percent. So I would humbly submit to Rangers fans that they will be just as interested in the Cowboys score as the Rangers score, whereas right now, the 49ers don't even exist."

Well, maybe the 2010 edition of the 49ers are just background noise for this World Series. But another 49ers team has shot into this conversation in a whole different way. That team would be the 1981 49ers—the first San Francisco professional sports team to win anything—and, still, "the gold standard of sports euphoria in San Francisco," Murphy said.

So the question dangling from every cable car this week is this: if the Giants were to win this World Series, could it possibly top the '81 Niners on the list of most powerful San Francisco sports experiences in the history of this particular universe?

The honest answer is probably no—if only, Murphy said, "because [that 49ers title] was first, and it made people in San Francisco feel like they'd never felt before."

But—and you knew there was a "but" coming, right?—"the Giants carry with them their own romance," Murphy went on. "Baseball carries with it its own romance. There's nothing that can beat the journey of a baseball season. And this would be their first. And they are deeply loved.

"So which would be bigger? I really can't tell you till we get there. The '81 Niners, for sheer euphoria, would probably top the Giants. But I don't know. If the Giants win it, we could be talking about a dead heat here. You know what I mean? So I don't want to diminish anything I'm feeling by even think-ing about the '81 Niners. Can't we just say we love our teams like we love our children? You love each one for his or her own qualities?"

Far be it from us to make that call. It's their love affair. It's their team. It's their town. But we recognize something special when we see it. And this is the real deal.

This baseball team has carried these people halfway to the stars. Now it's up to the wacked-out, spliced-together, who-ARE-these-guys 2010 edition of the San Francisco Giants to finish the journey—and life in their golden-gated city will never, ever be the same.

The Red Sox Are Going to Win the World Series

AUTHOR'S NOTE: Every year, right before Opening Day, I write a column doomed to go wrong—my fearless prediction on which team is going to win that year's World Series. It's a bad line of work. But in 2004, before anyone had played a game, I made a prediction I'm actually proud of. I predicted a team that hadn't won a World Series since 1918 was about to vanquish The Curse. And whaddaya know: it happened. I'm sparing you some of this column—the inside-baseball X's and O's that inspired me to make that pick. Just wanted to remind you all that every once in a while, I do get some of these right!

Can we even comprehend what life might be like if the Red Sox ever won the World Series?

Would it put an end to curses around the planet? Bambino? Billy Goat? *Sports Illustrated*? Indian Burial Ground? How 'bout the Sylvester Stallone Oscar Curse?

Would the monuments in Yankee Stadium all be persuaded by Boss Steinbrenner to come to life—and volunteer to play for the Yankees next year, for the minimum?

Would millions of Bostonians be consumed by so much euphoria, they would grab a shovel and volunteer to finish The Big Dig by hand?

Hey, who knows? If the Red Sox ever win the World Series, it's all possible. Anything.

Roseanne Barr winning the Boston Marathon. Weird Al Yankovic conducting the Boston Pops. Anything.

"I can't even imagine what would happen," says Red Sox first baseman David Ortiz. "I just don't want to be in the city when it happens. I'd be too afraid. If we win the World Series on the road, I'm flying straight from the World Series to the Dominican."

What? And miss the parade?

"I'd just say, 'Send me the tape,'" Ortiz laughs.

Ah, but some tape it would be. If the Red Sox ever win the World Series, imagine that parade. Think about piling the Rose Bowl parade, the Macy's Thanksgiving Day parade, and the Disney World New Year's Day parade into one big stampede down Boylston Street.

Then triple it.

But the hoopla wouldn't end there.

"It would be nonstop for the whole year," says center fielder Johnny Damon. "The merchandise would be flying off the shelves. I think the whole country is waiting for the Red Sox to win the World Series."

Well, that would be the whole country, minus certain pockets of the New York metropolitan area. But our message to the portion of America that doesn't include those pockets is this:

Clear your calendar for Halloween week, because this is The Year.

The Boston Red Sox are going to win the World Series. Really.

This year, Aaron Boone won't homer. Keith Foulke will let Pedro call it a night after the seventh. Bucky Dent will swing and miss. Bill Buckner will take himself out for defense. Whatever can go wrong, won't go wrong. This is The Year.

"The Red Sox," says one American League GM, "are the best team in baseball."

They might have been in 2003, too, by the way. Even the Yankees were terrified of them heading into that October. For good reason. There were even people inside the Yankees organization who thought the Red Sox were the better team.

But just as in all those other years, the Red Sox had That Fatal Flaw. And just as in all those other years, it showed up. Because it always shows up.

"I don't know how to explain it," says Johnny Pesky, a man who has been playing, coaching, and working for the Red Sox for most of the last 60 years. "We win a lot during the season. And then something always happens."

Yeah, we've noticed that. But not this year. Because this year, there is no fatal flaw.

Their Year is here. They can score. They can pitch. They can get those last five outs. And they can do more than overcome history. They can make some of their own. They see the prize in the distance. They have even written the script in their heads.

> **TRIVIA ANSWER**
> The 1972/1973/1974 Oakland A's and the 1959/1963/1965 Los Angeles Dodgers. (And yes, the Dodgers also won the Series in 1955, while they were still in Brooklyn.)

"Here's my script," Damon chuckles. "Winning the World Series—in four. I want it to be easy, man—because this Game 7 stuff is killing us."

ONE MORE AUTHOR'S NOTE: The Red Sox won that 2004 World Series—in four. Preseason prognostication at its finest.

Chapter 6
Legends

Pondering the Pete Rose Induction That Wasn't

The Hit King's Hall of Fame Induction Day never did arrive. But suppose it had.

August 2, 1992. We'd never have forgotten it.

Tom Seaver would have been there. Rollie Fingers would have been there. Hal Newhouser would have been there. It was their Induction Day, too. But everyone knows that, had the act of gambling never been invented, it would have been the Hit King's day.

Pete Rose had that way. Always had that way. He owned every room he ever entered. He was the magnetic force who stole every spotlight.

You couldn't convince your eyes to stop watching him play baseball. Your ears never got tired of listening to him speak the language of baseball.

So why are we still talking about him all these years later? That's why. Because Pete Rose was the most mesmerizing baseball figure of our lifetimes.

Back in 1989, I sat in that ballroom in Manhattan, listening to Bart Giamatti explain why he was banning "Mr. Rose" from baseball for life. I still remember the power of those words, the way they thundered through the room that day. And I still remember thinking how wrong it felt that the Hit King's career was coming to an end in a ballroom, not a ballpark.

More than two decades later, it still feels wrong. Not because Bart Giamatti made the wrong decision. Because Pete Rose made so many wrong choices to force the commissioner to make it.

It's the saddest baseball story I ever covered. And it keeps getting sadder—because we know now, all these years later, that the Hit King's Induction Day is never going to arrive.

What's the scenario now that could ever make that day a reality? I can't find one. I can't see one.

Bud Selig will never make it happen. I know that. I'd say you could bet the beach-house mortgage on it, except I'm pretty sure all gambling analogies were also banned from Pete Rose stories for life by Bart Giamatti.

But even if Selig somehow changes his mind, even if some future commissioner reopens this case, the Veterans Committee isn't ever electing Pete Rose. Ever.

Me, personally? I would vote for Pete Rose—Pete Rose the baseball player—for the Hall of Fame. I try to remind people all the time that the Hall's a museum. It's not the Vatican. So I wouldn't nominate the Hit King for sainthood. But it seems absurd to me that the man who got the most hits in the history of baseball doesn't have a plaque with his name on it in the ultimate baseball museum.

I've grown to recognize that there's a distinction between the crimes and the career. I'd want his plaque to tell us about both. But that plaque should be hanging in that gallery nonetheless.

That's the thinking that would drive my vote. But it's a vote I'll never get to cast. Pete's time to appear on the writers' ballot is up. And I don't see any scenarios ahead that could change that, either.

So how is this story ever going to have a happy ending? It can't. And it won't. But it could have. And that's the saddest part of Pete Rose's story, more than 20 years later.

He's had so many chances to save himself. He just never knew how. He could never say the words he needed to say. He could never make the changes in his life he needed to make.

He could never bring himself to do what seemed so obvious, even as recently as 2003, when his buddies, Mike Schmidt and Joe Morgan, practically drew a dotted line for him to follow.

My friend, Willie Weinbaum, produced a brilliant piece on Rose for *Outside the Lines*. In the course of working on that piece, he had long, fascinating, startlingly candid conversations with both Schmidt and Morgan about how hard they worked to get Rose a face-to-face meeting with Selig back then.

It was a meeting designed to capitalize on the national wave of sympathy for the Hit King that seemed to be building at the time, a meeting that was supposed to pave the way for Rose's reinstatement.

The meeting happened. The reinstatement never did. The aftermath still torments Rose's most loyal friends in the game.

Morgan actually shed a tear as he talked about his longtime teammate and what had become of his life. And Schmidt visibly agonized in frustration over Rose's inability to do and say what seemed so obvious to those of us not living inside the Hit King's skin.

"If it were me," Schmidt said, "and I had lived a lie for 14 years, and I went up to tell the commissioner that I was sincerely sorry for what I've done to my family, to the sport, etc., I probably would be back in baseball now and in the Hall of Fame—because I would have been a tremendously remorseful individual. And I would have felt the burden of that the rest of my life, in everything that I did. And I would have, in my travels, been a totally different person.

"My lifestyle would have changed. I would have felt an obligation to change and to become someone that the baseball world would once again learn to love after forgiving me. I would have been that guy. And I don't think Pete has been."

There were no promises made to Rose that day in 2003. But Schmidt went into stunning detail about the topics on the table in that meeting.

The men in that room actually talked informally, he said, about how Rose should go about holding a press conference to admit what he could never admit all those years—that he'd bet on baseball. They kicked around when he should hold that session. And where.

That press conference, of course, has never taken place—to this day.

But the men in that meeting also talked about the changes in lifestyle Rose was going to have to make. No more trips to Vegas. No more hanging out at the race track. That was going to have to stop.

And, of course, none of it ever stopped. Not then. Not now.

But the nature of the conversation tells you how much momentum was being built toward Rose's reinstatement. It may not have been imminent. But it was clearly within reach.

"So we were very confident," Schmidt said, "that once we left Milwaukee, that some phone calls would ensue, some emails and discussions with Pete's representatives and the commissioner's office, that a plan would be put in place."

But that plan never even made it onto a crumpled up sheet of scrap paper in Selig's office. And that was no one's fault but the Hit King's himself.

People in the commissioner's office are still muttering that Rose's first public stop after leaving Selig's office was an appearance at a Vegas sports book. It wasn't quite the reconfiguration of Pete Rose's life they had in mind.

After that, just about everything went wrong that could have gone wrong. And I guess I should confess I was mixed up in part of the undoing myself.

I got word of Rose's meeting with Selig, which was supposed to be private, and reported it on ESPN. And that leak, Schmidt says, reignited the furor swirling around Selig and turned up the heat from the anti-Rose crowd.

OK, maybe. But that heat wave was coming whether that news leaked or not. It was just a matter of when, not if. And even if it hadn't, we know now, without a doubt, that the big problem here was the Hit King himself.

He couldn't change. Or at least he didn't change. He knew—or should have known—what he had to do. He never did any of it.

He didn't avoid those sports books. He didn't swear off the track. He wasn't amenable to any compromises, wasn't willing to trade an ambassador-type job and spot on the Hall ballot for a concession that he'd never be allowed to manage again.

"Pete's interpretation of reconfiguring his life would be a lot different than our interpretation of reconfiguring his life," Schmidt said. "Pete's not doing anything illegal, and from that side of it, you know, you never know what could happen in the future. He's being prevented from earning a living in the industry in which he became a king. It would be almost akin to an actor being blackballed."

Yeah, almost. Maybe Bud Selig could have overlooked some of those transgressions. But there was zero chance he could overlook the way Rose chose to admit to the world that he had, in fact, bet on baseball.

Instead of a bare-his-soul press conference, Rose couldn't resist the sound of that cash register ringing. When he "told all" in a book, released it on Hall of Fame election week, and launched into a book tour instead of a press conference, he was cooked. Forever.

That may all be on him. But it's still a sad tale. The Hit King is more than 70 years old now. He has lived over two decades in purgatory. That's a lot of time to serve. And it has taken its toll, Morgan said.

"I feel that Pete's a different person now," Morgan said. "I think that's the other thing here. I think…he's different than he was. I think Pete always felt he was bulletproof before, and I think Pete feels now, or he has to know now, that he wasn't bigger than the game. He wasn't bigger than any situation. I think he realizes the mistake that he made.

"I think he realizes that he can never get those years back. I think he realizes that he doesn't want his legacy to be that he lied all those years and he never came clean. I think he's a different person now."

Only now it's too late. If he'd felt this way—sincerely felt this way—in 2003, you wouldn't be reading these words. If he'd just run the plays in the Schmidt/Rose/Selig playbook back then, his days as a pariah would be history.

Instead, his sentence now looks more like a life sentence every day. Which was just how Bart Giamatti portrayed it in that Manhattan ballroom in 1989.

Except back then, the permanence of it all hadn't set in. Now, though, it's hit us.

Now, many Hall of Fame Induction Days have come and gone. But the wait for the Hit King's very own Induction Day has never seemed longer.

How Great Was Chipper?

AUTHOR'S NOTE: There was only about a week remaining in the career of Larry "Chipper" Jones. We sat in the Braves' clubhouse one day, just the two of us, and tried to put that remarkable career in its proper perspective. The numbers I'd come up with were so staggering to Chipper himself, it turned into a conversation I'll remember for the rest of my life. So I've let this piece appear in this book, almost unchanged (other than a few numbers updates), just because it so accurately portrays Chipper's multi-tiered frame of mind as he found himself staring at the end of his career—and the beginning of the rest of his life.

All of a sudden, it's here. The End. The finish line. Not just of an unforgettable season, but of a unique and historic baseball career.

And now that he's arrived, at last, at the final week of his surreal journey—at least the regular season portion—Chipper Jones finds himself looking backward, looking forward, looking everywhere at once. It's a crazy time. And a beautiful time.

He has accepted all the lovely parting gifts. He has gotten "a little misty" over the ovations he's received, not just in ballparks where they've spent 18 years booing him but from the opposing players who play in those parks. He has clicked on the aerial photos of the giant No. 10 that has been carved in a sprawling Georgia corn field.

"My first-ever corn field," he chuckles.

A few more regular season games await him. And an emotional farewell ceremony in Atlanta on the final Sunday of the season. And then his final October, where Chipper Jones gets to write the last scene of one of baseball's most remarkable scripts of modern times.

And then?

Then comes peace. And serenity. And satisfaction. And, maybe most of all, a much-needed giant gulp of oxygen, after the most exhausting season of his life.

"I can't wait, to be honest with you," he says, leaning back in his chair in an otherwise-empty clubhouse. "I view the next couple of weeks to a month as a win-win for me, because when it's finally over, if you feel a big gust of wind come across you, it's probably me and the sigh of relief that I'm letting out."

But that's not all The End will bring, you know. What The End also brings, always, is the opportunity for the rest of us to experience That Moment—the moment of reflection when it all hits you, when you realize what it is you've been watching all these years as the great Chipper Jones has gone about his inimitable business.

Maybe That Moment hasn't set in for you quite yet. But that's why we're here. Somebody has to put this man's incredible career in perspective. It might as well be us.

So that's what we've set out to do—to sum up where the only "Chipper" in baseball history fits in the annals of the greatest third basemen, greatest switch-hitters, greatest No. 1 picks, and greatest winners who ever played. That's all.

To do that, we've enlisted the help of his teammates, his manager, his general manager, his overpowering numbers, and, of course, Chipper himself. Ready? Here it comes—the true meaning of the very special life and times of Chipper Jones:

Feat No. 1: Hitting .300 From Both Sides of the Plate

The Numbers: Jones hitting left-handed: .303/.405/.541. Hitting right-handed: .304.391/.498

What It Means: There have been 109 switch-hitters in history who came to the plate at least 5,000 times. Only two of them hit .300 or better from both sides. One was Frankie Frisch, whose career ended 75 years ago. The other: Chipper Jones.

Chipper's Take—Oh sure, it sounds impressive, Jones admits. "But not a lot of switch-hitters have been doing it since they were seven," he says. "That's 33 years. So if I don't have it somewhat down by now, something's wrong."

He laughs softly at his own quip. But he knows, he says, he couldn't have hung out with Frankie Frisch without the brilliant hitting coaches he had through the years—without Willie Stargell and Frank Howard to pass along their wisdom when he was young, without Don Baylor to prod him to reach that next level from the right side in 1999, and, especially, without a man named Larry Wayne Jones Sr., the father whose inspired idea this whole switch-hitting thing was in the first place.

"You know, it takes a lot of work," Jones says. "It takes twice as much work to be a switch-hitter as it does to be one-sided. But it certainly paid off. I can't imagine walking up to the plate and facing a Kevin Brown or a Pedro Martinez righty-on-righty, or a Randy Johnson or Cliff Lee lefty-on-lefty. I thank God every day my dad made me turn around in the backyard.

"We used to watch the Saturday game of the week on TV, with Joe Garagiola and Tony Kubek. And after the game was over, we'd go out in the backyard and imitate the lineup. Whenever a left-handed hitter came up in my lineup, I had to hit left-handed. My dad's standing 40 feet away from me with a tennis ball. And I've got a 32-inch piece of PVC pipe in my hand. And he's raring back and chucking it as hard as he can. That's how you learn to hit the fastball right there."

TRIVIALITY

No switch-hitter who ever lived can top Chipper Jones' 14 consecutive seasons with at least 20 home runs. Can you name the three other switch-hitters who hit 20 (or more) in at least 10 straight seasons?

Feat No. 2: Walking with The Mick

The Numbers: Jones' career on-base percentage: .401. His career slugging percentage: .529. His career homers: 468. All as a switch-hitter, of course.

What It Means: The list of greatest

switch-hitters in history obviously includes men like Frisch, Pete Rose, Eddie Murray, and even Lance Berkman. But only two switch-hitters are in that .400-.500-400 Club. One is Mickey Mantle. The other: Chipper Jones.

Chipper's Take: "I think, coming up, I knew what the standard was," Jones says. "I knew that Mickey Mantle and Eddie Murray were the two best switch-hitters of all time. While I never expected to hit 300 to 400 home runs in my career, the goal was still the same. I wanted to be mentioned, when I was done playing, if not with those two guys, then right behind them. And as I've gotten bigger and stronger and more mature mentally in my game, the numbers just kind of piled up. I've been able to play a long time. And now I'm to the point where every homer, every RBI, passes a Hall of Famer. It's been a lot of fun."

The Manager's Take: One of the problems with our modern-day reverence of on-base percentage, slugging, and OPS is that they're awesome metrics—but lousy measuring sticks. So as men like Chipper play into their twilight, it's the "counting numbers" that become their most magical, and memorable, mileposts. And why not?

When Jones passed Lou Gehrig on the all-time hits list in mid-September, for instance, it carried no powerful historic significance. But for his manager, Fredi Gonzalez, it was still a "goose bumps" moment.

"Somebody said, 'Hey when he gets his next hit, make sure to get the ball, because he's going to pass Lou Gehrig," Gonzalez says. "And I said, 'Whoa. Lou Gehrig?' You know, all season, every time he passed a guy, another name, you'd be like, 'Holy crap.' They're all guys you never saw play. But you see them in the history books."

But for Chipper, it truly hit him when he passed his all-time all-time icon, Mantle, on the career RBI list last year.

"When you start passing some of the great Yankees of all time, you really start to sit back and say, 'Wow,'" he says. "But the big one for me was passing Mickey in RBIs. For me, Mickey was put on such a high pedestal when I was a kid, from my dad, it's just hard for me to believe that I could pass him in anything, much less something as important as a run-production stat."

Feat No. 3: Topping Schmidt and Brett

The Number: 1,623 RBIs.

What It Means: In the history of baseball, only three players ever drove in more than 1,500 runs while spending most of their careers playing third base. Two were George Brett (1,596) and Mike Schmidt (1,595). You can learn all about them in Cooperstown, New York. But who's the all-time leader in RBIs by a guy who mostly played third base? Chipper Jones. That's who.

Chipper's Take: When Jones is hanging plaques in his own little third-base pantheon, he makes a point to pay homage to Eddie Mathews, "the model by which every Atlanta third baseman is going to be measured." But with all due respect to Brooks Robinson, Wade Boggs, Ron Santo, Pie Traynor, and the other great third basemen in history, Chipper's personal Hot Corner Hall of Fame begins with two men—Brett and Schmidt, the dynamic duo that comprises his definition of "the gold standard."

The three of them rank 1-2-3 in some order in a bunch of significant third-base categories. But when Jones found himself zooming past Schmidt and Brett in RBIs in the same week, in the middle of his final season, it was one of the most overwhelming experiences of his overwhelming year.

"When you talk about passing those guys in career RBIs in my final season, for guys whose primary position was third base, it was just one of those moments where you're like, 'Wow.' You can't really believe it," he says. "I grew up watching these guys. Never in a million years did I think I'd be mentioned in the same breath with them one day…It's really crazy. Whenever you do that, you just go home at night and sit in a chair in front of the TV and just say, 'Wow.' Never in my wildest dreams, when I was in my back yard in Pierson, Florida, did I ever think I would be in such elite company."

Feat No. 4: More Walks Than Whiffs

The Numbers: Here Jones is, after more than 10,000 trips to the plate, still able to say he has piled up more career walks (1,512) than strikeouts (1,409). Hard to do.

What It Means: At the time Jones retired, more than 130 active players had hit at least 100 homers in their careers—but only three of them had walked more than they'd punched out. Albert Pujols and Todd Helton were two of them. The other: Chipper Jones.

Teammate's Take: "A lot of switch-hitters, their swings are different from both sides, but not him," says Jones' clubhouse neighbor, Eric Hinske. "He's just so consistent. The number that sticks out to me is that he's got more walks than strikeouts in his career. To me, that's not even comprehendable."

Chipper's Take: "A lot of guys say that's probably the most impressive stat," Jones says. "I've heard a lot of guys saying they can't even wrap their heads around that. But you know, to be honest, I think if I have one regret in the course of my career, it's that I didn't swing the bat more when I was younger. Or else I'd be a heck of a lot closer to the 3,000 [hit] mark. But there's a reason I didn't: Because it goes against everything I believe in as an offensive player.

"When you walk to the plate, you need to go up there and be the toughest out possible. And in order to do that, you have to draw walks. You have to yield to the guy behind you in the lineup from time to time. The fact of the matter is, there are certain points during the season, during a game, that teams aren't going to let you beat them. And if you're smart enough to realize when those situations are, you're going to draw a bunch of walks. I've always thought that."

Feat No. 5: The Greatest No. 1 Overall Pick Ever

The Numbers: 2,726 hits and 468 homers—every one of them for the team that drafted him with the very first pick in 1990, the Atlanta Braves.

What It Means: Only one other No. 1 overall pick ever hit 400 homers for the team that drafted him: Ken Griffey Jr., who hit 417 for the Mariners. But here's what separates Chipper from Griffey and every other No. 1 in history: this guy did *everything* for the team that picked him. If you don't count active players, you know what the next-most hits and home runs is by a No. 1 overall pick who played his entire big-league career with the team that drafted him? Ummmmm…would you believe 25 hits and two homers, by former Mariners great Al Chambers? You can look it up.

The GM's Take: Maybe Griffey and ARod can stake their claims to the title of Greatest No. 1 Pick Ever. But at the very least, says Braves GM Frank Wren,

Chipper is the guy who's had "the greatest value to the organization that picked him. How about that? I think you could make that case, from a standpoint of, he's spent his whole career with one organization, and had a Hall of Fame career, whereas other guys haven't necessarily done that."

And that only happened, Wren says, because Jones "was always wanting to get something done so he'd stay here forever…And that's allowed him to have a special end to a career that wouldn't have existed if he'd chased the last dollar."

Chipper's Take: "I want to be identified with one team," Jones says, emphatically. "I don't want to spend the last two or three years in my career floating around the league, trying to attain a number. I've never wanted to play anywhere else. Atlanta fits my style and my speed. I've gotten a chance to play for Bobby [Cox], who I think is the greatest manager of all time, for 17 of the 19 years. I'm a Southern kid. I was born and bred in the Braves organization. And I want to stay here.

"The marriage between the Braves and myself has been a good one. It's been one with give and take on both sides. So I've never wanted to wear another uniform. And they've shown me throughout the years, by never even letting me get remotely close to free agency, that they want me here. And that means a lot to me. I wouldn't feel right going to the American League and DH-ing, just to get 3,000 hits or 500 homers…Do I think I could stick around for another two or three years and get 3,000 hits or 500 homers if I really wanted it? Yeah. No doubt. Because I still have the ability to be productive. But that would mean me probably having to go somewhere else. And it means more to me to spend 19 years in one organization, in one uniform, and nobody else seeing me in a different 'uni.'

"It'd just be too weird. It'd be weird for me. It would be weird for everybody who came out to watch. And heck, if I played for another team, I'd be running back and forth to the clubhouse checking how the Braves were doing. And I certainly could never see myself playing against an Atlanta team. That would just be way too difficult…I saw guys like [Tom] Glavine and Smoltzy [John Smoltz] do it, and I know it was hard for them. I know how difficult it was for them to play in our venue and play against us, to try and beat us. It's just something I wouldn't want to do."

Feat No. 6: 428 Games Over .500

The Numbers: Starting with the day Chipper Jones moved into the Braves' lineup to stay, on Opening Day 1995, they won 428 more games (1,662) than they lost (1,234). That would not be a coincidence, ladies and gentlemen.

What It Means: We've done the math. On the day Jones called it a career, there were only two active position players who could say their teams were at least 400 games over .500 in their time as regular players. One was (shocker) Derek Jeter (554 over). The other: Chipper Jones.

Chipper's Take: He knows this is a feat he didn't achieve alone. He knows he was just "one-ninth of the equation" every day he took the field. He knows the Braves "surrounded me with a ton of good players along the way." He gladly names many of their names. But that doesn't mean he wasn't part—maybe even the most important part—of a special team, at a special time.

"I'm proud that I'm the last guy standing from the old regime, that I'm still here and we're still competitive," Jones says. "We're still winning games. And I'm contributing to that. I think what when people talk about you, you want to be talked about as what? A winner. Ultimately, that's what it comes down to. People want to be known as a winner—and as a 'ballplayer,' because the people inside the game know what the term 'ballplayer' means. You can't argue with the success that we've had here during my tenure."

Yeah, he's heard all the garbage about how those 14 division titles the Braves won were tarnished by the fact they "only" won one World Series. But even as he gazes back on those years in the rear-view mirror, he sees nothing he feels he ought to apologize for.

"To be honest, '96 is the only one I look back on and have any regrets," Jones says. "That's the one I think we had the best team. I think we showed it the first two games [of that World Series] and then didn't show it from then on out. Every other year, I think that we got beaten by a better team at that particular time in the season. So yeah, it's 'only' one. But man, the body of work over that 14-year span, I don't think it'll ever be duplicated. I really don't."

Feat No. 7: The Best Farewell Season Ever

The Numbers: In the final season of his career, at age 40, here was the stat line of the great Chipper Jones: 112 games, 448 plate appearances, .287/.377/.455. Oh, and there's also this: he led his team—a team that made it to the postseason, by the way—in OPS (.832). Amazing.

What It Means: There have been many, many great players who played into their late thirties and early forties. Pretty much none of them had a final season to rival this one. With the help of the Elias Sports Bureau, we looked at all Hall of Fame position players since 1900 who finished their careers at age 37 or older. Exactly one of them had a say-good-night season that resembled Chipper's grand finale. That would be a fellow named Ted Williams, who hit .316/.451/.645 in 1960, at age 41—but in only 390 plate appearances. So it's Ted…and Chipper. Two guys who didn't just know *when* to turn out the lights. They also knew *how*. Did they ever.

Teammate's Take: He's been an MVP, an eight-time All-Star, a consistent run-production machine, and a man who hit third or fourth in every one of the 93 postseason games he played in. But there has been something especially magical about Chipper Jones' final season. And everyone around him is savoring the magic act.

"For me, the way he's playing, it's the best I've seen him play since I've been here—and he's won a batting title since I've been here," said Jones' friend and protégé, Brian McCann. "But for some reason, this year it seems like he's come up with more big hits than ever. He's been in the middle of everything…It's like he can see the finish line, and he's giving it all he's got, and it's great to see."

Manager's Take: It hasn't merely been the numbers that have made this final year so cinematic, though. "He's just got a way of rising to those moments," says Gonzalez. "There have been so many of them. Like, he missed the first six or seven days of the season because of his knee [surgery]. When he was ready to come back, I was begging him to go down [on a rehab assignment] to get some at-bats. He said, 'Just give me some BP. I'll be fine.' I said, 'You sure?' He looks at me and says, 'I'm sure.' Then he goes out there, his parents are in the stands, and he [singles] first at-bat, hits a home run next at-bat. And as he's going around the bases, Hinske is yelling at him, 'It can't be that easy.'"

Chipper's Take: The star of this show listens as we recite these numbers and pass along how his teammates describe him. What all this tells him, Jones says finally, is that "I've been productive when I've been in there."

"But the 'when I'm in there' is the catch phrase," he laughs. "I can't go to bed at night anymore and say for sure whether I'm going to play the next day. And that's not fair to Fredi. It's not fair to the guys on the team."

That, however, just explains why he's retiring. It doesn't explain why he has still been the best player on his team—even as he's cruising toward the exit ramp.

"It's just extremely gratifying to have not heard throughout the course of this year that 'you should have retired two or three years ago,'" Chipper Jones says. "And anything less than going out and hitting around .300 and doing some of the things that I've done this year, I probably would have heard that."

Without him having the year he's had, "we'd probably be back in the pack,

> **TRIVIA ANSWER**
> Mickey Mantle (11), Lance Berkman (10), and Mark Teixeira (10).

fighting with the Dodgers and the Brewers and those other teams just to get in [the playoffs]," Jones' manager says. And no one on his team would argue.

In fact, best we can tell, only the computer programmers would. According to baseball-reference.com, Jones was worth just 2.8 Wins Above Replacement in his final season, theoretically making him merely the sixth-most-valuable position player on his own team. But there are certain things, in life and in baseball, that you can't measure with decimal points. And Chipper Jones' grand-finale magic act is one of them.

"There have been so many cool things that have happened to me this year," he says. "The fans' appreciation and [opposing] teams' appreciation, that's been unbelievable in and of itself. And there have just been so many cool things that have happened on the field:

"My first five-hit game at home [July 3, against the Cubs]. I've never done that before…a couple of walkoffs [two homers that won games the Braves once trailed by six runs] at home. Man, that's the apex…home run on my [40th] birthday…home run in my first start of the season, with my parents in the stands…two homers on my bobblehead day…just some really, really cool moments where, as the balls are flying out of the park, I'm running down to first, saying, 'You have got to be kidding me. Did that just happen?'"

Seriously. Even in Hollywood, it would be hard to make up a story this good. Wouldn't it?

The No. 1 pick who batted third in the lineup in his very first start in the big leagues, spent the next 18 seasons chiseling his Hall of Fame plaque, and then would call it a wrap by batting cleanup in one last epic postseason baseball game—for the team that drafted him? You have got to be kidding. Did that just happen? In real life?

"It's movie-worthy," says Chipper Jones, at his Spielbergian finest. "Movie-worthy."

June, 2007

The Thumb and Bobby Cox

His rendezvous with history was about to arrive. With no warning, no *SportsCenter* countdown meter, no commissioners in attendance.

It may not have been a real romantic record that Bobby Cox was about to shatter. There were no plans to interrupt any regularly scheduled programming to show it. That's for sure.

And there was a 100 percent probability that the exalted longtime current record-holder, John McGraw, would not be rearranging his not-so-busy schedule to stop by.

But history is history. So as we typed these words, the great Bobby Cox found himself one wave of some umpire's thumb away from a record that may stand forever:

Most times ejected from a major league baseball game.

Cox's ejection collection stood at 130. According to research by the Society for American Baseball Research, McGraw sat atop this exotic list with 131 (14 of them as a player).

No other active manager (or player) was even within 50. So this may indeed be another one of those Records That May Never Be Broken. Please keep that in mind so you commemorate it properly.

It was hard to say exactly what the scene would look like when the Braves manager's Pursuit of the Boot pulled him even with, and then propelled him past, McGraw. But we know what it wouldn't look like.

This fellow wouldn't be shot-putting any bases into the outfield. He wouldn't crawl on the infield grass and toss any fake grenades. He wouldn't kick dirt on anybody's shin. He wouldn't be firing any PowerAde coolers into the upper deck.

Bobby Cox is funny like that. In this age of the Made For YouTube Tirade, the soon-to-be all-time master of ejection perfection never worked that way.

"I've seen him throw his lineup card in the air," said Cox's longtime general manager, John Schuerholz. "I remember he tossed his hat to the ground once. But that barely gets him on the measuring stick, compared to some other guys' histrionics."

Yeah, he's no histrionicist, that Bobby Cox. He's not exactly the P.T. Barnum of the Heave-Ho Show. So if you're looking for ejection style points in your managerial heroes, you've got the wrong man.

"We may have to subtract some [style] points for that," laughed former Braves president Stan Kasten. "I think all the *American Idol* judges scoring at home and texting in their votes would be quite disappointed. I think Simon Cowell would grade Bobby's efforts very poorly."

Ah, but don't take that the wrong way. That's actually a good thing. It's a good thing because it proves that all those ejections were never about him. They were about the guys who played for him and the team whose uniform he wore.

"He's so passionate about the game," Schuerholz said. "And he's even more passionate about protecting his players and sticking up for them, and getting the right shake, getting the right call, and having things done right."

Yep, it's all about truth, justice, and America's Team's way. And that's fine. You'd just think a guy who'd been asked to leave this many baseball games would have left more legendary ejection tales in his wake.

Nope. We asked around, asked men who had witnessed dozens of these ejectoramas to spin their favorite heave-the-manager yarns. They were all pretty much stumped.

"He doesn't do it with a lot of fanfare," said Royals manager Ned Yost, who spent 12 years as one of Cox's coaches in Atlanta.

"They all kind of run together," said Kasten.

"They're all pretty much alike," said Schuerholz. "They're all pretty much caused for the same reason. And they all end up with the same ending."

OK, we did hear one heart-thumping tale from the battle front. It came from Pat Corrales, a guy who spent 17 years coaching in Atlanta, the last eight of them as Cox's bench coach.

"I grabbed him one night," Corrales reported. "I could see him starting to blow. So I grabbed him around the chest. And he said, 'I'll fire you if you don't let me go.' I said, 'Then you're going to have to fire me, because I'm not letting go.' Then I just hung on until I realized he wasn't going to do anything."

But suppose he had let go? Would the scene that followed have been any more memorable than any of the 130 times when nobody stopped Bobby Cox? Of course not.

"He just walks out there like only Bobby Cox can, and you can tell by the walk he's going to get ejected," said former Braves assistant GM Chuck McMichael. "Once he gets out there, it never takes him long to get thrown out. He just gets in his piece and walks off. It's classic.

"I can't imagine," McMichael chuckled, "that John McGraw could possibly have been any better at getting ejected than Bobby Cox. It's hard to imagine anybody who was more classic than Bobby is at just going out there and making his point."

So if you hadn't known, thanks to people like us, that he was about to break this record, you'd never have suspected it, either, because *fiery* isn't a word you often hear folks use to describe Bobby Cox.

In fact, said Kasten, "I'm always amused that the No. 1 criticism you hear of him is that he's too laid back."

"He's the nicest guy in the world," said Yost. "Just don't get him mad at you. If he ever gets mad, he turns into Mike Tyson. He doesn't care who you are or what you are."

Heck, he doesn't even care if you're an umpire, apparently.

And that's the weirdest part of this record. Bobby Cox likes umpires. And umpires like him. Bobby Cox also respects umpires. And umpires respect him.

"He just has a real strong desire to protect his players," Yost said. "And when he feels one of them has been wronged, let's just say he's going to let it be known."

"One thing about Bobby," said former umpire Jerry Crawford. "He never rips you in the papers afterward. He gets ejected. Then he just goes about his business the next day. I've had times where he's gotten mad with me, and I've gotten mad with him. But we come out the next day, and everything's fine."

There was one time, way back many decades into their past, that things weren't so fine between Cox and Crawford. They were both working in the International League then, and Cox inadvertently sprayed Crawford with tobacco juice during a run-in—"and I probably said quite a few things to him that I shouldn't have said," Cox's "favorite" umpire reminisced.

But not only did they both move on and grow to like and admire each other, Crawford noticed something afterward: From then on, if Cox was chewing anything in the dugout—tobacco or gum—he always yanked it out of his mouth before he came out to argue.

"I believe I had a direct effect on that," Crawford said. "I don't think he wanted to do that at the time. It just happened. And after it happened, he probably was upset it happened, and he wanted to make sure it didn't happen again."

That might give you the impression, however, that Cox's eruptions were planned—or staged in some way for some greater purpose. But his friends say that's a myth.

"He doesn't do it for effect," said Corrales. "He just blows. He gets mad. And he doesn't do it to stir his troops up. He does it because he thinks he's right."

And when it was over, it was really over. No grudges. No feuds. No vindictive confrontations that get nasty and personal. He managed to accumulate all these ejections in a way that actually seemed to help him get more calls, not fewer. And that's no simple managerial art form.

"There are some sub-layers to it," Schuerholz said. "Maybe he doesn't win those arguments, but he wins their understanding. And it's a reminder to the umpires that, 'Hey, I'm in every game, and every play could be the difference between a win and a loss, and that's very important to me.'"

So when those calls started going the wrong way, and one call he didn't like turned into two or three or four, the veteran Cox watchers could hear a little voice in their head—a voice that said, "Uh-oh. Here it comes."

"I've been out there coaching third base, and I could see it coming," Yost said. "Normally, when I coached third, he and I were always on the same page, all game long. But when he'd start to get mad, we'd get off that page. And I'd be saying to myself, 'OK, Bobby. Let's calm down now.' But you knew it was only a matter of time before Mount Vesuvius erupted."

Well, it had erupted 130 times as he uttered those words. And there would be more eruptions where those came from. And history would be made.

The question to ponder, though, is what should we make of that history?

Should we applaud? Should we smile? Should we shake our heads in bemusement?

Should we salute this man? Or should we be telling our kids, "Please don't try this at home"?

Hey, if you ask us, it's a record that has been woven into the fabric of what makes Bobby Cox the greatest manager of his time. Cox himself called it "kind of embarrassing." But not everyone agrees.

"I regard it as a passionate byproduct of a guy who has given his soul to the game throughout his career, and gives it on every play, and has the passion to stand behind what he believes," Schuerholz said. "And when you get right down to it, what's wrong with that?"

Well, nothing, as a matter of fact. So if it's a record worth saluting, we have just one more question:

What should the Braves have given their favorite manager to commemorate this record properly? We asked the man in charge as the historic day approached.

"I'm not sure yet," Schuerholz laughed. "How about a brass thumb?"

March, 2013

Mariano's Last Spring

TAMPA, FLORIDA—He jogged to the mound at 9:35 on a sun-splashed spring training morning. A water bottle was clutched in his right hand. No. 99 in your program, Rob Segedin, awaited at home plate.

For the great Mariano Rivera, this was the beginning of his march toward history.

Right. More history.

You wouldn't think he'd have had much more left to do, much more left to prove, much more stuff he could accomplish to fill up anybody's history book. Would you?

Before he ever began this trek to the mound on this spring training morning, he had already saved more games, saved more postseason games, and turned more bats into kindling than any relief pitcher who ever lived. But this was different.

He was 43 years old, the same age as Steffi Graf, Brett Favre, and Jeff Cirillo. They'd all stopped playing—what, about a century earlier? But Mariano? Ehhhh, not so much.

Nearly 10 months after blowing out his right ACL on a warning track in Kansas City, he occupied this March morning by launching 20 of his fabled cutters past Rob Segedin and Kyle Roller (No. 98 in your program) on a gleaming diamond in Tampa.

It was the first time this man had delivered a pitch to a living, breathing hitter since the previous April 30, when Nick Markakis was cooperative enough to bounce into a game-ending double play at Yankee Stadium, to finish off career save No. 608. So this was a big, big day. For him. For that team that's enjoyed riding on his surfboard all these years.

So when this little session of "live BP" was through, and Rivera's golden right arm was still attached to his shoulder, life in the Yankees cosmos was finally back to—to use Joe Girardi's word of the day—"normal."

But that's where we need to step in and make a point:

This wasn't normal.

There was nothing normal about it. Nothing. What exactly was normal about a 43-year-old man, working on a blown-out knee, gearing up for another season of greatness?

Unless that man was Mariano Rivera, that is.

"I think, as everyone else gets older, he gets younger," said his one-time (ahem) heir apparent, Joba Chamberlain. "I don't know how he does it. I need to find his fountain of youth. Wherever it's at, he needs to share the wealth."

But the truth is, no one else has ever done it like The Great Mariano has done it. And it's hard to believe anyone ever will. So there's no map to his fountain that will be available to the rest of us anytime soon. Sorry about that.

If anyone else could possibly learn to throw That Pitch even remotely close to the way he's thrown it, someone would have learned it by now and done it by now. Right?

But apparently, there is nothing about this man that is humanly possible for the rest of the species to duplicate. So why would it ever occur to anyone who has ever been around him that he wouldn't come back, at 43, and pick right up where he left off?

On this team, in this clubhouse, that was actually looked at as a preposterous thought.

"He's just one of those ageless guys," said another of his bullpen amigos, David Phelps.

But it's time now for us to make another point we should all remind ourselves of:

No one is ageless. No one.

Not even Cher.

And not even the great Mariano Rivera.

This is where the historic part of this saga—his saga—comes in. We'd like you to make a list of all the 43-year-olds in baseball history who have achieved any level of "greatness." On any team. In any season. At any position.

It won't take long—it's a short list:

1. Knuckleballers

2. Nolan Ryan

No reason even to discuss the feats of 43-year-old hitters, because there hasn't been a single position player that old (or older) since 1900 who even was worth two Wins Above Replacement. (Carlton Fisk's 1.9 WAR in 1991 tops those charts.)

And when we start talking about the storied achievements of 43-year-old relievers, it's safe to say that won't take much time, either.

Hoyt Wilhelm knuckleballed his way to 14 saves in 1969. But other than him, since the invention of the modern save rule, you know what the record was for most saves in a season by a non-knuckleballer this old?

How about six—by Don McMahon, for the 1973 Giants.

Six saves? That's basically just another week in the life of Mariano Rivera.

So all he had to do was simply head out there for his final season and just play himself in this major motion picture, and he was bound for a place that no relief pitcher in history had ever gone.

Again.

But it was hard not to look at him, in this final spring, and wonder: suppose he didn't? Sorry. Had to ask.

There was always the chance, you know, that he would follow the path that pretty much every other earthling his age had followed in the history of his sport. Suppose he discovered that he, too, was human—and maybe his 43-year-old hamstrings started popping, or his 43-year-old elbow started throbbing, or his 43-year-old bones started aching?

Then what? That's not a development that anyone around this $210 million baseball team he plays for was ready to contemplate. There was no doubt about that.

We posed that question to the manager. And at first, Joe Girardi started conjecturing about moving David Robertson from the eighth inning to the ninth. Or doing it by committee. But finally, he said: "I try to not even think about that."

And that's the remarkable part of this remarkable story: no one in a Yankees uniform could even fathom the idea that this man could be anything less than great. Even at age 43. On a reconstructed knee.

Including Mariano Rivera himself, of course.

He sat in the dugout on this day, beads of sweat trickling down his face. And never once, for one moment, did he sound like a man with a doubt in the world about what lied ahead for him.

You'd think, for instance, that he might be concerned that he couldn't command his cutter again, with a hitter in the box, after all these months off? Yeah, right.

"That's one thing, thank God, I never worry about—command," he said. "I know if I do all the things I need to do, it will be there. It didn't take a vacation. It's still there. It hasn't gone nowhere, guys. Still there."

As the laughter died down, he was asked if he was ever nervous that it wouldn't be there. Wait. What? Rivera dismissed that idea with a wave of his arm.

"I don't think like that," he said, softly. "I always know that it will be there. Even if it's not, I always believe that it will be there."

And that, of course, is part of his secret. Because he has always believed so strongly and convincingly, everyone else around him believed. With the aura this man exuded, 24/7, how could they do anything but believe?

"I think the expectation is that he's always going to be Mo," said Girardi. "And I think the reason you're comfortable saying that is, that's all we've ever seen. Even when he burst on the scene in '96, when he didn't have much of a track record, he was great."

"Great—I don't even think that's the right word for it," said Chamberlain. "I honestly don't think that describes how good he has been. I don't think there's an adjective that can describe him."

So hold on here. There's a level beyond "great" somewhere out there, or up there where only Mariano Rivera resides? There has to be a word for that, doesn't there?

"I almost want to say immortal," Chamberlain said. "That's not far off."

Good one. But there's one slight problem with that word: when you're immortal, you can go on forever. When you're a 43-year-old relief pitcher, even the greatest who ever lived, you can go on only so long. And as Mariano Rivera couldn't stop hinting, that final cutter, that final save, were creeping ever closer every day.

So that's what made this slice of spring training life something to watch just a little extra closely. There he was, on one more glorious spring morning, back on a mound, firing away—that inimitable smile frozen on his face.

Asked if the time he missed the previous season made him appreciate a moment like this, The Great Mariano had to laugh.

"I always appreciate it," he said. "That's why I love the game of baseball. You don't know what will be the last day you play."

The Commish Drops By the Bonds Watch

MILWAUKEE—As we listened to the commissioner of baseball bob and weave his way around those Barry Bonds questions he loves so much on a potentially historic night, it finally hit us.

It was time to stop listening to the words coming out of Bud Selig's mouth. It was time to pay attention to the words that *weren't* coming out of his mouth.

For weeks, for months, we'd been waiting for the commissioner to make some kind of definitive statement about his favorite history-maker, right? We'd waited and waited and waited some more.

And then we figured it out: had it occurred to anybody he had already made that statement—that he'd been telling us exactly what he thinks of his man Barry?

It's just that the commish wasn't telling us with the stuff he said.

He was telling us with everything he didn't say.

He told us plenty again on this evening in Milwaukee, where The Traveling Home Run History Show had pulled into Bud Selig's home town—so the commissioner dropped by Miller Park to "watch the games."

And because it was "a beautiful night."

And because "it's a game that's important in the pennant race."

And because "it seemed like a very logical thing to do."

But hold on. There was a slightly different reason that all of us media luminaries had jetted in from every corner of America to pack the Miller Park press box on this night. It sure wasn't because it was "a beautiful night."

Let's put it that way.

If Barry Bonds' home run total was a draw for the commissioner of baseball, though, he hid it well.

In an eight-minute conversation, as ESPN producer Marc Weiner astutely detected, the commish didn't mention Bonds' first name or last name—not once.

He still refused to commit to attending a single Giants game played in a town other than Milwaukee.

He even said that any celebration of this momentous event was "in the Giants' domain—and they can handle it."

Sheesh. Ya think he could possibly have worked any harder to keep this magic moment at full Louisville Slugger's length? Doubtful.

So it was time to take the hint already.

If Bud Selig wanted us to celebrate Barry Bonds' home run record, *he'd* have celebrated it. At the very least, he'd have said he planned to celebrate it. Or he'd have said we should celebrate it. Or something to that effect. Don't you think?

Heck, he'd mention the guy's name every now and then, at the bare minimum.

But the commish never did anything of the kind. He never even hinted at anything of the kind.

He never, ever wavered. He said he'd decide whether to attend The Big Homer "at the appropriate time." And he kept on saying it.

He said it again on this night, even though it was theoretically possible he might already have been attending the game where The Big Homer was going to be hit.

At the appropriate time.

Well, this was the appropriate time. But Bud Selig's non-statement had turned into a statement in and of itself. That was the message. It was about time we all got it.

When he was asked whether his presence at this game made some kind of statement, listen to how he answered:

"I have to let everybody else make those kinds of judgments. I know what I feel. I know what I think. And I think it's the right thing to do."

So he wanted everybody else to make those judgments? Great. All of a sudden we were having no trouble making them—and no trouble reading him.

He was letting us know precisely what he felt. He was letting us know precisely what he thought. Just because he hadn't spoken his feelings or his thoughts into a microphone—or slapped them across some full-page ad in *USA Today*—didn't mean he wasn't communicating. The sounds of Bud Selig's silence had never spoken louder.

He was asked whether he thought fans disapproved of his refusal to say whether he'd be there when Nos. 755 and 756 came rolling off Bonds' assembly line. Not only did the commish not take that bait, he even patted himself on the posterior for not taking it.

"The more I think of it, I think it's been handled well," he said, with great satisfaction. "I'll do that at the appropriate time. Just like people want to know if I'm coming here. I'm here."

But even by being "here," he was able to draw a line between his presence and his approval. And that line had never looked bigger or thicker.

Asked if he felt Bonds' record would be a "legitimate" record, Selig could not have been more obvious about declining the opportunity to say yes.

"We won't get into that," the commish said. "We're here to watch to see whether he does it. And whatever else happens, I'm not passing judgment—nor should I."

Consider those words carefully. They were the seven biggest words of the night:

"I'm not passing judgment—nor should I."

This, friends, was the fattest batting-practice fastball of the night. And Bud Selig pounded it off of Bernie Brewer's slide—without even swinging at it.

There were a million ways to answer that question. A million. He could have talked about the unique majesty of baseball's numbers. He could have talked about how the numbers of every generation have had their own unique context.

He could even have mentioned the name, "Bonds." Or possibly "Barry."

But Bud Selig chose none of those answers, did he? He chose: "I'm not passing judgment."

And by not passing judgment, he passed all the judgment he would ever need to pass. Could he have been passing it any more clearly?

He wanted as little as possible to do with this man. He wanted as little as possible to do with this record. He wanted as little as possible to do with any celebration people want to bestow on this record.

You would never hear him say those words, because those are the kinds of words commissioners would look classless to utter at times like this. And granted, there would be those who thought that even to imply them would be classless. But if this was what Bud Selig truly thought—and clearly, it was—not saying them was about the highest road he could take.

On this night, that road led Bud Selig to Miller Park. And for the commish, it was indeed a beautiful night.

The man whose name he wouldn't utter came to the plate five times—and never trotted around those bases once.

Chapter 7
Philly!

A Tribute to Harry Kalas

PHILADELPHIA—He was so much more than the voice of the Phillies. Harry Kalas *was* the Phillies.

He didn't just describe the games. His voice took hold of those games and made them his personal amphitheater.

The home runs weren't officially home runs until Harry Kalas told you they were outta here.

The long outs didn't make Philadelphia's hearts flutter unless the volume on every speaker suddenly quadrupled and Harry announced they've *got…a… chance.*

Strike three wasn't strike three until Harry the K gave it that little chuckle and reported some Phillies pitcher had just struck some poor, overmatched schmoe with a bat "right on outta there."

And when the impossible happened, when a World Series title run erupted in front of his eyes, his town couldn't be totally sure this mind-warping event had actually happened until the great Harry Kalas' golden voice exploded with the words: "The Philadelphia Phillies are 2008 world champions of baseball!"

So here is what people like me, people who have lived most of our lives in Philadelphia, found ourselves wondering on the sad and tragic day when Harry Kalas left us:

How were we going to do this?

How were we going to go on in a world with no more "outta heres?"

How would we fill the un-fillable void that would hang over us forever now, as we tried to contemplate life, and baseball, without Harry Kalas?

Couldn't be done. Could it?

The games would go on. The sport would go on. Voices would crackle out of our TV speakers. That's the way it has to work. That's the way it's always worked.

But we didn't have to pretend it would ever be the same, because when you've spent 6,000 nights, over four decades, listening to Harry Kalas put his inimitable stamp on a baseball game, it's way too simple to say baseball would never *sound* the same.

Baseball in Philadelphia would never *be* the same.

I'm one of the lucky ones. I got to know one of the special human beings on this planet. It was one of the great thrills of my career.

Once, I was just one of the fortunate hordes who had the pleasure of listening to Harry Kalas. Next thing I knew, I was working alongside him.

Back when I was a rookie beat man for the *Philadelphia Inquirer*, and something memorable would happen on the emerald field below me, I'd often find myself thinking, *I wonder how Harry called that one?*

His voice, his presence, was that powerful. Even when you were witnessing something live, with your very own eyes, you still felt as if you were missing something—because you hadn't heard Harry Kalas describe it.

If it had only been me thinking those crazy thoughts, I'd have gotten therapy and tried to get that little voice out of my head. But it wasn't just me. Ohhhhh no.

Those *players* down there were way more addicted to that voice than I was.

Back on May 10, 2002, Phillies centerfielder Doug Glanville hit an inside-the-park home run, the only inside-the-parker of his career. You know what he remembers about it now? Harry Kalas' call of that magic moment.

The second he crossed home plate, Glanville said, "I wanted to hear him announce it. That was every bit as important to me as running around the bases."

Wait. Hold on here. You mean this man had just done something very few human beings have ever done, and all he could think of was the sound of That Voice? How can that be, you ask? Because it was Harry. That's how.

"Harry had that special gift," Glanville said. "Just with his words and the emotion in his voice, he could take you to that game and put you right in that moment. If I was trying to explain to somebody what it's like to hit an inside-the-park homer, I'd say, 'Just listen to Harry call it.'"

But it wasn't only him. When something big—especially something really, really big—came along, Harry Kalas' voice towered over the event like a thunderclap from the heavens.

Let me transport you back to April 18, 1987. It's a day I'll never forget. I got to see Mike Schmidt hit his 500th home run that day. But that's not the part I'll never forget.

The scene that is lodged in my brain forever was a scene that took place long after Schmidt's emotional home run trot. The interviews were over. The players were all dressed. The bus to the airport was almost ready to leave.

And then Harry Kalas entered the room.

It just so happened that he and his broadcast buddies had brought with them a tape of Kalas' still-indelible call. And so, right then, right there, life in that room screeched to a halt. Everything stopped. The bus could wait.

All 25 players gathered around the tape recorder. The play button was pushed. And here came That Voice:

"THERE it isssss. NUMMMMMMBER 500. The career 500th home run for Michael Jack Schmidt. And the Phillies have regained the lead in Pittsburgh 8–6."

They listened to it once, and they roared so loudly the walls shook. So then they listened to it again. And again. And again. And again. Screaming just as loudly every time.

That's when it hit me: even *they* didn't realize what had just happened here—not until they'd heard Harry the K put it into words.

Well, you know what? At least those words live. Still.

I heard them all over the airwaves on the day Harry Kalas died. It's the one consolation on days like that. Because Harry Kalas did what he did, because he uttered his special brand of poetry into a microphone, the words live on.

And we still need them. We need to hear those words again. And again. And again. And again.

We need That Voice, because it's been such a constant in all our lives for as long as most of us can remember. And not just at game time.

When I heard the sad news that Harry Kalas had died, I called my daughter, Hali—one of the great Harry the K fans on earth. Through the tears, she told me she'd just changed the ring tone on her cell phone—to the sound of Harry Kalas calling the final pitch of the 2008 World Series.

Later, my wife, Lisa, tried calling our neighbors, Bob and Karen Scheuer, because we knew they'd want to know. They weren't in. But their answering machine clicked on—and there was Harry Kalas' voice informing us that Bob and Karen had just gone on a lonnnnnng drive, and they were outa here…so please leave a message at the sound of the beep.

"The funny thing is," Bob told me later, "that in November, Karen finally said, 'It's time to change the tape.' So we did. But as soon as we did, my friends would call and say, 'Hey, what happened to Harry?' So when it was time for pitchers and catchers, we changed it back. It's one of the rites of spring. Harry's back."

I could relate to that feeling—totally. In fact, I could still vividly recall my last conversation with Harry Kalas during his brief trip to his final spring training. Pitchers and catchers had reported weeks earlier. The games had been going on for nearly a month. But for the first time ever, those games were going on without Harry.

He'd had some medical issues, described as nothing serious. So the Phillies were muddling along without him as best they could. And then, one day, I was walking down a ballpark hallway and there he was.

"It's a Harry the K sighting," I said. "Now we can finally get this season started."

He laughed. We shook hands. We talked a little baseball. He was ready to go. And now, so was I.

But I was only half-kidding. It wasn't baseball season without Harry Kalas—not for me. And not for millions like me.

So on the day he died, we couldn't help but ask: now what?

There *would* be a season. And in time, we knew, we'd be grateful for that season.

But it would take some getting used to—because, for millions of Philadelphians, Harry Kalas was what baseball sounded like.

If there's a rhythm to the heavens, if there's a script to every life, then we can take some solace in knowing there was an amazing finish to Harry Kalas' script.

In the final game he ever called, on an April Sunday in Denver, Matt Stairs gave him one final, dramatic, game-winning *outta here*.

Before the final home game Harry Kalas ever called, on the day the Phillies received their World Series rings, he was hand-picked by team president Dave Montgomery to throw out the first pitch.

And in the final postseason game he ever called, he got to tell all those people who loved him that the Phillies—his Phillies—were "2008 world champions of baseball."

That was their moment. But he made it his moment. And that's only fitting, because, for the people of Philadelphia, Harry Kalas didn't just describe their moments. He made their moments real.

Farewell to the Vet

PHILADELPHIA—You don't mourn the passing of places like Veterans Stadium, for the same reason you never hear anybody mourn black-and-white TVs, or mood rings, or the Macarena.

The Vet had its time. And it had its place. But that time isn't now. And that place is long gone. And whatever the Vet may have been in that time and that place, all we came to know now about it in its final years is what it wasn't.

Its crime, in the end, was that it wasn't Camden Yards. And it wasn't Jacobs Field. The ceiling leaked. The grass was plastic. And that aroma you smelled on the way in wasn't always hot dogs and popcorn.

So it's hard to imagine there was anybody left in the whole darned U.S. of A. who would miss this round mound of concrete now that it was gone. But that didn't stop 58,554 Philadelphians from showing up at the historic corner of Broad Street and Pattison Avenue, on the Vet's final day on the active roster, to say good-bye to a place where many of their most everlasting sports memories were manufactured.

Not necessarily their happiest memories, of course. This was, after all, Philadelphia, where the only thing harder to find than a championship flag was a kid familiar with the concept of a victory parade.

Nevertheless, more than 68 million people sat in the seats of the late, not-so-great Vet over its 33 years of life and watched the Phillies play baseball. And the sadness they felt on its final day didn't appear to have anything to do with the fact that this was, undoubtedly, the last game they would ever get to see on NexTurf.

Stuff happened at the Vet, you see. Great stuff. Historic stuff. Stuff even dynamite can't wipe off the face of the planet.

So it was only poetic that, on this final day, after one final ugly 5–2 loss to the Braves, the Phillies trotted out the men who did all that stuff, one after another after another, until tears flowed and throats were hoarse and memories came back to life.

More than 60 former Phillies—from Willie Montanez to Mickey Morandini—got to touch home plate and walk to the mound one last time. Then three generations of Phillies regulars got to hear their names announced by the great Harry Kalas and got to jog to their positions for the final time.

Then Steve Carlton toed the rubber, in his pinstriped No. 32, and threw one last invisible pitch. Let the record show he was as unhittable as ever.

And Mike Schmidt dug in at home plate, did one more little wiggle, unleashed that bat, and did one final home run trot.

And then, for the grand finale, the man who threw the final pitch of the only World Series the Phillies had ever won, Tug McGraw, was driven in from the bullpen in a long black limo.

When the doors opened, McGraw headed for his personal home office, that big pile of dirt in the middle of the infield. And once he was back on his mound, Tug McGraw said, "it all came right back."

Hey, how could it not? It was on this mound, 23 years earlier, that McGraw whiffed poor Willie Wilson, of those 1980 Royals, and kicked off a party Philadelphia would spend the next quarter-century forgetting how to throw. Well, on this day, all these years later, poor Willie Wilson would get to strike out yet again—and he wasn't even there.

"At least," McGraw laughed later, "that's the last time Willie Wilson is going to strike out on *that* field."

The Yankees had had 26 triumphant World Series moments like that one. Even the Minnesota Twins had two of them. But in Philadelphia, there had only been one. And maybe that's why the eruption that followed Veterans Stadium's final pitch ever seemed to rattle windows and shake billboards.

"I thought today was louder than anything I've ever heard before," said McGraw, still battling surgery to remove a brain tumor six months earlier. "I know 1980 was pretty loud. But today was a different kind of loud. A good-bye loud is different than a winning loud. I guess that's the difference."

In Boston and Chicago, in Atlanta and L.A., the good-bye *they* said to the Vet was more like good riddance. We know that. In all those other places, nobody remembers the good stuff that happened at the Vet. They just remember all the bad stuff. The embarrassing stuff. The stuff that made Philadelphia famous. The stuff that turned the Vet into America's least-beloved stadium.

It was at the Vet where Santa Claus got booed. It was at the Vet where the future governor of Pennsylvania (Ed Rendell) threw snowballs at Jimmy Johnson.

It was at the Vet where the Phillies' biggest free agent of the late 1980s, Lance Parrish, got booed for making an out in the *first* at-bat of his Phillies career. It was at the Vet, on the final day of its final season, where The Man Who Was Supposed to Be the Ace, Kevin Millwood, got booed off the mound for having the nerve to throw an 11-hitter on a day when everything was supposed to be perfect.

Wouldn't you love to calculate how many boos were uttered inside Veteran Stadium over those 33 years? It's possible we can't even count that high. But this writer and one of his all-time favorite 1980s Phillies, Don Carman, actually tried to figure it out.

We proposed a formula where we multiplied total attendance times losses. That came to nearly 82.8 billion boos, if you're interested. But Carman decided it was still low.

"I think you have to multiply it again times the games Schmitty played here," he suggested. "You could always count on Schmitty getting booed for not getting a hit or not hitting a home run."

So we tried that. And it came to more than 99 *trillion* boos. Which sounds about right—give or take a few trillion.

But as a surprisingly philosophical Millwood said afterward, "These people pay their money to come see a ballgame. They work hard to earn that money. So if they want to boo, they can boo. It's up to them."

And that's exactly how it works. Philadelphia is the birthplace of freedom. So if they thought Freedom to Boo was in the Bill of Rights somewhere, it's too late to convince them otherwise now.

But there *were* some happy times for these people at the Vet over the years. And just to make sure they remembered that, many of those times were replayed on Diamond Vision throughout the Vet's final afternoon.

The Phillies did win two National League Championship Series at the Vet—one in 1983, one in 1993. And the men who threw the last pitch of those two series—Al Holland and Mitch Williams—were both in attendance on this day.

Once upon another time, Pete Rose broke Stan Musial's all-time National League hits record at the Vet, too, back in August of 1981. Rose, of course, wasn't there. But a "We Want Pete" chant did rise up out of the seats, with or without him.

The Phillies once won a game at the Vet that ended at 4:41 AM (the back end of a July doubleheader against San Diego in 1993). And the amazing part of that one was not the six hours of rain delays that made it possible. It was that attendance actually *increased* between 2:00 AM and 4:40.

"There were more people in the stands at 3:00 am," the Padres' Andy Benes marveled at the time, "than we have in San Diego at our *regular* games."

There was a game in 1989 that the Phillies won after trailing the Pirates 10–0. Pirates broadcaster Jim Rooker will never forget that classic—because it was during that famous game when he said, "If we lose this game, I'll *walk* back to Pittsburgh." A few months later, he really did—for the sake of charity, if not for honesty.

And once, it was out there in center field at the Vet where so many Lenny Dykstra tobacco stains had preserved themselves in the Turf's archives that Pirates centerfielder Andy Van Slyke said: "It's like a toxic waste dump out there."

Stuff happened at the Vet that still makes you laugh—or at least hold your head. Kiteman crashed into the center-field stands at the Vet. Benny the Human Bomb blew himself up at the Vet. The legendary Jeff Stone got picked off at the Vet. The Phillies wound up on the wrong end of an unforgettable 15–14 World Series game at the Vet.

Those who cared to remember any of that could go on remembering it whether the Vet was still around or not. But they won't be able to peer way up into the right-field upper deck at the star that marked a 1971 Willie Stargell missile launch down an exit ramp that is still regarded as the Vet's longest homer.

And they won't be able to stare into the dugout, as ex-pitcher Larry Christenson often did, and think of how sore his butt used to get sitting on that rock-hard wooden bench.

And they won't be able to find that "spot right over second base" that Don Carman remembers because it was "where I hit that rocket off Storm Davis for my first hit"—after he'd started his offensive career by going 0-for-48. Of course, *rocket* might not be quite the correct word.

"Well," Carman said, "it was either a rocket or a 19-hopper up the middle. One or the other."

In five more months, when the dynamite was scheduled to go off, there would be nothing but their memories to keep those visions alive. But that's OK, too. Moving on, after all, is part of life.

"It isn't like we had a grass field here like Fenway Park or Wrigley Field or Yankee Stadium and they were never going to tear it down because of the memories," said Schmidt. "And I know *somebody* must agree with me on that, because they're going to blow it up."

"We can all leave with our memories," Schmidt rhapsodized. "But I also think we can all agree that now, we need to take our memories and get the hell out of here—before it falls down."

September, 2007

Phillies on the Verge of History

AUTHOR'S NOTE: Technically, the Phillies didn't "win" anything or "clinch" anything in Game 160 of the 2007 baseball season. But as I look back on it, this was the night when it became clear to the citizens of Philadelphia that something special was happening to their baseball team. One minute, that team was seven games behind the Mets with 17 to play. Then, just 15 games later, that same team was somehow leading the NL East. This was the night that team took first place for the first time all year—and changed everything about baseball in Philadelphia.

PHILADELPHIA—In Philadelphia, life was not supposed to work like this.

In Philadelphia, it was the home team that was supposed to make its own seven-game leads disappear.

In Philadelphia, it was the home team that was supposed to forget how to win at all the wrong times.

So in Philadelphia, what the mixed-up occupants of a heretofore star-crossed town found themselves witnessing, in this upside-down September of 2007, was practically an out-of-city experience.

They knew that miracles happen in sports. They had heard about them. They had read about them.

Except they always happened somewhere else. Everywhere else. Or that's how it had always seemed.

In Philadelphia, life was not supposed to work like this.

On September 12, 2007, the Phillies were seven games out of first place. With 17 games to play. This isn't normally how teams set the stage for their happiest ending to a season in 14 years.

But 15 days later, that seven-game Mets lead was gone. Vanished. Defunct. In 15 days. How was that possible?

And that brings us to this transcendent Friday night at shocking, rocking Citizens Bank Park. That brings us to the events that transpired on the glistening green field below and the suddenly friendly out-of-town scoreboard.

Phillies 6, Nationals 0.

Marlins 7, Mets 4.

Do the math. Check those standings. They didn't seem real, but they were.

Somehow, when those scores were final, it was the Phillies who led the National League East by a game, with two games left to play.

Somehow, it was the Phillies who were on the verge of pulling off that miracle that was always the specialty of someone else's house.

Somehow, it was the Phillies who had a chance to become one of those teams that people talk about for years, for decades, for centuries.

"I know that," said closer Brett Myers on this crazy night. "And it gives me chills to think about it. I mean, not to sound like a wimp or anything, but just seeing the fans and the way the town is lighting up, it makes you tear up, man, I mean, with happiness. It's just really cool to see this happen."

This was not what Philadelphia looked like, of course, back on April 20, when this same team was 4–11, just 15 painful games into such a hopeful season. More specifically, this was not what Philadelphia sounded like back then.

Four and 11—now *that* was a story they were familiar with. That was a story they knew exactly how to respond to. We bet we don't even need to spell that response out for you. Do we? Let's just say it rhymed with "blue." And "zoo."

"You know what?" Myers would say, all these months later. "I understand. We started 4–11. We deserved to get booed. I've said it all year. It's a love-hate relationship with these people. They hate it when you do bad, but they love it when you do well. And I think this year, in this clubhouse, we understood it more. It wasn't that they were booing us because we were a bad team. They were booing us because they weren't happy with what the results were."

Those results could have buried this team. That's the way it usually worked. And not just in Philadelphia. That's the way it usually worked everywhere.

In the 104 years since the invention of the World Series, only four teams had ever started a non-strike season 4–11 or worse and recovered to finish in first place—the 1914 "Miracle" Braves, the 1951 Bobby Thomson Giants, the 1974 Pirates, and the 2000 Giants.

But none of those teams had to do what this team had to do—not just recover from 4–11, but recover from those all-but-impossible seven-out-with-17-to-play mathematics.

No team in history had ever been seven out with 17 to play and lived to tell about it in October. But suddenly, after the results of this night, all it was going to take was one more Phillies win, one more Mets loss, or two more of either to finish off that tale—of the Mets' historic collapse, of the Phillies' historic reincarnation.

Asked if his team, amazingly, could suddenly smell that finish line, Phillies manager Charlie Manuel replied: "Yeah. Of course we smell it. And we want it. Matter of fact, we might want it bad enough where we've got to take it easy, just relax and just play."

Hey, great plan. But how the heck could a team relax at a time like this?

Its town had become a giant thunderclap. The rally towels were lighting up the night. The throats were hoarse. The eyes were glazed. Something crazy was happening here—something that had always happened to someone else. Not to this team. Not in this town.

Just 16 days earlier, this same Phillies team had gotten steamrolled by the Rockies 12–0 in its home park. Up the turnpike, the Mets had just won for the ninth time in 11 games. The lead was seven. The future didn't exactly seem ripe for fairy tales.

Asked if he could have envisioned this same group being this close to October, barely more than two weeks later, shortstop Jimmy Rollins couldn't resist a laugh.

"Yeah," he said. "For the wild card."

Undoubtedly, much of America was forever going to view what happened here as an epic suffocation by the Mets, not a miraculous resuscitation by the

Phillies. But these were parallel storylines, each of them monumental on its own merits, each one dependent on the other.

Yeah, the Mets had lost 11 of 15. But the Phillies had to win 12 of 15 to make that matter.

Yeah, the Mets' pitching, defense, and psyches had self-destructed. But you could argue it was just as big a story to chronicle how the Phillies' pieces had somehow magically morphed together—even pieces that never seemed to fit all year.

All of a sudden, at almost exactly the same time that the Mets' bullpen was unraveling, a Phillies bullpen that lit bonfires for five months finally found a formula that worked—J.C. Romero to Flash Gordon to Myers.

Half a season earlier, Romero was in limbo after getting dumped by the Red Sox. And Gordon and Myers were hurting members of the All-M.I.A. Team. So who could have foreseen them turning into the Phillies' version of Stanton-Nelson-Rivera at a time like this?

But here those three were, pitching just about every darned day in September. And of the 13 September games where all three of them had stomped out of that bullpen, the Phillies had won 11 of them.

And 16 days earlier, there was no Cole Hamels around to serve as the legit No. 1 starter every team needs at times like this, either. At the time, Hamels had been out for three weeks with a sore elbow. And no one was too sure if he'd be back before 2008.

But there he was on this night, in his third start back, practically toying with a Washington lineup that had just finished putting up 19 runs in three games at Shea Stadium.

Hamels gave up four hits to the first nine hitters he faced. Of the 21 hitters he pitched to after that, only seven even managed to *put a ball in play.* Thirteen of the other 14 whiffed.

"If he can keep going out there and pitching like that," said Myers, "there's not going to be anybody who's going to hit him."

Then again, the only way he could keep going out there, period, was if the Phillies tagged a happy ending onto this incomprehensible script and found themselves in the playoffs for the first time since 1993.

Now, normally in Philadelphia, there was no reason to think that a happy ending was right over the horizon, no matter how idyllic life may have looked at any given moment. But there was something about this group that didn't feel like all those other Phillies teams, that didn't play like all those other Phillies teams.

And maybe that's why this Phillies season didn't look as if it was going to end like all those other Phillies seasons.

"This is the best team I've been on. I know that," said Myers. "I know the past couple of years, we've come close. But—and I mean no disrespect to the guys who used to play here—it's just that now, as a unit, we're a better team. Our mentality, the way we go out there and attack the game, is: just have fun. There's no pressure. Nobody has to be a hero. We feel like you're going to be a hero if you go out and play relaxed.

"Hey, I know there's pressure, man. But we just take it as: let's just go out there and have fun, and see what we can make of this."

Huh? See what they can make of this? Heck, they could probably barely even comprehend what they had a chance to make of this.

They could make an everlasting mark on baseball history, for one thing. But that's not all.

More important, at least for that town they play in, they were on the verge of making a whole lot of ghosts disappear—the ghosts of all those seasons that ended just the opposite of this one. The ghosts of 2003. And 2005. And 2006. And, especially, 1964.

In 1964, the Phillies were the team on the wrong end of The Greatest Collapse in History. And then, 43 years later, they somehow found themselves just a win or two away from being the team on the right end of somebody else's Greatest Collapse in History.

In Philadelphia, life was not supposed to work like this. Everybody knew that. But apparently, this team never got that memo.

Phillies Pull Off a Game 4 Miracle

PHILADELPHIA—The magic is in the moment.

The frozen moment where a baseball soars through the night and your mind begins to understand what's unfolding before your eyeballs.

It all happens so fast in this sport. One instant, you are watching a team down to its final out, about to dig itself a mess of trouble. The next, the baseball flies off the bat, and the whole universe changes.

This was where the defending World Series champions, the 2009 Phillies, found themselves as the giant center-field clock ticked toward midnight on what was about to become a Monday night they would never forget.

One more out, and they were going to be tied with the Dodgers, at two wins apiece, in the NLCS.

One more out, and they were going to guarantee themselves a coast-to-coast plane flight they didn't want to take.

One more out, and their dreams of heading back to the parade floats were going to be in a serious state of muck.

And then it happened.

Jonathan Broxton's theoretically unhittable smokeball came roaring toward home plate at 98.8 miles per hour. Jimmy Rollins' bat flashed.

And as that bat met that baseball, everything you thought you knew about this National League Championship Series was about to become instantly defunct.

It all changed the moment that baseball began floating toward that patch of grass in distant right-center field where no one in a Dodgers cap was going to catch it.

It all changed as the two most unlikely track stars in town, Eric Bruntlett and Carlos Ruiz, began pumping around the bases.

It all changed as Rollins sprinted around first, stomped on the second-base bag, and shook his fist till the mob scene engulfed him.

It all unfolded in a matter of seconds. But once the meaning of it all sank in, you began to realize what you'd just witnessed:

Namely, an October baseball game that was going to be talked about for the rest of our lifetimes.

Try to understand what had just happened here. You can count the post-season baseball games that resemble what happened at Citizens Bank Park on this evening with two fingers. And those two fingers would be used to count games that can best be described with one word: *legendary*.

It was Jimmy Rollins' heart-thumping two-run double with two outs in the ninth that turned defeat into triumph, turned a 4–3 loss into Phillies 5, Dodgers 4. But now let's do our best to put that game-winning hit into historical perspective.

This was the 1,251st postseason game in baseball history. Only two others—two—had ever ended this way, with a walkoff extra-base hit by a team that was one out away from losing.

One was The Kirk Gibson Game—Game 1 of the 1988 World Series, Gibson homering off Dennis Eckersley, Jack Buck warbling: "I don't believe what I just saw."

The other was The Bill Bevens Game—Game 4 of the 1947 World Series, when Yankees pitcher Bill Bevens got within one out of the first no-hitter in World Series history, and then lost it all. Lost his win. Lost his place in immortality. Lost it on a two-run double by Cookie Lavagetto with two outs in the ninth.

And now here we are, still talking about it, more than six decades later. Why? Because the October dots connect it with this game. OK, now get the picture? This wasn't just another walkoff win that unfolded in South Philadelphia on this night. This was history.

And you'd be hard-pressed to find a ballplayer in this solar system who would rather have been heading for home plate with a chance to make that kind of history than Jimmy Rollins.

"He likes the moment," said his manager, Charlie Manuel. "He wants to be there, and he can control his adrenaline, and he can handle the moment. Those are the things that are very important when you get in the postseason... Jimmy Rollins—he thrives. The bigger the stage, the better he likes to play."

If you looked at Rollins' numbers in this particular postseason before he arrived in that batter's box in the ninth inning, however, you might have a tough time believing those words.

Heading into that at-bat, the Phillies shortstop was 3-for-18 (.167) in this series, 8-for-37 (.216) over this whole postseason. And normally, let's just say nobody would write any Mr. October poetry about a guy like that.

But look closer. Look at *when* Jimmy Rollins got those hits. This was his sixth trip to the plate in the ninth inning in this October—and he'd gone 4-for-6 (.667). So that made him 4-for-31 (.129) in innings one through eight—but a .667 hitter in the most important inning of the night.

Now, however, let's look closer still. In his five at-bats against two of the best closers in the National League—Colorado's Huston Street and Broxton—in this postseason, he had hit .800 (4-for-5). And three of those hits were right in the middle of magical game-winning eruptions—including this one. Think that's a coincidence? Yeah, sure it is.

"He thrives on moments like that," said Rollins' buddy, Shane Victorino. "Everybody wants to be that guy. But he really does thrive in that kind of situation. He's the kind of guy, he can be 0-for-40, and it doesn't matter...It just shows what kind of player he is."

But he also wasn't the only player in this mind-boggling script. And on this night, the Emmy for Best Supporting Actor in a Non-Hacking Role would go to...

Mr. Matt Stairs, ladies and gentlemen.

Now, you NLCS historians know all about Matt Stairs, of course. Just the year before, in Game 4 of another NLCS, he was the man who shook the universe, much like Jimmy Rollins would shake it a year later.

People in Philadelphia still talk so relentlessly about the game-winning, two-run, 9,000-foot, Game 4 homer that Matt Stairs launched in October of

2008, he sometimes feels as if it's still traveling.

And never more than on this night.

Because on this night, one October later, Matt Stairs would meet again with the pitcher who served up that homer—a fellow named Jonathan Broxton.

Their reunion would come with one out in the ninth inning and nobody on. Stairs was pinch-hitting for Pedro Feliz. Broxton was two outs from his most important October save ever.

Later, Matt Stairs would say he doubted seriously that the memories of that home run were still rattling around Broxton's head. Huh? Really? Us media skeptics weren't so sure of that. But either way, we asked Stairs, were those memories still in his head as he dug in to face Broxton again?

"Uhhhhhhhhhhhhhhhh," Stairs rope-a-doped, very briefly, before realizing he couldn't fake his way through this one,

"Yeah," he laughed. "Of course."

"As I was standing in that batter's box," he went on, "I had one thing in mind—and that was going for that Budweiser sign [which hangs from the facing of the second deck in right field]. But then again, that doesn't change—against anybody."

It was quite the scene, watching Stairs dig in. He kicked at the dirt in the box, tapped his spikes, waved his bat, looked straight at the man on the mound. Broxton glared right back from 60 feet and six inches away. The vibe in the ballpark was pure electro-shock madness.

Asked what it was like to sit around for 3½ hours and then find himself at home plate, facing a guy who throws rocketballs 100 miles per hour, Stairs answered: "Well, it's not something you want to do every day—but it's something I enjoy doing."

But Broxton would make sure there would be no reruns of Matt Stairs' home-run trot this October—by walking him on four pitches. Manuel admitted later he gave Stairs the old green light on 3–0. But ball four was so far outside (at 99 mph), even Stairs couldn't take a fly at it.

"I'm just glad he didn't throw me a 3–0 fastball [over the plate]," Stairs said, chuckling to himself, "because I was gonna swing as hard as I can and see what happens. I've never turned down a fastball, and I never will. I'll be swinging at fastballs till I'm 50. They might be slow-pitch fastballs, but I'll be swinging at them."

Not this time, though. Stairs trotted down to first base and gave way to a pinch runner, Bruntlett, as their stadium erupted. It wasn't quite The Walk Heard Round the Cheese Steak Stand. But it was close.

Next, it was Ruiz's turn. Broxton stretched, fired and…ouch…drilled Ruiz right in the elbow. The only good news for the plucky catcher was, at least he got nailed by a quasi-change-up—at a mere 96 miles per hour.

"Aw, he'll be OK," said always-sympathetic reliever Scott Eyre. "We got ice…The ice budget here is good. We've got plenty of ice."

What they also had at that point, though, was a big-time October rally in progress. Only twice in his career, according to the Elias Sports Bureau, had Broxton ever hit a batter and walked another in the same inning. But his timing, this time, couldn't have been worse.

He got to within one out of his destination by retiring pinch hitter Greg Dobbs on a looper to third base. But that just set the stage for history. As Rollins strolled toward home plate, he knew his body of work against Broxton wasn't real picturesque (1-for-6, counting the postseason, with the only hit coming two years earlier). But the shortstop also said: "I wasn't afraid."

"I've faced him a number of times before," Rollins went on. "And that always helps, when you're familiar with the guy, his movement, what his ball is going to do—and he's pretty much thrown me all fastballs."

So from first pitch to last, Jimmy Rollins was geared for the fastball, because he knew, in this situation, "he's going to give you his best. If he's going to lose, he's going to lose with his best."

The first smokeball came roaring toward him at 98.1 miles per hour, according to Inside Edge. Rollins fouled it back. Strike one.

The second pitch was even harder—98.5—but way outside. Rollins took it calmly. Ball one.

Broxton climbed back on the rubber and stared straight down at his feet, visualizing the pitch he was getting ready to fire. Rollins set himself, tapped the plate, rocked in the box. If there was anyone in this ballpark not standing, the only possible explanation was that they'd just passed out.

Now here came one last pitch—at 98.8 miles per hour. According to data compiled by Inside Edge, it was the hardest pitch anyone had thrown to Jimmy

Rollins *this entire season.*

"It was funny," Rollins recalled of the moment before that pitch left Broxton's hand. "Right before he threw it, I said [to himself], 'Hit a ball in the right-center-field gap…right over Broxton's head. That's at least one run.'"

And then it happened…precisely…like…that.

His bat flashed through the zone. The baseball took off toward that exact spot in the gap.

And for an instant, as you watched it, it was almost as if it froze in the sky. And then it hit you: the Phillies were going to—wait a minute, was this really happening?—win…this…game.

Bruntlett—whose pinch-running exploits the previous October had led him to score the winning run in two World Series games—loped home first. "I had the easy job," he said. "Just go out, turn around, and don't do anything too stupid."

But right behind him came Ruiz, a man in no danger of being voted the World's Fastest Human, or even one of the World's Fastest 1 Billion Humans. This time, though, he was chugging. He had to chug. There was no alternative but to chug.

"He was motoring," said Ryan Howard. "He knew, man. He knew what he had to do. He had to get going. Fastest I've seen him move since Clearwater, in rookie ball."

Ruiz pounded across home plate. Their ballpark shook with joy. And their teammates were thundering in all directions, not too sure whom to mob—Bruntlett, Ruiz, Rollins, or all of the above.

"I was going to third," Howard reported, "just to try to avoid the rest of humanity. I was the first one there—and then the first one on the bottom."

"The pile-up and the beat-down…that can be pretty dangerous," said Rollins, "especially when Ryan Howard is the first guy out there. But then I guess he's kind of like a shell at the same time—a little bit of protection.

"The only thing I didn't want to do," Jimmy Rollins announced, "was get crushed."

Well, he appeared to have virtually all of his appendages still attached as he spoke those words. So mission accomplished.

The bigger mission for his team, however, was not quite accomplished. It still needed one more win to make it to the World Series, and then four more after that to hop back on the parade floats. And these men understood how hard it would be to collect those five more wins.

But they were also a team that had developed this knack—to write these astounding scripts, to sculpt these October miracles that had become the specialty of their house.

It might not have seemed possible for them to top Game 4 of 2008. But they just might have done it on this night.

"Hey, that was last year," said Matt Stairs. "So we've turned the page.

"But fortunately," he said, "it was a real big page."

Remembering Tug

There are certain people you meet on this planet who leave a whole different mark than just about everyone else. Tug McGraw was one of those people.

I never met anybody, in my whole life, who had more fun doing what he did than Tug McGraw. Not just in baseball. In anything. Tug was a man who often bragged that he never worked a day in his life—because everything he ever did to earn a buck was just one more excuse to have a good time. And as you watched him dance through every day with a smile on his face, you knew he wasn't just saying that because it sounded good.

He was such a positive, charismatic human being, he transformed himself into a baseball icon in two different cities. In New York, he was the man who almost singlehandedly made an 82-win playoff team—those 1973 Mets— socially acceptable. Ya gotta believe? In *that* team? But he did. And they did. And any Mets fan who watched those Mets send the Big Red Machine home for the winter will never forget him for it.

And then came 10 years in Philadelphia, where he became one of the most beloved sports figures ever in a town not known for its love affairs with its heroes. On October 21, 1980, Tug McGraw did something no one else had ever done. He threw a pitch that won the World Series for the Phillies. Then he danced off the mound on the toes of his spikes, arms raised toward the sky, waiting for his friend and neighbor, Mike Schmidt, to leap into his arms. And the flash bulbs that popped at that moment recorded an image that still hangs on many a wall.

It was the greatest moment in Philadelphia sports history. And it allowed Tug McGraw to spend the rest of his life listening to literally thousands of people tell him exactly where they were when he threw That Pitch.

"What pitch was that?" he loved to ask them. "I played here 10 years, so I threw a lot of pitches."

But he knew. And they knew. And the stories came spilling out of them. Like the one about the guy who had a heart attack that night—but made the doctors bring a TV into the emergency room so he wouldn't miss That Pitch. Like the woman who went into labor—but almost gave birth in her car, because she refused to leave for the hospital until Tug threw That Pitch.

Of course, Tug McGraw *always* had stories for them, too. Here he was, two outs in the ninth inning, bases loaded, an entire stadium knowing another Philadelphia nightmare was on the way—and here's what the man with the baseball was thinking:

He was looking around, at all this madness around him. And he caught sight of one of those police horses that lined the warning track, choosing that moment to leave a little, eh, souvenir.

"And I thought to myself," Tug McGraw said, "*If I don't get this guy out, that's what I'm going to be in this town.*"

So if you ever watch the video tape of that inning, and you see a guy laughing to himself at a moment when he should have been shaking like a subway train, that was the Tug McGraw I'll remember.

It doesn't seem right that a man so full of life should be gone at age 59. But those of us who knew him will be laughing at his stories for the rest of our lives. It's hard to believe that Tug McGraw's journey is over so soon. But at least he left us knowing that That Pitch he threw in 1980 will be traveling forever.

Vuke: The Greatest .161 Hitter Who Ever Lived

CLEARWATER, FLORIDA—The AP news story moved on March 8, 2007. It told you that a career .161 hitter had just died. But for those of us in this world who were lucky enough to have our lives intersect with a beautiful man named John Vukovich, it felt as if we'd just lost Ted Williams.

I've never spent a sadder day at any ballpark than I spent that day in Clearwater, because it seemed as if everyone I met knew the end was near for our good friend, Vuke, only 59 years old. And how could that possibly have been true?

"I keep hearing his voice," said his buddy, longtime Phillies broadcaster Chris Wheeler. And I felt the same way.

John Vukovich had one of those voices that rose above the din, even if you were sitting in a stadium with 40,000 people and he was down there on the field, in the third-base coaches' box, 100 feet below you.

It was the strong, tough voice of a sheriff in a 1960s Western, with just enough edge to get your attention and just enough tenderness to let you know that the man you were listening to cared more than anyone else in the room, or the ballpark.

And it didn't even matter what the subject was.

Didn't matter if it was a baseball argument he refused to lose. Or a ballgame it had just pained him to lose. Or a conversation about our families or our mutual friends in a sport that had been so good to both of us. You were always riveted by the passion that came pouring out of his vocal chords.

If you were fortunate enough to spend time with John Vukovich, it was the most memorable slice of your day. Guaranteed. You learned something—always. You probably took some major abuse for *something*—always. And you walked away laughing—always.

Of the 31 years he spent with the Phillies, only one of them (1980) had the happy ending this man never stopped chasing. And those unhappy endings hurt him more than anyone else I knew—anyone.

He took those losses harder than he took any out he ever made at the plate. And he had a tough time abiding the people around him who didn't ache as much as he ached. Every once in a while, those people heard about it, too. Imagine that.

Sometimes, he'd even let them know how he felt without saying a word—like the night a few years ago he was so aggravated by one loss, he stopped the team bus, climbed off, and walked back to the hotel, smoke bombs wafting out of his ears, unprintable bombs erupting out of his mouth, every stride of the way.

I covered John Vukovich as a player. I covered him as a coach. I covered him the last couple of years in a role he had a tough time adapting to—"team executive." And as hard as I try to keep at least a little professional distance from the people I cover, it was impossible for me not to think of John Vukovich as a friend.

For most of the last 20 years, we stayed in the same building during spring training. We knew each other's wives and families. We met on elevators, in parking lots, in restaurants, even out on street corners.

And you could never just "run into" John Vukovich. You were going to have A Conversation. There was never a bad occasion to tap into this man's brain, because there was always something in there worth hearing.

I'm glad I soaked in as much as I did, because I still hear that voice, almost any time something unusual happens in a baseball game, explaining the way it's supposed to be done.

John Vukovich should have managed someone's baseball team. As recently as six months ago, his friend and mentor, Dallas Green, stopped me in the

Phillies' press room to ask me, please, to get this guy's name out there last winter, to connect him with somebody's managerial vacancy.

But just a couple of months later, our friend's health was already beginning to worsen. So he couldn't have taken one of those jobs even if he'd been offered one.

At least Dallas Green can say now he's the only man who ever hired Vuke to manage a big-league baseball team. That was in October of 1987, when Green was running the Cubs. If you don't remember how John Vukovich did in that job, well, there's a good reason for that.

Unfortunately for both of them, an hour later, Dallas Green and his bosses from the Tribune Company had a loud debate that was later described as a "philosophical difference." So Green wound up quitting, and John Vukovich's managerial reign ended before he even made it to the press conference.

It's still hard to believe he never got another chance to actually make it to some team's podium. Heaven knows the guy had enough friends in baseball. You'd have thought *somebody* would have hired him.

But he was just opinionated enough, just fiery enough, that, for two decades, GMs were too intimidated to hire him. It was pretty much that basic.

Yet there was such a soft, caring side to this man. Dodgers GM Ned Colletti couldn't help but wonder if he ever would have gone where he's gone in life without John Vukovich, "always steadying me and prodding and instigating me to make myself better."

They'd met each other 25 years earlier, with the Cubs. Their bond was forever. So Ned Colletti has never erased the voice-mail message from his friend, Vuke, the day he got that GM job—the one in which John Vukovich told him how proud he was, and that, "I love you, buddy."

I've known the guy even longer. I only saw him get 13 hits in the *three* seasons I covered him as a player. But I'll never forget him.

When I was just a young guy, learning to cover baseball, I can't tell you how many times John Vukovich would take me aside, put his arm around my shoulder, and start teaching. About how players think. About how coaches and managers think. About how baseball is meant to be played. About the life lessons baseball never stopped delivering.

There were many, many times we disagreed about the course of events in his universe. He let me know about just about all of them, too. But he had a way of sending his messages.

He'd let me know exactly how wrong I was. But by the end of the lecture, he'd be telling me, "You're too smart to write that crap. You're too good to say that baloney." And I'd know the truth. The reason he just spent all that time yelling at me was the same reason he'd spent all that time teaching me the game when we were both a lot younger: Because he was too good, too caring, a human being to do anything else.

On New Year's Eve, 1999, my phone rang. It was a friend of mine—and fellow John Vukovich fan—in the baseball-writing business. He had just read my end-of-the-baseball-century column in that morning's newspaper. One of the items in that column was a rundown of The Five Worst Hitters of the 20th Century.

"How'd you leave Vuke out of *that* list?" he wondered, laughing.

Well, it took some doing. I admitted to that. I had to make sure I raised the minimum at-bats to qualify for the list above the 559 career ABs John Vukovich got. But I did that—for him.

Not because I didn't want to subject myself to the earful his inclusion would have inspired, either.

It was because it didn't do justice to the great John Vukovich to sum him up as just some guy who batted .161. It didn't then. It doesn't now. And it never will. Ever.

Jamie Moyer Just Can't Stop Pitching

CLEARWATER, FLORIDA—The easy way to find the definition of ageless is to click over to dictionary.com.

But here's a better idea. You really want to find the definition of ageless? You merely had to locate the pitcher's mound in Bright House Field, where a man named Jamie Moyer was still showing up for work in the spring of 2010, whether the rest of the planet thought he should or not.

He might have been the most amazing story of that spring training. And just about nobody seemed to notice.

This would go down as his 26th spring training—yeah, his 26th. The calendar told us he was eight months away from his 48th birthday—yeah, his 48th. He'd had three surgeries—yeah, three—since the previous September. And as he headed for another season in the Phillies' rotation, all we could say was: alert the historians.

Want to know the last team before the 2010 Phillies to start a season with a pitcher as old as Jamie Moyer in its rotation? You'd have to travel back in time nearly a quarter-century.

That team was the 1987 Cleveland Indians, proud employer of 48-year-old Phil Niekro. Except Niekro, as a couple of thousand still-aggravated hitters will recall, was a knuckleball king. So let's rephrase the question:

What was the last team to start a season with a *non-knuckleballer* as old as Jamie Moyer in their rotation? Now you've got a much longer journey in the old wayback machine.

That team would be those 1931 Brooklyn Dodgers, who started 47-year-old Jack Quinn on opening day—and then never started him again. So let's rephrase this question one last time:

What was the last team to start a non-knuckleballer older than Jamie Moyer more than *once* in a season? Any season? And the answer to that was: you couldn't find one. Ever.

But all of that was about to change, because it was already clear the Ancient Ex-Mariner was *going* to be a member of the rotation of the defending NL champions. What a tale.

He was four years older than the next-oldest starting pitcher in the big leagues (that knuckleballing Tim Wakefield)—and nearly 10 years older than the next-oldest left-handed starter (Andy Pettitte). But when that nasty word, *age*, came up in the conversation, Moyer was having none of that. As always.

> ### TRIVIALITY
> Even though it seemed as if Jamie Moyer pitched forever, three left-handed pitchers in the expansion era (since 1961) actually started more games than he did (638). Can you name them?

"I don't think age really comes into play with me," he said, perfectly serious about this. "I think the media in general will use that however they want to use it. Some people will say, 'You're too old. Why are you doing this?' Hey, I'm doing it because I *can*. I feel like I *can*. You know what I mean?

"I've always said this. The game is going to tell me I can't…And right now, I don't feel like the game has told me I can't."

Not that the game hadn't sent him a few messages he wasn't real fond of over the last year. He got bounced out of the Phillies' rotation the previous August, for instance. That wasn't exactly his favorite message ever.

Then he crumpled to the ground one night in late September, after tearing three tendons in his groin and abdomen. And not only did that wipe out any shot he had of becoming the first 46-year-old in eight decades to pitch in October, it kicked off a painful barrage of medical misfortune that sent him to the operating room three different times in three months.

So if this were anyone else—and we do mean anyone—we can almost guarantee the only sport he'd have been playing five months later would involve a pitching wedge. But in the case of Jamie Moyer, we're talking about one of the most unique human beings ever to play any sport.

Almost two decades earlier, you'll recall, the Cardinals had given him a little career advice: bag that crazy idea that he could pitch for a living and become a pitching coach. Nearly two decades and 224 big-league wins later, it was time for him to give us a little advice:

Quit trying to tell him what he can't do.

"When I go back and look at 1991, when I was told it was time to quit and become a coach, I didn't feel like it was time," Moyer said. "And right now, I feel the same way. I don't feel like it's time."

Only a few months before, though, no one was too sure what to think— including him—when the trips to his friendly neighborhood surgeon just kept on coming. First there was the groin/abdomen surgery in October. Then a second operation to control a post-operative infection a few weeks later. Then a third surgery in January to repair a torn meniscus in his left knee.

None of those issues would have been viewed as career-threatening if he were 27, or possibly even 37. But at 47? Who *wouldn't* assume the worst?

"I had to sit and watch the playoffs, and then the World Series," Moyer said. "And then I had to ponder, all winter long—'What if? What if? What if?'—not really knowing anything…wondering what was going to happen."

Well, he wasn't the only one.

"When he went down with the [groin] injury, it turned out to be more serious than I thought it was at the time," said his manager, Charlie Manuel. "And when he kept having problems, I was very concerned about him."

So the manager had no idea what he'd see the following spring, either. Which means he was as surprised as anybody when what he saw was "the same old Jamie."

Naturally, it was Moyer who became the first Phillies pitcher to throw three innings in any game all spring, even though it came in a 10:00 AM "B" game. Naturally, he then didn't miss a drill—any kind of drill—all spring. And naturally, said his friend and protégé, Cole Hamels, "he blows by us every single day out there" on the practice fields.

Uh, wait a second. Did he really just use the expression, "blows by us?"

"Yeah, that's kind of a funny figure of speech," Hamels laughed, "considering he only throws 80 miles per hour. But it makes him feel good about himself."

At Moyer's age, though, he had no choice but to keep blowing by those young whippersnappers, because when you're 47 years old, the reality of life is this: you're always going to be one lousy start away from hearing, "You're done."

But the oldest non-knuckleballer of modern times wouldn't have it any other way. His motto about stuff like this is: attitude is everything.

"A lot of what we do in life," he said, "is in how we approach things."

So how was he approaching what had a chance to be his final spring? By savoring every moment.

"I've thought about this a lot this spring," he said. "People say, 'Why don't you retire? Aren't you tired of playing?' But honestly, I've played a long time. And I've played on many, many, many talented teams—but also, many of those teams were not very successful.

"And right now, I have an opportunity to continue to play on a very successful baseball team. These guys know how to act. And they know how to win. They're very professional. And it's very exciting to be a part of it. And maybe that's some of what I don't want to let go. And I feel like I can add something to it."

TRIVIA ANSWER
Steve Carlton (709), Tommy John (700), and Tom Glavine (682).

If he could, that was fine with everyone around him. If he couldn't, then they'd all just have to figure out a way to make the final chapter of this remarkable saga turn out as happy as possible.

But as we'd all find out, it was way too soon to start typing that chapter—because the Ancient Ex-Mariner had some history to make.

10,000 Losses

Ten thousand losses.

I was somewhere above Ohio, sitting in seat 6-D of US Airways Flight 912, the night the Phillies lost their 10,000th game.

I had lots of people say to me they couldn't believe I wasn't going to blow up my busy schedule to be there for No. 10,000. My reaction was: why?

After 21 years of covering baseball in Philadelphia, after spending most of my lifetime living in Philadelphia, I'd witnessed enough of those 10,000 losses to get the hang of them.

I saw that game in 1979 when the Phillies got blown out by the Expos while wearing all-maroon uniforms that Greg Luzinski said made them look like 25 bell hops playing baseball.

I was the courageous writer who watched an 11–3 wipeout to the Cardinals, three games after the end of the 1981 players' strike, and thought I'd lighten the mood in the manager's office by asking my good friend, Dallas Green, if this meant the pitchers weren't ahead of the hitters anymore. Green kicked off his not-so-amused answer with the immortal words, "[Bleep] you, Jayson," then tossed out many more endearing phrases just like that one for the next 4½ minutes.

I also personally witnessed a 1992 road trip to San Francisco and San Diego in which the Phillies lost eight straight games leading into the All-Star break. Then they compounded that euphoria by packing up the uniforms of their two All-Stars—John Kruk and Darren Daulton—and shipping them back to Philadelphia. So Kruk and Daulton showed up at the All Star Game in San Diego with no uniforms and no caps—and when they sent a clubhouse guy out to try to buy either of them at the souvenir stands, they were told the Padres didn't carry any Phillies gear, because what sane person would ever buy it?

So if I haven't quite seen it all, it's close. I was there for Mitch Williams versus Joe Carter in October of 1993. I was there for the nine straight losses that ended the 1984 season. I was there, sitting in the stands with my dad on October 7, 1977, when "Black Friday" unfolded in front of us. And I could tick off more memories like those for the next 11 hours.

So why the heck would I have to be there for Loss No. 10,000? In life and in baseball, it's the journey that really matters. And I witnessed enough of this journey to know I didn't need Mapquest to figure out where it was heading.

Ten thousand losses.

Great. Congratulations to everyone responsible—from Hans Lobert (distinguished managerial record: 42–111) to Doc Prothro (distinguished managerial record: 138–320), from Russ Miller (a pitcher who went 0–12 for the horrendous 1928 Phillies) to John Coleman (who lost 48 games all by himself in 1883).

You know, there are many more culprits where those came from, and many more fun-filled facts and figures I could haul out there. But I'll save that for some other time.

I'll save it because the easy thing to do at times like this is to look backward. But I'd like to propose something much more constructive to all the citizens of the town I grew up in:

A catharsis.

Ten thousand losses. We've been there. We've done that. Now let's move on—to something better, something sunnier, something more uplifting and constructive. It can be done.

"These aren't really losses. They're tests of character," said always-amusing ex-Phillies pitcher Don Carman. "That's what the coaches always tell you, right—that losing builds character? Well, if that's true, then people in Philadelphia have more character than any other city in America. The other thing you hear is that you learn more from losing than from winning. So that means they've also learned more than any other city.

"So I think this should be the dawn of a new age. Turn the page. Start anew. Write a whole new chapter. Heck, maybe even write a whole new book."

Exactly. Maybe we could call it: *10,000 Reasons Not to Boo Anymore (Unless Brian Sanches Gives Up Four Homers in Two Innings Again).*"

I'm not sure how we'd pull this off. But repeat after me: it can be done.

And for guidance as to exactly how, I called on a man far more ingenious than I am—longtime Phillies outfielder/visionary Doug Glanville. Here was his plan:

"You call upon the world to share in this momentous occasion," Glanville proposed, "and ask for a union of all the sports figures and teams that understand the pain of losing.

"Across the world, people with the longest losing streaks in history unite to purge the world of defeat. Select people will be chosen to carry the torch from city to city in a worldwide effort: Brian Kingman, Anthony Young, Eddie The Eagle, Al Gore. They will make famed stops at Columbia University; Prairie View A&M; Queensland, Australia, [site of a 67-year drought in men's rowing eight]—all to end in a city parade that we will call a 'boo-fest.'"

Wait. A boo-fest? Maybe you, like me, thought that's what has been going on in Philadelphia for the last century, anyway. So why would they need Anthony Young or Brian Kingman to lead another one?

But it turned out Glanville had a deeper, more powerful event in mind.

"A boo-fest," he said, "is similar to a ticker-tape parade—except that instead of tape, Philly faithful can throw symbols of the objects they have thrown in disapproval over the years, in hopes to forever rid themselves of the desire to throw them again…This would include AA batteries, half-eaten chicken wings, Michael Irvin bobbleheads, and elves from Santa Claus' toy factory."

Hmmm. Not bad. We might have to rewrite a few city ordinances—especially that elf-throwing ban. But this could work.

A catharsis, remember, is what we're after here. We'd like to see 10,000 losses represent not just another Philadelphia debacle, but a cleansing. An inspiration. An impetus to seek better times through the miracle of positivity.

And why not? All that booing, all that negativity, all that wallowing in the misery—what has that accomplished, when you get right down to it? Not a whole lot—outside of more booing, negativity, and misery. So why not try it the other way? What would anyone have to lose?

Just as the 2004 World Series freed Red Sox Nation of its demons, why can't 10,000 losses be The Benchmark That Sets Philadelphians Free?

It can be done.

"To be sure this occasion is forever preserved in Philly history, the mantra, 'City of Brotherly Love,' will be no more," Glanville decreed. "It will be replaced with 'The City of Ten Thousand'—representing the day that Philadelphia forgave every loss in its sports history. And the day the 10,000th loss was recorded, from now to eternity, will be a celebration of love, prosperity, and amnesia."

Love? We can handle that. Prosperity? Can't turn our backs on prosperity. But amnesia? Hoo boy. That won't be easy, not without the destruction of miles and miles of video tape. But face it. That booing act has gotten older than Julio Franco. So I'm urging all Philadelphians to repeat after Doug Glanville: It can be done.

At least until the next blown save, anyway.

Chapter 8
Just for the Fun of It

August, 2013

The True Story of Glove Talking

Once, there was a time in baseball when gloves were just gloves, and talk was just talk, and it was actually possible to employ one without the other.

So much for those days.

Now, in this neurotic age we live in, it's apparently no longer safe or feasible for anyone to carry on a conversation on a baseball field without placing a big old hunk of leather—among other obstacles—in front of their mouths.

You see it every night. The scene goes something like this:

A pitcher—let's say Junichi Tazawa in Boston—runs into trouble out there. So…

Catcher, pitching coach, and interpreter scramble to the mound. Pitching coach talks into his sleeve—in English. Interpreter talks into his hand—in Japanese. Pitcher talks back into his glove—in Japanese. Interpreter talks back into his hand—in English. Catcher talks into his glove *and* mask.

And they actually understand each other?

"Oh yeah," said Red Sox catcher David Ross. "It's a special language all its own. Everybody speaks glove."

Boy, that's for sure. And they don't just speak it. They're flat out addicted to glove—because *everybody* does it these days.

"Here's what I'm waiting for," said Cubs broadcast-witticist Jim Deshaies. "The manager goes out to argue a call. Then he and the umpire both whip their gloves out and start screaming into their gloves."

Hey, at this rate, would it shock you if that really happened? Wouldn't stun us in the least. So as we've watched this glove-talking epidemic spread across the baseball landscape over the last few years, we've asked ourselves many times:

How did it come to this? Does glove-talking actually accomplish anything? Are there lip-readers in every dugout—or possibly CIA agents?

Are scouts watching? Are hitters watching? Are the video machines rolling? And what's glove got to do with it, anyway?

So we set out to dig for these important answers. Please alert the Pulitzer Committee, because this is a story that has never been told:

The true story of glove-talking in the 21st century.

Why They Do It

Why do grown men talk into their baseball gloves? C'mon. Why do you think?

"It's just paranoia," said Braves pitcher Paul Maholm. "I think every pitcher and every catcher are just paranoid, so we throw our gloves up."

And what exactly are they paranoid about? Ehhh, pretty much everything. And anything.

"They've got Tivo these days," said Rays pitcher David Price. "They can rewind, fast-forward, slow it down. So they can read our lips. And they can do it many times."

Can they? Sure. But do they? Hmmm. No one is too certain about that.

"The whole thing is funny to me," said Red Sox pitcher Ryan Dempster. "I watch it all the time. While they're out there glove-talking, little do they realize we're sitting in the dugout, not even paying attention. Look at the hitters when [the catcher and pitching coach] go out there. They're usually talking to the umpire, messing with their bat, checking their uniform out to make sure they look good. I watch it all the time. It makes me laugh."

So Dempster is one of the proud, the few, the courageous in this sport right now. He refuses to glove-talk.

He's been known to wriggle his glove around 75 times before he throws a pitch. He's been known to take aim at his good friend, A-Rod. But talk into his glove? No chance. Doesn't see the point.

"It would be interesting to see how many times in a game guys cover their lips," he said. "Somebody should really count them up some night—and then how many times, after they cover their lips, do they get the out? We need a stat. You've got FIP and X-FIP. How about X-LIP—the X-LIP Factor?"

Beautiful. Somebody get FanGraphs on this immediately, OK? But more on whether glove-talking actually accomplishes anything later in our show. First, however, we need to play the role of history professor and examine…

The Real History of Glove Talking

There has to have been a time, somewhere in the history of American innovation, when man spoke words—and probably curse words—into his glove for the first time. Was it Thomas Edison, perhaps?

"Edison—he was a noted glove-talker," said David Ross. "That's the rumor, anyway."

Unfortunately, though, we don't have the videotape to prove it. So we set out to examine what we could prove. Which brought us to…

Greg Maddux.

Legend has had it, for quite some time now, that the always-innovative Maddux was the true Father of Glove Talking. It's right there in Pete Morris' book, *A Game of Inches: The Story Behind the Innovations that Shaped Baseball*.

The way this tale goes is this: in Game 1 of the 1989 NLCS, Maddux was about to face Will Clark with the bases loaded in a one-run game. Maddux's catcher, Rick Wrona, and pitching coach, Dick Pole, trotted to the mound for a conference with Maddux and his infielders.

Meanwhile, from the on-deck circle, Clark supposedly read Maddux's lips as he mouthed the words, "Fastball, high inside." You can watch the whole thing on YouTube if you want to relive this life-changing moment.

Clark then whomped a grand slam, off an up-and-in first-pitch fastball. And, theoretically, glove-talking was born, approximately four seconds later.

But was it?

In Morris' book, Clark's teammate, Bob Brenly, expresses doubts about the truth of that story, although you can see in the video that Clark watched the scene on the mound very intently.

And what about Maddux? His longtime friend and ex-teammate on those Cubs, ESPN's own Rick Sutcliffe, has a different recollection of how and why Maddux turned into one of the first of the glove-talkers—if not *the* first.

"I talked to Mark Grace [also a member of those Cubs] about it," Sutcliffe said. "And we both think Greg was the first we ever saw put his glove over his mouth."

But…

It was *not* to prevent future Will Clark–type subterfuge, Sutcliffe said. At least not at first.

One reason, he said, was that Maddux would sometimes get the catcher's sign and "mouth [the pitch] he was going to throw." So deep thinker that he is, Maddux began hiding his lips as he looked in for the sign, Sutcliffe said.

"Also," he said, "Greg was a guy who used some profanity from time to time. And finally, his wife told him, 'If you're gonna say those things when you're on TV, at least cover your mouth.'

"So Greg was the first one I remember doing that," Sutcliffe reported. "But honestly, he did it more to hide the profanity."

Just to double-check, we tracked down Leo Mazzone, who became Maddux's pitching coach in Atlanta a few years later. Mazzone laughed uproariously at any suggestion that Maddux was at the forefront of paranoid glove-talking.

For one thing, Mazzone said he "never covered my mouth—not one time" when he talked to Maddux, or anyone else on that awesome Braves staff. For another, he said, Maddux was so dominating, he practically eliminated the need to hold mound conferences.

"One time," Mazzone laughed, "he said to me, 'Come on out and visit me. I haven't seen you [on the mound] in a couple of months.' He said, 'You know, Leo, it gets kind of lonely out there. So why don't you come out and visit me in the sixth inning.'

"So sure enough, he's shutting out the Mets, and he looks in the dugout with one out in the sixth. And Bobby [Cox] says to me, 'Mad Dog is looking for you. Go out there and make sure he's all right.' So I go out there and he says, 'I'm glad you came out. My catcher doesn't speak English. I'm tired of talking to Chipper. So it was nice of you to come out here. You got anything you need to ask me?' And I said, 'Yeah, you planning on going seven tonight or all nine?'"

And none of that was uttered, Mazzone swore, with a glove over anyone's mouth. Or so the story goes. Too bad there were no lip-readers in the park to verify that, right?

So if Maddux is truly the Father of Glove Talking, it's news to his old pitching coach. What did happen, Mazzone is pretty sure, is that another pitching coach had his lips read on the mound one night in the '90s—"and it might have been Joe Kerrigan," he theorized.

Which meant it was time to track down Kerrigan, the former pitching coach for the Expos, Red Sox, Phillies, and Pirates. But Kerrigan was quick to nip that rumor in the bud.

"I know you're looking for that Watergate break-in moment," he told us. "But I ain't got it for you."

In fact, he said, every time he sees people glove-talking on the mound in modern-day America, he asks himself: "What's the point?"

So if it wasn't him and it wasn't Maddux, who was the first glove-talker in history? It took some heavy-duty reporting. But we're pretty sure we found him.

One of our many reliable glove-talking sources nominated another member of our deep ESPN pitching staff, Curt Schilling. And when we ran that by Schilling, we were shocked when he said, almost immediately: "I think I might have invented that."

He even remembered exactly when and where. It was Game 5 of the 1993 World Series. He was on the way to an epic 147-pitch, Series-extending shutout. And with two on and nobody out in the eighth inning, and Rickey Henderson heading for home plate, out came catcher Darren Daulton to talk it over.

> **TRIVIALITY**
>
> Since this is a piece about gloves, here's a Gold Glove question: Only five players in history have won 13 Gold Glove Awards (or more). Can you name them?

As they started to talk, "I remember thinking, *They're looking at me. They can read my lips*," Schilling reminisced. "I was just paranoid."

So he placed his glove over his mouth, said what he had to say, then got a huge out at the plate on a comebacker to the mound. And after he'd finished dancing out of trouble and finishing that shutout, he thought to himself: *I don't ever remember seeing anybody do that.*

"I watched baseball my whole life," Schilling said. "And I don't know if I was the first or not. I'm sure I probably wasn't the first. But I don't remember anybody doing it before that. And I do remember people talking about it after I did it. Then everybody was doing it."

So we asked Schilling if he wanted us to stamp him as the first known pioneer of the soon-to-be heavily populated glove-talking frontier.

"If I can take credit for it, absolutely," he said, delightedly. "That would be a legacy I'd be totally proud of. This game is over 100 years old. There aren't many firsts anymore."

So there you have it. Thomas Edison…Alexander Graham Bell…Curt Schilling: Inventors who changed the world, forever and ever and ever.

But What Has He Wrought?

All right, so glove-talking is upon us. And spreading at an even more rapid rate than A-Rod's law firms. We acknowledge that. But here's the ultimate question:

Is this a brilliant, important, and unavoidable development in this crazy, espionage-laden, high-tech age? Or is it the most overblown, out-of-control, maniacal exercise in paranoia ever to sweep the planet?

Even the "inventor" of this phenomenon knows the answer. Are there lip-readers and sign-stealers and edge-seekers everywhere in baseball? Of course. But is *this* degree of nonstop, never-ending, glove-talking really necessary? Be serious.

"Oh, this is way over the top," Schilling admitted. "Like the Army building a fake army for Patton before D-Day. There's a level of paranoia involved. No doubt about it."

Hey, ya think?

Brad Ausmus caught in the big leagues for 18 seasons, from 1993 to 2010. He watched glove-talking erupt all around him. He eventually became hooked himself. And he always told himself if it merely made the difference in one game, and that game turned out to be the margin between making the playoffs and missing them, it was worth a try.

But even he concedes he has no evidence it actually worked—ever. Heck, he's not even sure if the pitchers were talking to the correct object.

"If you're going to talk to something," Ausmus chuckled, "and you had a choice between the ball and the glove, I'd pick the ball, because the ball's the one going to home plate."

Excellent point. But that wasn't the only innovative spin on glove-talking that he pondered in his day. As a Dartmouth grad and noted creative thinker, Ausmus tried out actual variations on the glove-talking concept, for variety's sake if nothing else.

"Ironically, I remember going the other way," he said. "I'd go out to the mound, pull my mask off, not cover anything, and turn toward the hitter and say the word, *fastball*, hoping they could read my lips. I'd say something like, 'I don't think fastball'—and then turn my head back to the pitcher—'is a good idea.' It was just a little exercise in reverse psychology. Just trying to bait the hook. I have no proof it worked."

And of course, we have no proof that glove-talking, in its most basic form, truly works, either. But face it. It isn't even about whether it works anymore. This, says Deshaies, is a classic example of "the herd mentality" run amok. It was glove at first sight—an outbreak born, he says, almost totally out of the logic that "if Maddux is doing it, I'd better do it."

"It reminds me," Deshaies quipped, "of the old *Get Smart* Cone of Silence: 'Chief, we need the Cone of Silence. We must talk into our gloves.'"

Well, if that's their directive, some pitchers take it about as literally as it can be taken. Matt Garza, for example, "goes full cover," said Dempster, his former teammate in Chicago. "He covers his entire face. It's incredible. I don't know how they even hear him. He's, like: 'Fastball down and away right here.' And the catcher is going: 'I don't even know what he just said.'"

Dempster's other favorite glove-talking over-reactor is Carlos Marmol, who is "always covering. He covers as soon as the catcher starts to come out—just in case he says something."

But we have to admit that the ranks of player-kind that exceed the limits of glove-talking logic are hardly confined just to those two. And not only to pitchers, either.

"I've seen catchers leave their mask on and cover their face," Ross said. "And I think, *How secretive can you be?* But I don't think most guys even think about it. I don't even think we know what we're doing half the time."

And does anyone ever even question anymore whether half of this counter-espionage stuff is really necessary? Some degree of caution obviously is. But most of it? Get a grip.

"I don't do it," said Phillies shortstop Jimmy Rollins. "I'll usually go in and put my head down. And if we need to change the signs or something, then I might do it. But if it's just casual conversation, I don't bother. I know my lips are big. But if guys can read them from that far away, they're pretty good."

Maybe, Dempster suggested, "teams need to sign lip-readers. I think that's where we're headed. In fact," he said, motioning toward his team's Japanese interpreter, C.J. Matsumoto, "it wouldn't surprise me if C.J. over there isn't really an interpreter at all. I think he's actually a professional lip-reader. I bet he doesn't even speak Japanese."

All right, yes he does. But could official team lip-readers be just over the glove-talking horizon? Why the heck not?

"If you're fresh out of college, and looking for a job in a tough job market, this might be the way to go," Deshaies said. "Colleges can start offering programs in baseball lip-reading. Maybe they'll give out scholarships for kids who can read lips through glove-talking."

Hey, don't laugh. How could we rule out that—or numerous other potential innovations on the glove-talking front?

"I could have an off-season camp for catchers," Ausmus mused. "Major League Glove Talking Camp. Forget receiving, blocking, throwing, game-calling. It's time to teach glove-talking."

"Maybe," said Deshaies, "instead of glove-talking, each club can come up with their own dialect, their own glove-talking language. Then they could just talk at will, and the other teams would say, 'What on earth are they saying?'"

"Could we do it with cell phones?" Ausmus wondered. "Maybe guys could start texting instead of talking. Glove-texting gloves. That could be this year's hot product."

Yes, it could all be right around the corner if the glove-talking epidemic keeps mushrooming. But it's time to ask, does it have to mushroom? Really?

"I think we should start a movement, to stop all glove-talking," said Deshaies, who boasts that he never glove-talked once in a 12-season big-league pitching career. "The only thing is, we'd need an elite player to step forward, to be our spokesman."

Hmmm. But who? Luckily, Deshaies knows just the guy for the job.

"What about Mariano Rivera?" he proposed. "It could be his last great act, his last great contribution to sporting life. He can let it be known that, for the final month of his career, he will not speak into his glove, that he has no fear of that—because, by golly, they have no idea he's going to throw a cutter."

This, friends, is a movement we could seriously get behind: The Mariano Rivera Stamp Out Glove Talking Movement. Now what about you? Can we make this happen, please? Double-please?

It might be our only hope to restore the art of simple, unfettered conversation on a mound near you. So sign us up right now. This has to happen—for the glove of the game.

"Take Me Out to the Ball Game"

We always knew we covered the greatest sport ever invented, even before the National Endowment for the Arts and the Recording Association of America came along to prove it.

But now, thanks to them, there can be no doubt.

Thanks to them, we now know baseball is cooler than Ray Charles, more influential than Britney Spears, more harmonious than the Righteous Brothers, more lyrical than The Beatles, and hotter than Madonna.

How can this be? you ask.

We don't have any idea, we answer.

All we know is: "Take Me Out to the Ball Game" is No. 8 on the charts.

And amazingly, you don't even find those charts in the Intensive Care Ward.

No, we're talking about the charts that list the top 365 "Songs of the (20th) Century," as determined recently by the National Endowment for the Arts and the Recording Association of America.

Neither of which, incidentally, is in any way related to Bud Selig, Ichiro, or the Elias Sports Bureau. As far as we know.

The deal was this: the Recording Association of America put together a list of 18,000 songs from the 20th century. It cut that down to 1,100 before opening day. Then it sent out 1,200 ballots to an influential cast of voters that included Bill Clinton, Paul McCartney, a bunch of governors, and numerous other people who clearly have bought way too much peanuts and Cracker Jack.

And when the results were in, "Take Me Out to the Ball Game" wound up No. 8 on this list.

OK, obviously if this song doesn't win, it's a shame. Does this unforgettable work really deserve to be ranked below the No. 1 song of the century—uh, "Over the Rainbow?" Or "White Christmas" (No. 2), "This Land is Your Land" (No. 3), and the dubious likes of "American Pie" (No. 5) and "Boogie Woogie Bugle Boy" (No. 6)?

That, music lovers, is an outrage.

But we'll take it. After all, it still beat Elvis by 60, and it was 20 higher than The Beatles, 51 better than Springsteen, 84 in front of Bob Dylan, 153 places above Madonna, and an even 100 on top of Whitney Houston.

Who'd have thunk it?

So we assembled some of our favorite baseball music critics to attempt to discern whether this timeless tune was ranked too high or too low, and, most importantly, what this ranking said about baseball and its place in the melodies of every-day American life.

Too High or Too Low?

"That," said noted song bird Curt Schilling, "depends on which version of the song they were ranking. Was it the New York version, which usually features two brawls and three arrests during the chorus? Or was it the L.A. version, which has 32,000 of the 40,000 fans singing as they walk out of the stadium during a 0–0 double-no-hitter?"

Hmmm. Sounds like Schilling has some other agenda working here. So we turned, for a second opinion, to former Angels GM Bill Bavasi.

"First of all," Bavasi said, "I am shocked and dismayed that 'Shake Your Booty,' by KC and the Sunshine Band, didn't crack the top 125. The lyrics alone make it a classic. And where, in the name of all that is holy, is 'Freebird?'

"Second, it doesn't seem like 'Take Me Out to the Ball Game' should be in the 'song' category. It might belong with themes. You know, like the themes from *The Jetsons* or *The Flintstones* or *Car 54 Where Are You?*

"But the fact that 'Take Me Out to the Ball Game' is considered a song *and* beat the likes of No. 16, 'Satisfaction,' No. 53, 'Stairway to Heaven,' and No. 57, 'Louie Louie,' is truly impressive," Bavasi said. "Demented...but impressive."

Dementia notwithstanding, though, this man never did answer our question. Neither, for that matter, did longtime first baseman Rico Brogna, who was shocked to see that "Yankee Doodle Dandy" was ranked as high as No. 70.

"Haven't they had enough success the last few years?" Brogna wondered, apparently referring more to Joe Torre and his band than Vess Ossman and the band responsible for that ditty.

So we thought maybe a distinguished Ivy Leaguer, like Penn alum Doug Glanville, could provide his usual worldly perspective.

"It should be higher," the loquacious Glanville pronounced. "It should be seventh—for seventh inning. They messed up there."

Rather than look at this musically, see, Glanville took sort of an arithmetic approach.

"The ranking should go with the number," he said. "Like 'Take Five,' by Dave Brubeck [unranked, by the way]—that should be No. 5. What are they doing?

"And a song like 'Georgia on My Mind' (No. 42)—they've got to find out what number state [in the union] Georgia was and place it there. 'Hotel California' [a stunning No. 46]—they've got to find the address of the hotel, and that's where that should go."

Glanville is so convinced, in fact, that there's a numerical order to these matters that he proposed: "What baseball should do now is pair the song with the inning. In the first inning, play 'Over the Rainbow.' In the second inning, play 'White Christmas.' And if we happen to get to the 55th inning some night, play 'When You Wish Upon a Star.'"

Nah, if anybody ever gets to the 55th inning, they ought to play, "I Just Wanna Go Home." Because, at that point, if any living organisms were actually left in the stadium, they sure as heck *would* care if they ever got back.

So perhaps we need to look at this from a slightly different tilt. As in…

What the Heck Were These Voters Thinking?

Let us think about this question this way: in a world that has provided us with artists as brilliant and diverse as Weird Al Yankovic and Pearl Jam, and with songs as infectious and indelible as "La Vida Loca" and "Play that Funky Music White Boy," what on earth is "Take Me Out to the Ball Game" doing in the top 10 of any chart?

"Hey, a lot of people know that song," said Jim Deshaies. "I'm a senti-mentalist when it comes to that song. Now, I don't know, if you're a true artist and you're talking music, whether it should be up there. I don't know if it's a particularly difficult song to sing or what. But it paints a picture, by golly.

"It's the only song, other than the national anthem, that people stand up for. That gives it pretty lofty status. Did you ever try to sit through that song? You can't do it. You can try and sit there for a little while. But pretty soon, you're saying, 'Aw, all right. I'd better get up.'"

And this is true. This is a song that makes people rise up unlike any other, a song that literally halts the lives of everyone within range when it is played.

"When you think that every game stops in the middle for people to sing a song," said left-handed musicologist Terry Mulholland, "how can it not be up there? It's a game-stopper."

Therefore, Mulholland concluded, that No. 8 ranking is simply "too low. It should be No. 1—because it's the greatest game in the world."

He'll get no argument from us on that point, naturally. But is this really about games? It's about songs. Right? So is this really a greater song than "Over the Rainbow," featuring Oz's cute little Dorothy and Toto and the Tin Man?

"Hey, how many little kids went to bed and had nightmares because of that movie?" Mulholland retorted.

All right. Maybe they did. But what about those other songs that finished ahead of it? How about "White Christmas"? What negatives could possibly be attached to "White Christmas"?

"They've got elves and things in there," Mulholland said. "We don't have elves. We don't have munchkins. We don't have scary characters. We don't have houses falling on witches. And if something scary does show up in the game—like Derek Bell's baggy pants—someone in the commissioner's office says he can't wear them."

Of course, we do occasionally have strikes in our game. And lockouts. And 18-year-old draft dodgers fleeing to the Northern League. But this isn't the time or place to talk about those minor glitches.

The reason, clearly, that "Take Me Out to the Ball Game" ranked so high is more cultural than musical. Baseball is America. Those other sports aren't.

You'll note there are no football, basketball, hockey, lacrosse, curling, or Nordic combined tunes on this list. So either this says something about baseball's place in American life or there was some sort of Florida-like vote-counting procedure.

"I don't see a hockey song," Glanville said. "There's no 'Buh-buh-ba-da, buh-buh-ba-da' on there. And I don't see a football song. Like 'Who Dat Trying to Beat Dem Saints'—I thought that would be in there someplace.

"But 'Take Me Out to the Ball Game'—that belongs. Baseball is an integral part of America. So it deserves its place—in the seventh inning."

Yup, it's official now. So next time, instead of heading for the men's room or one last beverage when you hear that inspirational melody, savor the greatness of "Take Me Out to the Ball Game"—No. 1 in our hearts, No. 7 in our innings, and No. 8 on the ballot of Clinton, McCartney, and the National Endowment for the Arts.

Duane Kuiper's
Unforgettable Homer

You think it's hard to hit 755 home runs? Let's talk about a feat that's just as hard:

Hitting *one* home run.

And only one.

In 3,379 at-bats.

Now, you may think we're only tossing a crazy statement like that out there as some cheap stunt to get your attention. But this is one cheap stunt we can back up with actual facts.

And the actual facts tell us there are more members in the 750 Homer Club (two) than there are in the One Homer in 3,000 At-Bats Club (one). Feel free to look that up.

So at a time when we were interrupting pretty much all our regularly scheduled programming to commemorate a man who hit more home runs than anyone else who ever lived, shouldn't we be fair? And just? And balanced?

Shouldn't we devote at least one minor piece of literature to the man who has made history in the most diametrically opposite way possible?

Well, of course we should. So here's to the King of *Not* Hitting Homers. Here's to Duane Eugene Kuiper—for 12 seasons a sure-handed, not-so-power-packed big-league second baseman, and now (irony of ironies) a terrific broadcaster for those San Francisco (Home of Barry) Giants.

The Home Run Made Duane Kuiper Famous. So mark your calendars. Who among us will ever forget it?

OK, so the answer to that is: just about everybody. But not Duane Kuiper himself, naturally. He has retold this tale a whole lot more than 755 times since then. That's for darned sure.

He was playing second base for the Indians back then, in only his third full season in the big leagues. He stepped in to hit against White Sox pitcher Steve Stone in the first inning of a game at old Cleveland Municipal Stadium. Only 6,236 witnesses were on hand. We're sure millions more wish they were.

"I remember I hit it, and I saw Wayne Nordhagen, the right fielder, running after it, and I saw his number," Kuiper reminisced. "And I *never* saw a right fielder's number. I saw him running back, and I said, "You know what? This is going to go out.""

That's a thought that didn't exactly race through Kuiper's brain every time he swung the bat, you understand. So pay attention—because, in fact, this ball did go out. Way out. Deep into the third row. Or possibly the fourth.

But the precise location isn't important now. What's important is that the historic baseball clattered off (what else?) an empty seat and caromed back onto the field.

So Wayne Nordhagen, astutely recognizing that this was a guy who was capable of playing eight more seasons without ever hitting another home run, picked up the ball and fired it toward the Cleveland dugout. Which means Duane Kuiper got to save the baseball.

But that's not all he saved.

As he was leaving the dugout to head for the plate a second time that night, his teammate, Bill Melton, said to him, "You're not going to use that bat again, are you?"

"So I said, 'Yeah, why not?'" Kuiper recalled. "He said, 'You may not hit another one. You ought to put that one away.' Well, I didn't know he was telling the truth. But I tried to bunt for a hit my next time up, and then I did put my bat away. Never used it again."

Instead, he gave the bat and the ball to the equipment manager, who had them mounted together, with a plaque that read DUANE KUIPER'S FIRST MAJOR-LEAGUE HOME RUN. A few years later, a clairvoyant teammate grabbed a marker and added the fateful words, "and only," on there. But that's not important, either.

What's important is that Kuiper has the ball *and* the bat. You'd think he'd have sent them off to Cooperstown years ago. But mysteriously, Cooperstown has never asked. So Duane Kuiper knows just where to look any time he wants to savor his magic moment.

"Yeah, in the attic," he laughed. "It's mounted in the attic. It would probably take me 10 minutes to get to it, but I have a general idea where it's at."

Meanwhile, we still have the general idea that you, our loyal audience, don't yet comprehend the cosmic significance of the home run that plaque has preserved. So let's pause for a brief history lesson:

- In the 62 seasons since World War II, no other members of the One Homer in Their Whole Darned Career Club have even come within 1,000 at-bats of Duane Kuiper's lifetime total. And just two one-homer men even made it to 2,000 career at-bats: Woody Woodward (one in 2,187 at-bats) and Al Newman (one in 2,107).

- In that same time span, *every* other player who batted as many times as Kuiper managed to hit at least five home runs—with the exception of longtime pinger Frank Taveras (who hit two).

- And even if we take in all of baseball's eras—live-ball, dead-ball, gloves-without-fingers, mound-45-feet-from-home-plate, etc.—you'd still have to go back to 1886 (to the retirement of the mysterious Davy Force) to find another player who hit just one homer and came within 450 at-bats of getting as many shots to hit one as Kuiper did.

So there. Impressed yet?

No wonder Kuiper hung onto the bat and the ball—and the seat, too, for that matter. The Indians gave him the seat after they traded him to the Giants in 1982. And where can you find that historic seat now? In his garage, where it has been residing since he hauled it in from his yard because the paint started cracking.

"I like to say that I hit it so hard, the ball cracked the top of the seat," Kuiper quipped. "But it doesn't look like that happened."

At the time that home run hit that seat, it was too early in Kuiper's career for him, or anyone, to have the proper perspective on what that mighty blast represented. That home run left the yard in 1977. But Kuiper didn't leave the playing field himself until 1985. So he racked up another 1,997 at-bats in his day, every one of them 100 percent trot-free.

In all that time, he said, there were barely even any close calls. But there was one near-miss he'll never forget—a triple off the top of the fence in 1981. And the reason Kuiper will never forget it is because the pitcher who gave it up happened to be the same guy who had served up The Homer—Steve Stone.

"I remember standing on third, looking at Stoney's face, and I realized that [having the second ball not go out] was a good thing," Kuiper said, at his sympathetic best. "To have two in your whole life—and have them both off the same guy—that would have been rough. Plus Stoney was born in Cleveland. His parents lived there. He did not need to hear all that crap."

Nope, sure didn't. So instead, all the crap was reserved for Kuiper himself. As the seasons and at-bats mounted—but the homer total didn't—he heard it all from America's most compassionate fans, folks who obviously didn't sufficiently appreciate the art of not homering.

But Duane Kuiper appreciated it. And that's what mattered. He knew exactly what he was and exactly what he wasn't. And while Hank Aaron reincarnate was what he wasn't, he never did see any problem with that.

"You know, when I got to the big leagues, [manager] Frank Robinson pulled me aside," Kuiper said. "And he said, 'I'll give you 10 at-bats. If you hit more than two balls in the air, I'll send you back to Triple A.' I kind of laughed. And he said, 'This is not a joke. I will send your ass back to Triple A.' Because I could run, and his whole idea was: hit the ball in the hole and make the shortstop throw you out. And that was the stroke that kept me in the big leagues.

"Of course," Duane Kuiper couldn't help but add, "I kind of had that stroke anyway."

Did he think about what he might do or say if he ever hit another homer? Sure he did. But does it bug him, even a little bit, that he never hit another homer? Not for one second.

"There's something special about one," Kuiper philosophized. "There's not a whole lot special about two. I mean, nobody ever keeps their *second* major league hit."

So this is our chance to recognize that he's special in his way, just as Barry Bonds' little rendezvous with history was special in a whole different way. But there's something totally cool about the way the earth managed to spin, in its own crazy path, to bring them together around this momentous baseball event.

What, after all, were the odds that baseball's all-time Home Run King would have the biggest homer of his life called by a play-by-play man whose specialty was not hitting homers? A billion to one? A trillion? A zillion?

"You know what?" Duane Kuiper said, as Bonds' historic homer approached. "I keep saying that, at the end of Barry's career, I want a picture of just him and me. And whatever his total is, let's say it's 765, that will be my Christmas card.

"It's going to say: COMBINED, WE'VE HIT 766 TOGETHER."

And that, too, would be an actual fact. Feel free to look it up—and take a moment to salute the fact that the singles hitter's total was just as unique as that other guy's.

Fewest HRs Since World War II (min: 3,000 at-bats)

		HR	AB
1	Duane Kuiper	1	3379
2	Frank Taveras	2	4043
3	Roger Metzger	5	4201
4	Dal Maxvill	6	3443
T5	Doug Flynn	7	3853
T5	Jerry Remy	7	4455
T5	Sonny Jackson	7	3055
T5	Greg Gross	7	3745
T5	Bud Harrelson	7	4744
10	Hal Lanier	8	3703
11	Jose Lind	9	3677

Most At-Bats Since World War II—One HR or None

		AB	HR
1	Duane Kuiper	3379	1
2	Woody Woodward	2187	1
3	Al Newman	2107	1
4	Floyd Baker	1929	1
5	Emil Verban	1816	1
6	Jayson Tyner	1358	1
7	Don Sutton	1354	0
8	Pepe Frias	1346	1
9	Bob Randall	1325	1
10	Tom Glavine	1323	1

The World Series That Wasn't

It's amazing how much in life can be summed up by just the right Casey Stengel quote. So it's time to cite one of our favorites.

Back when the late, great Casey was managing the worst team on earth, those '62 Mets, he was brilliant enough to point out that we actually *need* losers in this world.

Why? Because "without losers," Casey philosophized, "where would the winners be?"

This is a true fact. And without the '62 Mets, where would the 2003 Tigers be?

If it weren't for those '62 Mets and their legendary 40–120 record, think how many people in 2003 would have been calling the Tigers the worst team in modern history. And they wouldn't much want to hear about those 1935 Braves or 1932 Red Sox or 1969 Padres.

But the great thing about this world we live in now is, we don't have to argue about this. We have computers. And they've got *all* the answers, right?

So as the Tigers were closing in on the Mets' not-so-coveted record of 120 losses, we convinced the inventors of the best computer-simulation baseball game around, the geniuses at Diamond Mind Baseball, to simulate a seven-game "World Series" between Ol' Casey's '62 Mets and those 119-loss 2003 Tigers.

We gave the Tigers home-field advantage—based on the results of the 2003 All-Star Game, of course. We brought the Polo Grounds back to life (on a

297

minimal budget, too), so the Mets *could* go home again. And because baseball in 1962 was a slightly different animal than baseball in 2003, Diamond Mind averaged out playing conditions over the 48 years in between to make this fair.

Then, to make this really fun, we brought in the great Rod Kanehl, the funniest '62 Met we knew, to provide official color commentary. For the record, Kanehl said at the time he didn't want the Tigers to lose 121.

"Hell, it would be a travesty," Kanehl said. "Our team, we didn't have any farm system. We didn't have 100 years of background. And we didn't have any pitching. The only people we had were people other teams didn't want… So I want us to keep the record. At least we have an excuse. If they catch us, everybody in their front office ought to be fired.

"Who's that guy who won three games for them in the '68 World Series? Mickey Lolich. They should bring him back. Bring back Denny McLain. Get him out of jail. He can beat somebody. I don't want to see them do this. They should bring in some ringers."

Well, the Tigers never did bring in some ringers for September. And they weren't allowed to bring anybody but themselves to our computer World Series, either. So not surprisingly, that made for a sensational and dramatic series that went right down to the final hitter in Game 7.

So don't turn that page. Here come the fabulous details of the greatest "World Series" never played.

Game 1 at Comerica Park

Tigers 7, Mets 5

Not your prettiest game. But that's probably not surprising, considering many of these Mets were dead at the present time.

The teams combine for eight errors—five by the Mets, three by Tigers third baseman Eric Munson. The Mets take an early 3–1 lead against Tigers starter Mike Maroth, then serve up six unanswered runs. An error by second baseman Charlie Neal in the fifth leads to the go-ahead run. The Tigers wind up scoring six unearned runs. And even though the Mets come back in the eighth, thanks to a passed ball and Munson's third error, Danny Patterson nails it down with a 1-2-3 ninth.

Kanehl on those six unanswered runs the Mets gave up: "Sounds familiar."

Kanehl on whether the Mets might have been rusty after 41 years off: "Rusty? We shoulda been at our best. We were well rested, wouldn't you say?"

What Stengel once said about catcher Chris Cannizzaro, who went hitless: "He's a great hitter—until I play him."

Game 2 at Comerica Park

Tigers 4, Mets 3, in 11 spectacular innings

The Mets trail in the seventh 2–1, then tie it against reliever Steve Sparks on a leadoff walk by Richie Ashburn, an Elio Chacon single, and Frank Thomas' RBI ground ball. After that, this gets crazy. On the way to leaving 17 on, the Mets have the winning run thrown out at the plate in the eighth, leave the bases loaded in the ninth, and waste a leadoff double by Cannizzaro in the 10th. But in the 11th, Munson makes his fifth error of the series, leading to a Mets run. Then it's time for Stengel's big decision of the day:

Starting pitcher Al Jackson (8–20, 4.40 ERA) has pitched all 10 innings and has thrown 123 pitches. But Casey sends him out for the bottom of the 11th. Uh-oh. Dmitri Young singles. Carlos Pena hits the second pitch out. Tigers up, two games to zip.

Kanehl on those 17 runners left on by the Mets: "Sounds like us."

Kanehl on Stengel leaving Jackson in to try for an 11-inning complete game: "It doesn't surprise me, because we had *no* relief. Of course, that was before they had 'saves' [officially]. But we didn't have any, anyway."

What Stengel once said to Marv Throneberry, who went 0-for-3: "We was gonna get you a birthday cake, but we figured you'd drop it."

Game 3 at Polo Grounds

Mets 5, Tigers 1

A mere 39 years after being obliterated for a housing project and playground, the Polo Grounds springs back to life for the cleanest game of the series. Not one error. And the Mets ride ace Roger Craig (10–24, 4.52) to their easiest win in decades.

It's a 1–1 game after five innings. Then Jim Hickman whomps a three-run homer off Nate Cornejo. The Mets take a four-run lead into the ninth. But Craig Anderson (3–17, 5.36 ERA) comes out of Kanehl's favorite bullpen to load the bases—before getting Bobby Higginson to ground out for the final out. Hickman raises his average for the series to .462 with three hits and a walk.

Kanehl's reaction as Anderson comes in to pitch the ninth: "Oh, [bleep]."

What Stengel once said about the Polo Grounds: "Just when my fellas learn to hit in this ballpark, they're gonna tear it down."

Game 4 at Polo Grounds

Mets 7, Tigers 4

The big story is Mets starter Bob L. Miller, whose win in this game gives him as many wins in the (ahem) "postseason" as he had all season (one). Miller had started the year 0–12 but beat the Cubs in the next-to-last game of the year. So it took him 41 years, but he'd just won himself two decisions in a row (sort of).

Tigers starter Matt Roney gets pounded for six runs in 4 2/3. The Mets coast into the ninth up 7–1 before Dmitri Young's three-run homer off reliever Bob Moorhead makes it look like a game. Mets third baseman Felix Mantilla commits his fourth error of the series. Choo Choo Coleman thrills the crowd by committing a passed ball. Marvelous Marv Throneberry thrills the crowd with one of his rarified triples.

Kanehl on Throneberry's triple: "Oh, I know he could hit a triple in the Polo Grounds. Remember the famous story about how he hits a triple and gets called out for missing second. Then Stengel goes out to argue and the umpire tells him, 'Don't bother. He missed *first*, too.' And Casey says, 'Well, I know he didn't miss third. He's *standing* on it.'"

Kanehl on Bob L. Miller's only regular season win: "The thing I remember about it is, all the writers who covered us took off and went to the track, and left one writer to cover for everybody. So here Bob Miller lost all those games, and there'd be 10 writers there after all the losses. Then he finally wins a game, and there's one writer there. But hell, it was Chicago. Nobody wanted to go to the games if they could go to the track."

What Stengel actually said once about the immortal Choo Choo Coleman: "I had 15 pitchers who said they couldn't pitch to him—and it turned out they couldn't pitch to *nobody*."

Game 5 at Polo Grounds

Mets 5, Tigers 3

The home team wins for the fifth straight game in this Series. But in "pivotal" Game 5, the Tigers are a mess. Dmitri Young drops a fly ball in left in the third, leading to the go-ahead run. Munson commits another error, his sixth of the series. The Tigers undo a decent effort by Maroth with four errors. The Mets take a 5–1 lead in the seventh and, as always, hang on.

The big star is starting pitcher Jay Hook (8–19, 4.84 ERA). He not only pitches 8⅔ innings. He gets *three* hits, helping the Mets to lead the series for the first time, three games to two.

Kanehl on Hook getting three hits. "I don't remember him getting *one* hit."

What Stengel once said to Hook after he won a game and singled in a run: "I might pitch you every day. But you didn't hit as good as I expected."

Game 6 at Comerica Park

Tigers 6, Mets 5

Every Game 6 is required to be a classic. And this one qualifies. Tigers starter Jeremy Bonderman, who was minus-21 years old when the '62 Mets were in their heyday, outpitches Al Jackson. And the Tigers take a 3–2 lead into the ninth...

At this point, we interrupt our saga for this question from Rod Kanehl, who failed to sneak into any of the first five games: "When," Kanehl wonders, "do I do something?" When we inform him Game 6 would indeed be the game, he retorts: "Let me guess. I pinch-run, right? (Right.) And I tie the game, right? (Right.) Happened all the time. He put me in to pinch-run, I'd steal second and score."

OK, back to the action. The Tigers are one strike away from winning. But Kanehl, the potential tying run, is on third. And Richie Ashburn, having a fabulous series (.448 on-base percentage), then beats out a ground ball to short. Kanehl scores. Tie game. The Mets then score two more runs and take a two-run lead. But in comes Craig Anderson again. And you know what happens.

He walks the leadoff hitter (Kevin Witt). So Stengel gongs him for left-hander Ken Mackenzie. A double by Pena puts the tying run in scoring position. But a sac fly and ground ball bring the Mets to within an out of winning the series. Oops. They're the *Mets*. So Cannizzaro commits a passed ball on the next pitch to tie the game. Then Mackenzie drills Ramon Santiago, who charges the mound and starts a brawl. Both are kicked out, so in comes seldom-used left-hander Willard Hunter (1–6, 5.57). Two hitters later, Shane Halter singles, and the Tigers win.

Kanehl on Cannizzaro's passed ball: "Oh, [bleep]. *That* brings back memories. I thought he knew better than to throw one low to Cannizzaro. Cripes, what was he *thinking*?"

Kanehl on the heartbreak of having the game and Series get away when the Mets were one strike away from winning it: "Heck, we were one out away all the time in '62. I mean, you're talking about a team that lost 120 games. So one out away and losing—that happened *every* day."

What Stengel once said about Cannizzaro: "That Canzoneri...he's the only defensive catcher in baseball who can't catch."

Game 7 at Comerica Park

How 'bout *this* drama?

The Mets go back to their ace, Roger Craig, a man who would actually spend a week of spring training with the '03 Tigers as a guest voice of wisdom. The Tigers score first. But Cornejo gives up a two-run double to Throneberry in the third and a solo homer to Gene Woodling in the fourth. And Craig hands a 3–1 lead to Mackenzie in the eighth.

But it's Mackenzie's sixth appearance in seven games, and (naturally) he tires in the ninth. Craig Monroe homers with one out, and it's 3–2. Pena then crushes one 410 feet to dead center, but Ashburn makes it back to the track and hauls it in. So down to their final out, up steps Munson, who has more errors in the series (six) than hits (five). But it's his chance to make up for all of that, and he mashes one to center—deep, deep, deep. Ashburn reaches the wall, leans back against the 420 sign...and catches it.

Mets win! Mets win! Mets win!

Kanehl on the thrill of victory: "We won the booby prize. We won the Futility Cup. I don't think they'd let us drink the good champagne, the Veuve Clicquot, after that. We could drink that purple stuff. We'd have to drink Cold Duck."

What Stengel once said after winning a World Series: "I couldn't have done it without my players."

The 25 Greatest Home Run Derby Moments

AUTHOR'S NOTE: *It's funny how you can develop certain niches in life without even meaning to. Well, here's one of mine: I've become Mr. Home Run Derby. Nobody in the history of baseball writing has written more about the Derby than I have. And I'm not even sure how that happened. But whatever. So in 2010, on the eve of the 25th Home Run Derby in All-Star Game history, I decided to rank my 25 greatest Home Run Derby memories. So here they come.*

1. Josh Hamilton, Yankee Stadium, 2008

It was the Last Great Homer Show in the old Yankee Stadium. And it forever transformed Josh Hamilton into a magical baseball figure. OK, so officially, he may not have "won" this Derby. (Justin Morneau did.) But when Hamilton launched 28 home runs *in one round*, he deposited a Derby performance in our memory banks that ranks above all the others.

Before he reached the batter's box, only one man (Bobby Abreu) had ever hit 28 homers in all three rounds *combined*. Then Josh Hamilton got rolling. He hit a home run on 13 swings *in a row*. And 16 of 17. And 20 of 22. And 22 of 25. He crushed five balls into the upper deck. He pounded another off the facing of the mezzanine, and two more into the seemingly unreachable black seats in center. And he mashed three 500-footers, including a 518-foot space shuttle that might have hit the Statue of Liberty if the top of the third deck hadn't gotten in the way.

"Obviously, I've never experienced a groove like that before," he said afterward. To which we can only ask: has anyone?

2. Mark McGwire, Fenway Park, 1999

We take you back to another time, a different era, when Big Mac was still baseball's most beloved, almost mythical figure. Nine months after crashing through the 70-homer barrier, he turned Fenway into his own personal Derby stage.

He, too, didn't "win" this Derby. (Ken Griffey Jr. did.) But in the first round, McGwire terrorized New Englanders from Kenmore Square to Kennebunkport, with a then-record 13-homer round that amounted to 5,692 feet worth of bomb-age. His ultimate highlight: a 488-foot mortar that whooshed beyond the Green Monster, cleared the street, soared over a parking garage, and hit a billboard above the train tracks, right next to the never-reached Massachusetts Turnpike.

"Once he got in his groove," said his personal pitcher that night, Tim Flannery, "it was like feeding the Great White Shark."

3. Bobby Abreu, Comerica Park, 2005

In his regular life, Abreu is a man who has never hit more than 31 home runs in one season. So it's safe to say he wasn't your official Best Bet in Vegas to go out and hit 41 Derby homers in one *night*.

But stuff happens sometimes in Home Run Derbies. And it sure happened this night. Of Abreu's first 14 swings, 10 left the park. One hit the facing of the upper deck. Another landed in the Pepsi Porch by the upper-deck foul pole. The last one traveled 517 feet, and nearly came down in somebody's rib platter at the Montgomery Inn, across the concourse in the right-field upper deck. And that was just the beginning.

Abreu would have 14 more bombs in him, just in that round. Which were followed by 17 more in the next two rounds. And at one point, as he was on the way to a Derby-record 41 homers, his Venezuelan countrymen—Melvin

Mora, Cesar Izturis, and Miguel Cabrera—actually raced to the plate and wrapped him in a flag. And that was *before* he won this thing.

"He might be the king now," Abreu's teammate, Jimmy Rollins, said afterward. "The king of Venezuela."

4. Mark McGwire vs. Barry Bonds, Veterans Stadium, 1996

There were no big, black PED clouds swirling over either of these men back in 1996. But there sure were a lot of home runs swirling around old Veterans Stadium in Philly, as baseball's two preeminent mashers put on maybe the greatest Derby duel ever.

Before they came along, the Derby was just another All-Star sideshow. They almost personally catapulted it into the must-see baseball event it is now, with a back-and-forth bomb-a-thon in which only the oohs outnumbered the aahs.

McGwire led off the second round with nine transcontinental homers. Bonds stepped in next and pounded 10. That elevated them into the finals, where Bonds got within one out of losing—and then crunched three spine-tingling homers in his final three swings. But while McGwire lost, he did hit two baseballs where none had ever traveled before—into the altitudinous 600 level of the Vet's upper deck.

Asked afterward if he could remember the last time he'd hit a ball like that, McGwire joked: "I'd say in spring training—with my new titanium driver."

5. Sammy Sosa, Miller Park, 2002

He was 87 miles up the interstate from his home turf. And Slammin' Sammy Sosa knew just what he was there for. So he took over Milwaukee's first and only Derby as only he could back then.

In the first round, Sosa squashed 12 home runs. And while that was only tied, at the time, for the third-biggest round ever, this was one round you needed to measure in mileage, not homer counts. Those 12 home runs traveled an *average* of (no kidding) 477 feet. And it seemed like more.

Sosa clattered a home run off Bernie Brewer's slide, another that sailed over the humongous center-field scoreboard, and three more that *exited* a domed stadium (through the windows, that is). Seven of those home runs carried 500 feet-plus. Nine went 490-plus. So even the eventual "winner" that day, Jason Giambi, couldn't stop talking about Sosa.

"I don't think anything can hold him," Giambi said, "except Yellowstone."

6. Cal Ripken Jr., Skydome, 1991

Any time you hear somebody in baseball whine about how the Derby screws up a guy's swing, we want to refer you to the great Calvin Edwin Ripken Jr. Anyone remember who the MVP of the American League was in 1992? It was Ripken, all right. And he openly admitted that, in the course of hitting a then-record 12 home runs in 22 swings on the way to winning this Derby, he found something—namely, the stroke that drove him all the way to an MVP award.

But don't take that to mean those 12 Derby homers didn't shock him: "It's not easy to hit home runs, even when you're trying to hit home runs," Ripken said that day. "It's not easy to hit home runs, period. I just got halfway through, and I thought, *This is kind of unbelievable. Am I really doing it?*"

7. Ryan Howard, PNC Park, 2006

Hey, as long as we're on that Derby Curse is a Myth rant, what better time to bring up Ryan Howard? This was the year he joined Ripken and became the second man to win a Derby and an MVP trophy in the same season. And he, too, might not have won his MVP award if it weren't for his triumph in the most water-logged Derby ever. On a Pittsburgh night when 15 baseballs wound up in the Allegheny River, Howard was responsible for splashing six of them—two on the fly, four on the bounce.

"I was hoping he was going to kill some fish out in that river," said his personal Derby pitcher, Phillies coach Ramon Henderson. "And he did."

8. Ken Griffey Jr., Coors Field, 1998

It was the only Derby ever held at an altitude normally reserved for Boeing 767s. But what we remember most about it—even now—was a transformation that took place at an altitude of 75 inches. That would be the approximate location of Griffey's brain lobes. And it was there that a very famous lightning bolt hit—and led Griffey to wind up winning this Derby.

Beforehand, our man was insisting—as he had for weeks—that he had no interest, none, in taking part of this Derby. Even though he was an esteemed icon, on the way to a 56-homer season. Even though he was the leading vote-getter of all the players in this All Star Game.

Next thing he knew, he found himself running around on Workout Day, getting booed for every move he made. Whereupon, in possibly the greatest triumph by boobirds in the long, frustrating history of boo-a-thons, he changed his mind, agreed to take part, and won the whole thing, with 19 homers in 42 swings.

"I don't like to get booed," Griffey said, after magically converting those boos into a standing ovation. "I don't think anybody does. This is not a time to get booed—the All-Star Game." Hey, good point.

9. Frank Thomas, Three Rivers Stadium, 1994

You know you've hit a memorable home run when the place where it landed is preserved, even though the stadium it was hit in lost a rendezvous with dynamite years ago. And that's a 100 percent true story in the case of the home run Thomas launched in this Derby—an upper-deck lunar orbiter to left-center, *nine* sections over from the foul pole.

It was estimated at 519 feet, the longest ball ever hit in Three Rivers. It was such a momentous blast, the Pirates put a star on the seat, later had Thomas and the coach who served it up, Rich Donnelly, sign the star, and then auctioned it off before they blew up the stadium.

"Frank Thomas is just too big," laughed Gregg Jefferies afterward. "If you're over 260 pounds, there should be a rule—that you have to play football."

10. Lance Berkman vs. Miguel Tejada, Minute Maid Park, 2004

A funny thing happened to this Derby, which was supposed to feature every active member of the 500-Homer Club: it came down to two guys who didn't own 500 homers combined.

It was the winner, Tejada, who would set records for most home runs in one round (15, in Round 2) and most in one Derby (27). But it was the hometown hero, Berkman, who set an unofficial record—for most home runs that came down on the streets of an otherwise-innocent American city. That would be five (in seven swings), after the roof was opened for Round 2.

Asked afterward if he was worried he might hurt somebody outside, an innocent-sounding Berkman replied: "I'm pretty sure they had a disclaimer hanging out there: STAND OUT HERE AT YOUR OWN RISK. Something like that. And even if they didn't, how would they know who hit it? It could have been me. Could have been someone else. They wouldn't even know who to sue."

11. David Ortiz, Comerica Park, 2005

It's funny how nobody except Big Papi seems to remember this. But just minutes after Abreu finished putting on his 24-homer show in the first round in 2005, Ortiz had himself what would have been viewed as The Greatest Derby Round Ever—except that it wasn't even The Greatest Derby Round of That Particular Derby Round. Nevertheless, the Papster's 17 homers still rank No. 3 on your handy-dandy list of most prodigious rounds in Derby history. And what we particularly admire is that he never, ever whines about the Derby fouling up his stroke.

"It don't affect *me*," he said. "I swing from my butt all the time anyway."

12. David Wright, PNC Park, 2006

Ryan Howard won this thing, as we might have mentioned someplace. But Wright's 16 homers in the first round still ranked, years later, as the fourth-biggest Derby round ever—an especially amazing feat in a park with a gigantic left field. And in a move nobody saw coming, the "pitcher" he chose to serve them up was his teammate, catcher Paul LoDuca—who was so proud of all those home runs he threw, he announced afterward: "When my career's over, I'm going to come back as a special Home Run Derby BP thrower."

13. Ken Griffey Jr., Camden Yards, 1993

Back in 1993, the Derby was still a one-round team competition—National League versus American League. But Griffey and Juan Gonzalez forced the first mano-a-mano grand finale by tying for the individual lead (with seven each). Eventually, Gonzalez won their little mash-off. But it was Griffey who left us with the most memorable moment—cranking the first ball ever to clank off the fabled B&O Warehouse, on the other side of Eutaw Street, on the fly. There's still a plaque on that warehouse that marks the spot.

14. Cecil Fielder, Skydome, 1991

We'll concede that for most of the planet, the big memory from this day was Ripken's 12-homer extravaganza. But for some folks (like us, for instance), our favorite moments from this Derby were provided by Big Cecil—who crushed not one but two home runs that came down in the Sight Lines bar, way, way, wayyyy out there in the third deck in center field. We've also never forgotten possibly The Greatest Home Run Derby quote ever—from A's quipmeister Dave Henderson—which was inspired by those bombs.

"Ever heard that saying, 'There's a fly in my soup?'" Henderson laughed afterward. "Well, there was a *fly ball* in that guy's soup."

15. Prince Fielder, Busch Stadium, 2009

There has only been one father-son combo to take part in a Derby. And that's the Fielders. But unlike Cecil, his kid Prince actually won a Derby, in 2009 in St. Louis. Unlike his father, however, Prince didn't hit a single home run that came down in anybody's piña colada.

Nevertheless, he did pound 10,087 feet worth of homers—which was enough to win this thing. And one of them was a 503-foot satellite that cleared the right-center-field bleachers and was later described this way by his personal pitcher, Sandy Guerrero, in an apparent bid to narrate a future potato-chip commercial: "It sounded like a cannon," Guerrero said. "Not as loud, but very crispy."

16. Sammy Sosa, Turner Field, 2000

To most people, Sosa's signature Derby was the 2002 show in Milwaukee. But this one still ranks as the personal favorite of the only real Derby historian we know—the Sultan of Swat Stats, legendary home run historian David Vincent. As the Sultan ducked for cover in the auxiliary press box out in left-center field, Sosa fired eight NASA shots that either landed in the upper deck or hit the facing. And he punctuated his only Derby title with a 508-foot monster mash over the home of the center-field TV cameras, which we're still pretty sure was located closer to Savannah than home plate.

17. Jason Giambi, US Cellular Field, 2003

Giambi didn't win this Derby. He just saved it. After the first seven contestants threatened to nod most of America to sleep by averaging a whopping three homers apiece in Round 1, up stepped Giambi to whomp 10 in 12 swings, on the way to 23 in all. We've always had a soft spot for guys who unabashedly love the Derby. And Giambi loves it more than any player we've ever met. He pumped 68 Derby homers in three years (second all time to Griffey's 70), and once reached double figures in four different rounds in 2001–02–03.

"I just enjoy it," he said. "I like to go out there, have a good time. And it's not really much different than my swing out of my shoes in the games."

18. Albert Pujols, US Cellular Field, 2003

Giambi didn't merely wake up the crowd that night in Chicago. He also woke up Sir Albert. This was Pujols' first Derby. And he scuffled in the first round, hitting four and barely advancing. But then he got matched up in a one-on-one with Giambi in the second round. And he knew what to do when he got out there.

He slashed 14 homers in his first 20 swings, a record for any round at the time. And the cool, Pujols-esque part of that display was that he hit them to every part of Chicago except Pizzeria Uno—six to left field, six to right, and two to center. Eventually, he lost in the finals to (no kidding) Garret Anderson. But this may have been the night Albert Pujols proved to America he was the greatest, most complete hitter on earth.

19. Darryl Strawberry, Astrodome, 1986

It was the first truly memorable Derby homer. In the second Derby ever staged, Strawberry unfurled one of those trademark uppercut hacks of his—and lofted a baseball so high and so far to right field that it did something only one other fair ball had ever done in the history of Houston's fabled, cavernesque Astrodome: clank off a speaker hanging from the roof.

That speaker was located 350 feet from home plate in deep right-center field, 140 feet above planet earth. And there are folks who will claim that this ball was still going up when that speaker got in the way. Those folks could be making that up, of course. But who cares? If we're still talking about that homer, all these years later, it had to be pretty darned cool.

20. Bill Murray, Wrigley Field, 1990

Yeah, we're talking about *that* Bill Murray. The guy from Caddyshack. He wasn't actually allowed to compete in the only Derby ever held at Wrigley. But he was allowed to serve as the P.A. announcer. And it was a good thing, because otherwise, this would have been the least interesting Home Run Derby ever. Only five home runs got hit *in the whole derby*. But that just enabled Murray to take over and serve as the Babe Ruth of this day.

He introduced Ryne Sandberg as "perhaps the greatest Chicago second baseman since Tony Taylor." He announced Matt Williams as "a man who wears no sunblock." He said Strawberry was a guy who "hit 21 home runs last week." And after a Fielder blast landed on the warning track, Murray announced: "Cecil, that's a home run in Osaka, right?"

21. Round 1, Coors Field, 1998

You bring the Home Run Derby to pre-humidor Denver, and you know what's coming: Namely, a whole lot of baseballs soaring toward distant mountain tops. And that's what we got at Coors, in a 53-homer first round that still ranks as the third-most-prodigious Derby round ever. Javy Lopez crunched one that cleared an exit ramp in center field. Jim Thome oohed-and-aahed a ball halfway up the *third* deck in right. And of course, McGwire mashed one of his standard 510-footers.

"Halfway through the first round," said then-Marlins coach Rich Donnelly, who pitched to three of the eight contestants, "we had to call Budweiser and say, 'Get that blimp up about 100 feet.'"

22. Cove 1, Derby 0, AT&T Park, 2007

Never in Home Run Derby history have so many kayaks floated in vain. Even though Barry Bonds balked at including himself in this Derby, held in his very own home park, that didn't stop approximately 4.8 trillion kayak paddlers—a group that even included Arizona outfielder Eric Byrnes—from cramming themselves into McCovey Cove.

Alas, the three left-handed bombers in this thing—Howard, Fielder, and Justin Morneau—left them all sailing around for naught. We counted 45 swings by that trio, but zero baseballs bobbing in the Cove. "What can I say?" Howard said, sadly, afterward. "Uh, sorry."

23. Vladimir Guerrero, AT&T Park, 2007

At least the Man from Vlad didn't have to apologize that night in San Francisco. Somebody had to win this Derby, in the least home-run-friendly park ever to host one. And it might as well have been a guy who A) hits right-handed, and B) swings as hard as he can at every pitch. And that was Vlad. Every time it looked like he was in big trouble, he'd do stuff like crunch five home runs in seven swings. And eventually, he was the last masher standing. "I was just trying to swing the bat hard," he said, "like I always do." Good idea!

24. The Zero Heroes—Mike Piazza, Jason Bay, and Bret Boone

In truth, these three guys aren't the only men who ever hung a bagel on the scoreboard in a Home Run Derby. It's happened many times. In 1990, for instance, more contestants (five) didn't homer than those who did (three). But these three just happen to be the most famous Zero Heroes in Derby history.

Piazza went homerless in 1993 and never took part again, even declining an invitation to be Team Italy's representative in the 2005 edition that was supposed to promote the first World Baseball Classic. Bay, on the other hand, agreed to be the Team Canada contestant that night, went 0-for-10 (thanks, clearly, to spectacular goaltending), and announced later: "I'm probably not the ideal Home Run Derby guy."

And then there was Boone, the only member of the Boone family ever to take part in a Derby and, undoubtedly, the last, after firing 10 blanks in 2003. Afterward, Boone revealed he'd heard immediately from his brother Aaron, who, shockingly, "told me I stunk. And my son told me I stunk. And I haven't even dealt with the wife yet."

25. The Dawn of the Derby, Metrodome, 1985

All these years later, it's hard to believe an event this humongous could really have started this quietly. But in an attempt to answer the NBA and its slam-dunk extravaganza, baseball decided to stage a simple little long-ball contest—NL versus AL, five hitters from each league, 10 swings apiece. The AL won 17–16. Dave Parker led the pack with six homers.

The special admission charge for what used to be looked at as a low-key workout day? Two bucks. For charity. Nowadays, we don't know anyone who remembers anything about that day. But just look what it started—one of the most memorable baseball events on the calendar. And it doesn't even count.

Does Anybody Know the Rules?

Does anybody out there know the rules of baseball? Seriously.

If ever there was a year that made you wonder about that, 2013 would be the year.

We saw Jean Segura run the bases backward in Milwaukee—and actually steal *first* base (sort of)—only to learn five days later that wasn't exactly legal.

We saw an entire umpiring crew in Houston forget a basic rule on when a manager can change pitchers and when he can't.

We saw Luke Hochevar save an 11–4 game for the Royals—and admit afterward he had no idea that the save rule had just applied to him.

And on and on and on. So the more we saw, the more we got to thinking. Which is always a precarious development for the rest of civilization.

Suppose we gave a little quiz, we thought. A rules quiz.

We'd let players take it. We'd let coaches take it. We'd let any managers who were interested take it. And of course, we'd take it ourselves.

It wouldn't quite remind anyone of, say, the bar exam. Just 10 questions— all true/false—compiled by esteemed baseball rules expert Rich Marazzi.

And when the results were in, we'd have our answer. We'd find out how much all of us really know about the most convoluted book ever published— the Rules of Baseball.

It ought to be a sacred book, The Almighty Rules of Baseball. Don't you think? Hallowed. Worshiped. Revered. Memorized. Heck, some of these darned rules go back more than 150 years. Back to a time that predates even Jamie Moyer.

Instead, what we've learned—and what we suspected we'd learn from this quiz—is that many of these rules defy comprehension. Not to mention common sense. And some of the smartest people we know in this sport are out there every night, having their fates decided by a bunch of quirky rules that most of them have never read.

"Yeah, I read it," Marlins manager Mike Redmond said of the Almighty Rulebook. "I never used to read it when I was a player. But I read that book all the time now. I like to know about all the stuff that comes up every game. So I'm always thumbing through it.

"But let me tell you, it's kind of a dry read. It's not one of those books you pick up and read for 20 minutes because it's so interesting."

Heh-heh. No kidding. It isn't quite *The Da Vinci Code.*

So you'd think an avid reader of the rulebook like Mike Redmond couldn't wait to take this quiz, right? Uh, wrong.

"Oh, no," Redmond said, through a you've-gotta-be-kidding-me grin. "I want no part of that."

Luckily, though, we did find 32 courageous folks who were willing. Some of them wondered afterward why they'd ever gotten themselves into this mess. But when the results were in, here was the verdict:

- We had 20 of the most astute players in the game take the quiz. Their average score: 5.5 out of 10.

- Four coaches and one manager (John Farrell of the Red Sox) joined the fun. They averaged 6.6 out of 10. Farrell represented America's managers in exemplary fashion. He got nine out of 10.

- And seven of us media know-it-alls tried our luck—six ESPN baseball "geniuses," plus Twins broadcaster (and longtime former player) Dan Gladden. You'll be shocked to learn our average score was a spectacular 4.4. Then again, we were dragged down a little by our otherwise-all-knowing friend, Aaron Boone, who somehow got one out of 10. (Full disclosure: I took this thing, too—and put a six on the old scoreboard. I'll take it.)

BASEBALL RULES QUIZ
BY RICH MARAZZI

Following are 10 true/false questions. Number your paper from 1 to 10 and swing away!

1. The Phillies have Ben Revere on second base and no outs when Michael Young hits a shot to Reds third baseman Todd Frazier, who is playing at normal depth. On the pitch, Revere attempts to steal third, and while sliding into the base he is hit by the batted ball. Even though Revere was on the base when struck by the ball, he should be called out because he interfered with Frazier from making a play. True or false?

2. The Indians have Michael Bourn on first base and one out when Nick Swisher launches a fly to deep center field. Bourn rounds second but then retreats to first, thinking the ball will be caught by Yankees center fielder Brett Gardner. But Gardner can't reach the ball, and Swisher heads to second and is about to pass Bourn, who is returning to first base. Realizing the ball was not caught, Swisher pushes Bourn toward second and he reaches the base safely while Swisher returns to first. Swisher should be called out for making contact with Bourn and assisting him on the bases. True or false?

3. The Cubs have Starlin Castro on second and Welington Castillo on first and no outs when Darwin Barney bunts the ball about 20 feet in the air. Mets pitcher Matt Harvey allows the ball to fall to the ground untouched and starts a 1-5-4-3 triple play. The umpires should have called the infield-fly rule to protect the runners. True or false?

4. The Astros bat out of order in the first inning as they do not follow the lineup card submitted to the plate umpire prior to the game. Dodgers manager Don Mattingly does not appeal since no runner reached base. Astros manager Bo Porter can correct the mistake and have his team bat in proper order the remainder of the game without penalty. True or false?

5. The Pirates have Neil Walker on third base and one out when Pedro Alvarez hits a fly ball near the stands along the third-base line. Rangers third baseman Adrian Beltre makes a leaping catch and falls into the stands, holding on to the ball. The catch should count but as soon as Beltre fell into the stands, "Time" should have been called and Walker should be sent home and allowed to score. True or false?

6. The Angels have the bases loaded and no outs. The Royals infield is playing in when Josh Hamilton hits a shot that gets by Royals first baseman Eric Hosmer and hits Albert Pujols, who is immediately behind Hosmer and headed to second base. Even though the ball struck Pujols, he should not

be called out because no other infielder had a chance to make the play after the ball got by Hosmer. True or false?

7. The Twins have the bases loaded and two outs when Justin Morneau wallops a grand slam. Josh Willingham, the runner on first base, misses second base as he circles the bases. The A's appeal that Willingham missed second base and the appeal is upheld. Willingham is called out. The Twins should score two runs on the play. True or false?

8. The Red Sox have Dustin Pedroia on second and no outs. David Ortiz is the batter facing White Sox pitcher Jose Quintana who does not make a complete stop in his set position. Umpire Dale Scott calls a balk but Quintana delivers the pitch anyway, which Ortiz crushes for a home run. The umps send Pedroia to third but because Quintana balked, the ball is dead and the home run should be nullified. Ortiz must remain in the batter's box with the same count before the balk occurred. True or false?

9. The Blue Jays are playing the Padres. In the eighth inning, Jays manager John Gibbons goes to the mound to remove R.A. Dickey. He brings in Chad Jenkins. Gibbons walks back toward the dugout and crosses the foul line, then decides he wants to add further instructions to Jenkins. Gibbons should not be allowed to do this because it would give Gibbons two trips to the mound with the same batter at the plate. True or false?

10. The Orioles have Nick Markakis on third and no outs when Chris Davis hits a ground ball to Mariners second baseman Nick Franklin and is out 4-3. Markakis scores from third on the play, but plate umpire Todd Tichenor calls catcher's interference on Seattle's Jesus Sucre. Tichenor carries out the penalty of the rule and sends Markakis back to third and awards Davis first base. O's manager Buck Showalter informs Tichenor that he wants to take the play instead of the penalty; this means that Showalter trades the out for the run. Tichenor does not allow Showalter to do this, claiming the ball is dead the moment Davis' bat made contact with the catcher's mitt. The umpire is correct. True or false?

Marazzi told us he considered six out of 10 to be a "passing" grade. By that measure, only 13 of the 32 participants passed—eight players, two coaches, our designated manager, and two media "geniuses" (including this author, he slipped in there nonchalantly).

But some guys had this nailed. Our valedictorian was Diamondbacks reliever Brad Ziegler. He was the only quiz-taker in his class to drill 10 out of 10. When informed of his honor, Ziegler said: "I'd say it's not as prestigious as being valedictorian of your high school class. I don't get a scholarship out of it, or anything like that."

Wow. That's for sure. Or his own autographed rulebook, either. In fact, Ziegler wasn't even allowed to give a valedictory speech. But he did thank his father, who used to grill him on the rules as a kid when he was just minding his own business, trying to watch TV. See how that fatherly wisdom can sometimes pay off in life?

"I'm going to guess that if you quizzed all 750 [players] in the big leagues, there would have been a lot more 10s," Ziegler said, humbly. "All it means is that I've got way too much useless information in my head. I tell guys about stuff like this all the time. And they always say, 'Why do you know that?' And '*How* do you know that?'"

Well, we can think of two players who would definitely ask him that. That would be two of the headiest players we know—Sam Fuld of the Rays and Michael Young of the Phillies—who answered exactly three questions correctly apiece.

"I used to think I knew the rules," Young said. "But over time, I began to learn I didn't know them as well as I thought. One time in a game, they called the infield-fly rule, and I wasn't sure why. So afterward, I went over to the ump and said, 'Don't ever tell anybody I said this, but what's that rule again?'"

The ever-erudite Fuld, meanwhile, was pretty much mortified by his score.

"It was humiliating," he said, with a laugh that suggested he'd get over that humiliation somehow. "I would have done better if I'd closed my eyes and picked randomly. It's pathetic to think that my three-year-old son could have done better than that.

"Of course," he said proudly of three-year-old Charles Fuld, "he knows his baseball."

Fuld—who graduated from Stanford with a degree in economics and a GPA of 3.14—even admitted that before he submitted his quiz, he "collaborated" with his father, Kenneth Fuld, dean of the College of Liberal Arts at the University of New Hampshire. And his dad was so devastated by their score, "it took him about a day to get over it."

"If you questioned about a hundred five-year-olds, they'd get five out of 10," the Rays' human highlight reel said, dejectedly. "And my dad and I got

QUIZ ANSWERS

1. True (With the exception of the infield-fly rule, the base does not provide a sanctuary for the runner if struck by a batted ball while on the base).

2. False (A runner can assist another runner as long as he did not score or was already put out. A runner can actually *carry* a teammate around the bases).

3. False (Bunts are not included in the infield-fly rule).

4. True (The offensive team can correct the error at any time during the game).

5. True (When a fielder carries the ball into dead-ball territory and controls the ball, he is credited with the catch but all runners are awarded one base on the play).

6. True (When a runner is struck by a batted ball, he should not be called out if no other infielder has a chance to make a play. This applies only if the ball has passed an infielder).

7. False (No runs can score when an inning ends in a force out. Because Willingham was "forced" to go to second on the play, the appeal resulted in an inning-ending force out).

8. False (When a balk is called, the play is not necessarily dead. If all runners including the batter advance at least one base on the play, the balk is nullified).

9. False (Gibbons was within his rights to return to the mound. He had not yet made a visit to Jenkins since the original visit is charged to Dickey, the pitcher being removed from the game).

10. False (The ball is not dead when catcher's interference is called. If all runners including the batter advance one base, the infraction is ignored. However, if that does not happen, the manager of the offensive team can elect to take the play instead of the penalty—sounds like football! In baseball, however, the manager must initiate the conference with the umpire. If he doesn't, the umpire will carry out the penalty aspect of the rule. In the play in question, Markakis would be returned to third since he was not forced to advance on the play and Davis would be awarded first base).

a three."

Now think about this. Sam Fuld has to be one of the brightest human beings in baseball. He got over 1400 in his SATs. He understands stuff like matrix methodology. But even he has a hard time understanding the rationale behind the rules of baseball. And can you blame him?

"Most of these rules are just illogical," he said. "I tried to base my answers on logic and reason…But baseball and logic don't mix very well, in many respects."

And that, ladies and gentlemen, is one of the biggest lessons that came out of this quiz extravaganza:

The rules may be the rules. But that doesn't mean they have to make much sense.

You should have heard the complaining from players about stuff like the balk rule…and the mysteries of why some wild throws give runners two extra bases while others are only worth one base…and on and on.

That, Marazzi admitted, is because the rulebook "is one of the worst-written documents ever published." It's way too complicated, he said. It's hard to navigate. And all in all, "it's terrible."

And that terrible-osity is exemplified by the actual existence, in that very book, of Rule 8:02 (a) (6) (a-b-c-d-e), which is then followed by two differ-ent official "comments" that attempt to explain what they've just defined. No kidding.

So Fuld proposed: "I think we should take a collection of the smartest people in baseball and have them completely rewrite the rulebook, so, for the next 100 years, we'll have completely logical rules."

Well, guess what? That'll never happen. So despite pleas from rational people like Ziegler that the rulebook "needs to be altered and brought into the 21st century—or even the 20th century," who the heck would want to take on that job? W.P. Kinsella? Ken Burns? Crash Davis? Whichever Molina brother happens to be free that week?

So what really needs to happen is a whole different approach:

Maybe somebody should actually explain these rules to the people who have to live and play by them. How 'bout that?

Somebody kind of like Rich Marazzi, for example.

"Almost nobody in the game has ever been taught the rules. They learned the hard way," said Marazzi, who works with the Red Sox, Yankees, and Blue Jays to help improve players' knowledge of the rules. "And because there are so many rules, people don't talk about them and general managers don't bring in rules consultants to help their teams with them. Everybody thinks they know the rules. But they don't know the impact of them, or how to maximize their understanding of the rules to help them win games."

So Marazzi, who spent 23 years umpiring in college, high school, and independent leagues, gives video presentations to the teams he works with, plus quizzes—much like the one we gave our contestants—that open their eyes in many ways. And that got us to thinking again, about another momentous question:

How would it change baseball if everyone (gasp) knew the rules?

"I think it actually would be detrimental," Ziegler said, totally seriously. "Not to the way players play the game, but to the relationship between players and umpires. All of a sudden, players would have a lot more knowledge, so they wouldn't always take the umpires' word for it."

Boy, that sure sounds like trouble. But maybe not. The last thing we're advocating is a development that would take us from, like, two player-umpire tiffs per game to 2,000. But you know what? In reality, ignorance is not bliss. Ignorance actually costs teams games.

Ask John Farrell. His team brings Marazzi in every spring for a little rules seminar. And he's convinced it has helped the Red Sox.

"We're talking about stuff inside the game," Farrell said, "that can affect the outcome of a game. Plays like interference, some of which can be initiated by the base runner."

Marazzi swears the teams he's worked with have used these rules to win more games. And he says teams that don't know the rules really do lose games because of it.

For instance, "most baseball people don't know the difference between a Type A and Type B obstruction," he said. "Both are fairly common. Lack of knowledge of this rule, in my opinion, cost the A's the 2003 Division Series versus the Red Sox."

Hmmm. To be honest, most of us wouldn't know Type A interference from Type A blood plasma. But we'll spare you the definitions, because that's not important now. Trust us on that. What's important is what we've proven here today:

That it's totally mind-blowing how few people who play or work in baseball can make sense of the gobbledygook in that rulebook.

Not that it's their fault. Not that we blame them. But now that we've made that clear, what should we do about it? Well, we have several options.

There's education, says Rich Marazzi. That's a good one. Or there's the update-the-book-by-a-century-or-so school of thought, as espoused by Brad Ziegler. Or maybe…

"What we need is a rules guru," said Sam Fuld. "One guy that MLB pays a bunch of money to, to be the rules guru, so every time one of these things comes along, he can figure it out, instead of everyone having to flip through 1,000 pages in the rulebook to figure out which one applies.

"All we need is one guy who would know every rule," Fuld went on. "Then we could just Skype him in every time we need him. He could be in Hong Kong for all we care, as long as he'd materialize on the scoreboard every time we needed him."

Wow. Beautiful. One all-knowing Rules Guru who would always be available, 24/7, to clear up, well, everything? Perfect. We can start the line for applicants at Jean Segura's house.

"Just," Sam Fuld laughed, as we pondered this brilliant idea, "don't expect me to volunteer."

2001–13

Strange But True Feats of the Millennium

What's the best thing about baseball? It's stranger than Lady Gaga's wardrobe, stranger than *My Big Fat Obnoxious Fiancé*, maybe even stranger than Brian Wilson's beard. The impossible becomes possible every day of every season. The madness never ends. And we can't stop watching—or loving every minute of it.

So here they come, my favorite Strange But True Feats of the 21st century (so far):

Strangest But Truest Home Run of the Millennium

Haven't we always suspected that nobody was a bigger threat to stretch a home run into a single than that fabled sprint champ, Bengie Molina? Well, on September 26, 2008, the Giants' always-innovative catcher did something even more impossible:

He hit a home run—*but didn't score a run.*

So how'd he become the first man in major league history to pull that off? It took a rare, Molina-esque combination of muscle, leadfoot-itude, and modern technology. But it happened, all right. Here's how:

In the sixth inning of this game, Molina lofted a fly ball that looked as if it hit the top of the right-field wall at AT&T Park. So Molina stopped at first. Emmanuel Burriss pinch-ran for him. And nothing seemed amiss—until Omar Vizquel told Giants manager Bruce Bochy he thought he'd heard the ball clank off the metal roof just above the wall.

So Bochy asked the umpires to use replay. And whaddayaknow, the call was reversed and Molina had himself a two-run homer. But the umps wouldn't let Molina come back to finish his trot because Burriss was already in the game and couldn't exit. So Burriss finished circling the bases. And Molina wound up with a box-score line that went 3-0-1-2—on a night he hit a home run.

Want to know how impossible that is? When official scorer Michael Duca tried to enter this sequence into his computer, the computer program wouldn't let him—because every computer ever built knows a guy can't hit a home run without scoring a run. Right?

So even the box scores of this momentous event are all mixed up. Retrosheet has it right. But our friends over at baseball-reference.com still can't make their box-score program believe this happened. But it did. In actual life. And all of us Strange But True Feats of the Millennium fans will be eternally grateful that it did.

Strangest But Truest Base Running Feat of the Millennium

On the fateful evening of April 19, 2013, we finally found baseball's version of Leon Lett.

We're talking about Brewers shortstop Jean Segura, who, like the mixed-up grandma who made a U-turn on a one-way street, performed an act of base running madness that he'll be seeing, on scoreboard video-screen blooper reels, for the rest of his life.

To even try to describe this adventure is almost as challenging as actually doing it. But basically, here's the simplest way to sum it up:

This guy stole second. Then he tried to steal third but somehow wound up on first. Then he got thrown out trying to steal second again. All in a span of five pitches.

Just try that on your PlayStation sometime. Excellent chance smoke starts pouring out of it within seconds.

"Bizarre," umpire Tom Hallion said afterward. "Technically, he stole second, stole first, then got thrown out stealing second."

Well, "technically," he didn't, to be honest, because that's impossible. But in real life, here's what actually happened:

On a 2-2 pitch to Ryan Braun, in the eighth inning of a game against the Cubs, Segura stole second. On the next pitch, Braun walked. So far, pretty standard stuff. But not for long.

Three pitches after that, Segura broke for third. But his first mistake was, he forgot to wait until the pitcher, Shawn Camp, delivered the ball.

So Camp whirled and got Segura hung up between second and third. That led Braun to follow Baseball 101 protocol and roar into second base. Which was proper and cool—until Segura scrambled back to the bag to join him.

The Cubs started tagging everyone in the vicinity. And the rules say it was Braun who was out. But that was news to Segura, who thought he was the one who was out. So he started trotting toward the dugout.

Along the way, though, he got the memo that he wasn't out after all. So he pulled back into first base. And first-base coach Garth Iorg wouldn't let him leave.

Not until two pitches later, anyway—when Segura burst toward second again and, in take two, got thrown out.

So there you have it—a man who stole second and was caught stealing second in the same inning.

Without his team batting around.

This was another play the computers of America weren't ready for. The baseball-reference.com play-by-play account lists him as "advancing" to first base—from second. The MLB.com box and play-by-play don't even bother explaining how any of this happened. And the official ruling, at the time, was that he was caught stealing third, even though he actually slid into second (three different times, in fact), just because there was no way to make a computer understand how he wound up on first.

It was such a mess, it took three days for baseball's umpiring gurus to step in and say he should have been called out the first time. But by the time that happened, some of my favorite creative thinkers had so much fun kicking this around, they decided this could trigger a whole new way to liven up the sport.

Former Brewers third-base coach Rich Donnelly (who will be heard from again in this piece) devised the perfect plan: once a year, he proposed, baseball should liven things up by having everybody run the bases backward. Hitters would run to third instead of first. And then they'd just keep going, left to right instead of right to left. Hmmm, why not?

"Who said that when you hit the ball, you have to go to first?" Donnelly wondered. "Abner Doubleday? No, he didn't. The important thing is, you have to get home."

"It's like when we were teenagers. All your parents said was, 'You have to be home.' They didn't say which way you had to go. Did they?"

Strangest But Truest Grand Finale of the Millennium

I still can't believe this happened, but millions watched it unfold with their hearts pumping.

It was the final night of the 2011 baseball season. Remember?

The Red Sox were one out away from beating the Orioles…the Rays trailed the Yankees 7–0 in the eighth inning…and then…

Amazingly, it was the Rays who wound up winning and making the playoffs. It was the Red Sox who wound up losing and completing the most epic collapse of all time. And it all happened. In real life.

So here come the Strange But True developments that sum up the monumental improbability of that turn of events:

- Until that night, the Red Sox were 89–0 in games they led in the ninth inning or later. Yep, 89 and 000000000.

- The man they had on the mound, Jonathan Papelbon, had blown one save since May 9, had struck out the first two hitters in the ninth, and had two outs and nobody on with the No. 8 and 9 hitters coming up.

- Meanwhile, in Tampa Bay, the Yankees hadn't blown a seven-run lead in the eighth inning or later in any game they'd played, against anybody, since August 18, 1953.

- All the Rays were trying to do was become the first team in history to find themselves seven runs down—at any point—in their final game of the season and then come back to win a game that launched them into the postseason.

- The Red Sox would lose this game on a walkoff single by Robert Andino—who before that moment was hitting .170 in the ninth inning,

.196 with two outs and runners in scoring position, and .239 against all AL East teams not known as the Red Sox. But amazingly, this was his seventh Red Sox–killing RBI against Boston just in the last nine days of the season.

- The Rays would tie their game on a two-out, two-strike Dan Johnson pinch homer. Before that swing of the bat, Johnson was hitting .108 and hadn't had a hit in the big leagues since April 27.

- Then the hit that finished off the Red Sox—and one of history's strangest but truest comebacks—was Evan Longoria's 12th-inning walkoff homer. And where'd that home run leave the yard? It barely cleared the left-field fence in a spot known as "The Crawford Cut-out"—because the Rays had lowered that section of the wall to help Carl Crawford rob home runs. Instead, incredibly, it wound up robbing Crawford and the Red Sox of a trip to October.

Strangest But Truest Blowout of the Millennium

This was the real score, of an actual major league game, played on August 22, 2007:

Rangers 30, Orioles 3.

"I kept thinking about the announcers all over the country giving the scores during their games," Orioles first baseman Kevin Millar told me after the most lopsided baseball game of modern times. "They had to be saying, '30–3? That's gotta be a misprint.'"

Ah, but that was no misprint. And all these years later, I'm still trying to digest a game that couldn't possibly happen—but did.

- Four Orioles pitchers gave up six, seven, eight, and nine runs apiece. And that was the first time four pitchers on one team had ever allowed six-plus earned runs in the same game.

- The Orioles' bullpen gave up 24 (yep, 24) earned runs in this game—a record for any bullpen, any time, any place, any season.

- The Rangers' No. 3 hitter, Michael Young, drove in *none* of his team's 30 runs. But the Rangers' eighth and ninth hitters, Jarrod Saltalamacchia and Ramon Vazquez, knocked in seven *apiece*—the first time any 8-9 hitters had ever done anything like that in the same game.

- The Rangers hadn't scored 30 runs in any series in their last 54 series, then scored 30 in one game.

- They also hadn't scored 16 runs in any of their previous 371 *games*, then put up 16 just in the last two *innings*.

- And somehow, they scored those 30 runs in a game in which they had more innings where they *didn't* score (five) than innings where they did (four).

"The last time I was on a team that gave up 30, I was playing high school football," Millar laughed. "Our secondary defense was terrible that night."

Strangest But Truest Delay of Game of the Millennium

It was a game only Samantha Bee, BB King, and the late great Bea Arthur could have loved. The Bee Gees should have sung the anthem. And why B.J. Surhoff wasn't recruited to throw out the first pitch, I have no idea.

Normally, when there's a buzz in the ballpark, that's a good thing. But it wasn't such a good thing in San Diego on July 2, 2009—when the Astros and Padres got stung by the longest bee delay in modern baseball history.

They spent 52 minutes watching thousands of bees mistake the left-field ballgirl's Padres jacket for a rhododendron bush, or something. And it wasn't until their friendly neighborhood bee-keeper showed up and provided his own special brand of outfield extermination that they actually got to finish their little ballgame.

"You know, it's so ironic to have this happen in San Diego," then-Astros broadcaster Jim Deshaies told our Strange But True investigative force, "because they're never going to have a rain delay. I don't even know if they have a tarp. But they have a bee-keeper on speed-dial."

If you somehow stumbled onto the feed of this game on the MLB Extra Innings package, you know that Deshaies was the true MV-Bee of that telecast—providing 52 minutes of hilarious bee quips and info. So we've called on him to fill in our bee-sieged readers on just what they missed:

On the bee-keeper's extermination techniques: "I was thinking, if this were you or I, we'd just go out there with a couple of cans of Raid and blast away. But with the bee-keeper, I expected something greater, something different—like maybe he herds them back into the comb somehow and leads them off to safety. But no, the bee-keeper shows up and just does the same thing you or I would do: PSSSSSSSSSSHHH."

On how bizarre it was that this could happen to an Astros franchise known for its killer bees (Jeff Bagwell and Craig Biggio): "We should have tried to get Bagwell and Biggio on a satellite hook-up, so we could ask: 'Who are the *real* Killer Bees?'"

On the most important fact he learned from the "bee quiz" that he sprung on partner Bill Brown during the delay—that all worker bees are females: "So the question Brownie asked me was, if the worker bees are females, then what do the male bees do? And my theory is: all the males just sit at home in their little bee recliners with a beer, watching *SportsCenter*. I can see them now. They're watching E-S-B-N, drinking a honey-rum lager."

10 More Awesome Strange But True Feats of the Millennium

1. How good was Luis Sojo at hanging on forever? In 2003, he played for the Yankees in a regular season game *and* their Old-Timers Game.

2. Whatever you do, don't say the Mariners "hit" into a triple play back on September 2, 2006, against Tampa Bay. Why not? Because this was one trifecta that got turned without a ball being put in play. So how'd that happen? It wasn't easy. Raul Ibanez got called out on strikes for the first out. Adrian Beltre got nailed stealing second for the second out. Then Jose Lopez bolted for the plate and got thrown out at home for the third out. Try that one on your Xbox sometime.

3. Has there ever been a stranger (but truer) hitting streak than Dan Uggla's out-of-the-blue 33-gamer in 2011? Let the record show that:
    On the day this streak started (July 5), Uggla was hitting .173. That was worse than Russell Branyan (.200), Jack Cust (.215), and Bill Hall (.214)—three guys who hit so badly, they got *released*.

That .173 average enabled Uggla to accomplish something during this streak that nobody has ever done, according to Strange But True streak guru Trent McCotter: the guy started out so low, he was able to raise his batting average in 27 games in a row!

And by the time his streak finally came to an end, nearly a month and a half later, Uggla was still only hitting .231—after a 33-game hitting streak. Not only was that the worst average in history at the time a streak that long ended—but nobody else was within 66 points of him.

4. On September 8, 2010, after 16 long years in the minor leagues, 33-year-old Dodgers rookie John Lindsey finally made his long-awaited big-league debut—by playing in a game he never played in. True story. He was announced as a pinch hitter. The Padres switched pitchers. Andre Ethier then pinch-hit for him. And that, according to the record book, was the entire story of John Lindsey's major league debut.

5. In the Strange But True postseason classic that was Game 6 of the 2011 World Series, the Cardinals trailed by scores of 1–0, 3–2, 4–3, 7–4, and 9–7—and won. Just so you know, the Cardinals had played 19,387 regular season games in their history at that point. Not once, in any of them, had they won a game in which they trailed five different times.

6. There have been many, many insane baseball games in the 2000s. But for seven mind-boggling hours of pure, cue-the-*Twilight-Zone*-theme-music strangeness, you couldn't beat this classic: Mets 2, Cardinals 1, in 20 seemingly never-ending innings, on April 17, 2010.

- This game began with neither team scoring for 36 consecutive half-innings—after which, of course, the same two teams scored in three half-innings in a row!

- How 'bout this: the Mets won this game even though precisely one of the first 37 hitters they sent to the plate got a hit.

- The winning pitcher (Francisco Rodriguez) was the only guy on his team who gave up a run—in 20 innings.

- This was the first game since 1979 in which a pitcher (emergency Cardinals outfielder Kyle Lohse) recorded two putouts in a game he wasn't pitching in.

- The Cardinals needed to point two different position players (Felipe Lopez and Joe Mather) to the mound to get nine outs as pitchers.

- And fittingly, it was the first game in the history of baseball in which a position player (Mather) took the loss, a closer (K-Rod) got the win, and a starter (Mike Pelfrey) wound up with a save. Of course it was!

7. How allergic to scoring runs were the 2010 Mariners? All you need to know is that Ichiro Suzuki—the guy who was first in the American League in hits that year—still managed to score fewer runs (74) than Mark Reynolds (79), the guy who was last (among qualifiers) in the National League in hits. We kiddeth you not.

8. Thanks to the miracle of suspended animation—or at least a suspended Nationals-Astros game in 2009 that started on May 5 (in Washington, D.C.) and didn't end until July 9 (in Houston)—the Astros managed to lose a game on a walkoff hit in their home park. (First team to do that since the 1975 Twins). And Washington's winning pitcher was Joel Hanrahan, who had been traded to the Pirates during that two-month intermission. So he was actually taking a nap at the moment he was awarded that win. "You know," quipped Rich Donnelly, a Pirates coach at the time, "if he'd have gotten a good eight hours in, he might have had a chance to win 20."

9. Ever played that card game, Crazy Eights? The 2012 Mariners obviously had. In a May 30, 2012, game in Texas, they mysteriously awoke from their perpetual offensive funk to put up eight-run innings in two innings in a row. Before that, naturally, they'd scored eight runs (or more) in precisely one of their previous 5,277 innings. And afterward? Well, as this book went to press, they'd played another 2,490 innings since that game. You know how many times they'd scored eight runs (or more) in any of those innings? Right you are. None.

10. Finally, the ultimate proof that literally anything is possible in baseball appeared before our eyes on September 18, 2006, when the Dodgers entered the bottom of the ninth inning of a game against San Diego, trailing by four runs. And then:

    • Hit four home runs *in a row* to tie the game.

    • And did it in a span of seven pitches.

    • And hit them off two pitchers (Jon Adkins and Trevor Hoffman) who had given up three homers all season to the previous 432 hitters they'd faced.

    • And then, after falling behind in the top of the 10th, hit *another* homer in the bottom of the 10th to turn a loss into a win.

    • Oh. And one more thing we forgot to mention: the Dodgers were last in the league in home runs at the time.

"It might be the most amazing thing that ever happened in sports," said Rich Donnelly, who was coaching third as all those Dodgers trotted by. "It's like the Stanford band thing—without the trombones."